THE HISTORY OF
FORMULA 1

THE HISTORY OF
FORMULA 1

igloo

igloo

First published in 2009
by Igloo Books Ltd
Cottage Farm
Sywell
NN6 0BJ
www.igloo-books.com

ISBN 978-184817-397-2

Project managed by BlueRed Press Ltd
Cover designed by Stephen Croucher
Designed by Jason Anscombe
Author Martin Derrick

Printed and manufactured in China

Contents

Foreword

Cutting-edge cars. Great circuits. Tight teamwork. Danger. Glamour. Bright lights. Deafening roar. Adrenaline rushes. Pounding, punishing, power, passion.

Welcome to the world of F1.

And F1 is a world – a world of people who dare to not only dream the dream, but to live it. The drivers, owners, sponsors and followers are dedicated to the point of obsession. The stakes are high; the risks for everyone are life-changing. Nothing exists outside the speed and supremacy of being the fastest and the best, almost regardless of cost.

The raw excitement of a Formula One race is unlike any other sporting spectacle. The almost deafening roar of the engines as they accelerate from 0 to 100 mph (160km/h) in under five seconds; the almost super-human skill of the drivers as they push themselves and their cars to perform to their very limits in pursuit of sporting glory. The undeniable glamour of the venues, from the grandeur of the Monaco street circuit to the ultra-modern track in Bahrain – all these things help make Formula One the greatest show on Earth.

For the drivers, a Grand Prix race provides the ultimate test of courage, speed and skill, where the consequences of a tiny error can be fatal. For those fortunate enough to witness the drama first-hand, it is an adrenaline-fuelled experience that overwhelms the senses.

The first Grand Prix was held in France in 1906, and was won by the Hungarian Ferenc Szisz in a Renault. After that, Grand Prix developed from a sport enjoyed by a handful of wealthy people and a few early motor manufacturers, into a major spectacle, with races held at different venues around the world. Then, as motor sport became increasingly popular, Formula One was created in 1950 – as the world's foremost and most prestigious motor racing series.

Since then, Formula One has evolved to become the ultimate global glamour sport. It offers the unique mix of superstar gladiatorial drivers competing in an undoubtedly dangerous arena, with high speed, cutting edge technology, wealthy owners, high-rolling sponsors and glamorous followers.

Everyone involved in this sport, from the engineers who create and maintain the cars, to the owners and backers who empower the races to take place, to the drivers, who risk their lives every time they push the cars and themselves to the limit, make Formula One the dynamic sport that it is.

Welcome to the world of F1.

LEFT: *Sebastien Bourdais (Toro Rosso STR04 Ferrari) in action during the 2009 Chinese Grand Prix.*

INTRODUCTION

No sooner had the first motor cars been developed at the end of the 19th Century than drivers started competing to see who could go further and faster. In 1894 the Paris to Rouen trial saw 21 cars competing for a 5,000 Franc first prize, which was awarded jointly to Panhard-Levassor and Peugeot for displaying the best combination of safety, economy, and ease of driving. It was a popular event and the following year, 1885, what is now held to be the world's first motor race was devised.

The 750 mile (1,200 km) course stretched from Paris to Bordeaux and back and the race was won by Pierre Levassor in a Panhard-Levassor. He completed the run in 48 hours 48 minutes at an average speed of just 13.13 mph (21.14 kph).

Over the following years motor racing took off and events were held all over Europe as well as in the USA. As time went by, manufacturers realized that good results in racing could, and probably would, result in improved sales of their products. Certainly Mercedes got a major boost when it won the 1901 Nice-Salon-Nice race, finishing a full half an hour before the second placed car. As a direct result its Simplex car that had evolved directly from the racing car became a major success. Racing performances were soon becoming increasingly important both in demonstrating the potential of the motor car and in publicizing the most successful models.

Racing could also publicize other business. Gordon Bennett, a wealthy American press baron, arranged annual road races from 1900 to 1905 purely to promote his own newspapers. The first of these was between Paris and Lyon in France and was won by Fernand Charon driving a Panhard with a Daimler engine. The same car won the following year, while the 1903 Cup—held in

LEFT: *Sebastian Vettel (Toro Rosso STR03 Ferrari) in action during the 2008 Japanese Grand Prix at the Fuji Speedway.*

ABOVE: *Nico Rosberg of Williams during pre-season Formula One winter testing in 2007 at the Monteblanco Circuit in Seville, Spain.*

Ireland, because motor racing was banned in Britain—was won by Camille Jenatzy in a Mercedes.

The first-ever Grand Prix was organized by the Automobile Club de l'Ouest in 1906 at Le Mans, which would later become famous for its annual 24-Hour race. It was won by François Szisz from Hungary driving a 90 horsepower Renault. The first Targa Florio race in Sicily was also held that year and victory went to Alessandro Cagno in an Itala.

Numerous manufacturers, including Daimler, Peugeot, Fiat, Benz ,De Dion Bouton, and Panhard-Levassor were involved with motor racing from the earliest days and all enjoyed the fruits that success brought. But the growing race scene was facing a dilemma: it was becoming increasingly dangerous to race on public roads. What was now needed were purpose-built circuits where the increasingly higher speeds the cars were now capable of could be achieved in relative safety. And that was exactly what Hugh Locke-King, a man with an immense personal fortune and the vision to create what was to become the world's first purpose-built motor racing track, set about providing. On his Brooklands estate in Surrey, southern England, Locke-King's dream took shape as thousands of workmen, hundreds of horses, and massive steam engines were employed to carve out a 2.75 mile (4.42 km) oval track that involved the construction of a special

branch railway line from the London to Portsmouth main line and the diversion of the River Wey in two places. Amazingly, Brooklands was built in just nine months and as soon as it opened it became the hub of British motor sport. The main race of the first meeting held at Brooklands on July 6, 1907, was won by a Mercedes driven by J.E Hutton at an average speed of 82 mph (132 kph) and Mercedes cars continued to dominate that first season's racing, winning more prize money than any other make.

Around the world, others saw the success of Brooklands and soon bespoke motor racing venues were developed elsewhere. The famous Indianapolis Oval saw its first race in 1909, while Monza in Italy was completed in 1922. Sitges,, near Barcelona in Spain, began hosting races in 1923, though the track was quickly abandoned because its banking was so badly designed, while one of the greatest venues on the Grand Prix calendar—Nürburgring in Germany— opened in 1927.

As more tracks were completed and it became safer to go faster, so the manufacturers responded with quicker and quicker cars, culminating in the brutally powerful Mercedes-Benz W154, the rear-engined Auto Union Type D, the supercharged Maserati 8CTF, and the Type 308 Alfa Romeo of the late 1930s, when power outputs were up to some 490bhp and top speeds were close to 200 mph (320 kph).

Motor racing came to a halt during World War II, but started again very soon after. An important milestone was 1947 when the Fédération Internationale de l'Automobile (FIA) established new regulations for Grand Prix racing and for the first time introduced the term 'Formula One'. Just three years later, in 1950, the World Drivers' Championship was instituted and Giuseppe Farina was crowned the first victor, driving what was—that season—the literally unbeatable Alfa Romeo Type 158. With Farina, Juan Manuel Fangio, and Luigi Fagioli at the wheel the car won all eleven races.

Since then, Formula One has gone from strength to strength. Today, it is perhaps the world's pre-eminent sport. It offers a heady mix of glamor, excitement, speed, high-rolling sponsors, state-of-the-art engineering, pioneering design, and gladiatorial drivers. No wonder just under 600 million people from all around the globe are estimated to tune in to Formula One on their televisions each year. Over the years, budgets had also risen with the number of fans. It's estimated that the average team budget in the 1990s was under £80 million a season, but had become nearly £300 million by 2008. With money from sponsors becoming increasingly tight, that kind of annual spend was not sustainable and efforts are now being made to cap the total amount of money the teams can spend to a—still dizzying—£40 million per season.

Perhaps one of the most important developments in Formula One has been in terms of driver safety. In the 1950s, 1960s, and 1970s motor racing was a highly dangerous occupation as the statistics so vividly show: 15 drivers died in the 50s, 12 in the 60s, and 10 in the 70s. Four died in the 80s and two in the 90s.

However, since the last fatal accident—that of Ayrton Senna at Monza in 1994—there has not been a single death in Formula One. The reason is that the FIA, the Formula One teams, and the drivers themselves have worked together to agree a succession of measures aimed at reducing the risk to both drivers and spectators. Accidents will always happen in motor racing but Formula One has proved that the consequences of those accidents can be contained. Some of the measures have involved changes to tracks, with larger run-off areas, wider verges, and ensuring the spectators are kept at least three meters (10 feet) from the action, behind fencing. Others saw the tightening up of driver licence demands, better fireproofing of overalls, better seat belt harnesses, and ensuring all helmets are approved. Most recently, the HANS head and neck protection device has been made compulsory. Finally, the cars themselves have been better designed to absorb far more energy in crashes, so that the driver's tub remains undamaged whatever the severity of the impact. The results speak for themselves, and while no-one involved in Formula One is ever complacent, it's a matter of some pride to all involved that since the Ayrton Senna tragedy no driver has lost his life in a Formula One car.

Formula One may be safer than ever before but it's no less exciting for that. It's still the world's greatest motorsport series. It's colorful, exhilarating, prestigious, and the only championship that is genuinely global in its reach. The leading drivers are household names around the world. Today, as it always has been, Formula One is the ultimate expression of automotive and individual endeavor and achievement.

ABOVE: *Ralf Schumacher (center, Toyota TF107) spins on the first lap during the 2007 Chinese Grand Prix.*

THE CIRCUITS

Formula One is the premier, international racing series, so hosting the races in different countries demands suitable circuits for the drivers to play out their championships. Over the course of Formula One's history, the circuits have been agreed by royals, heads of state, governments, television and media producers, and even key sports people, but always through the Fédération Internationale du Sport Automobile (FISA) and in conjunction with the FIA.

While it may not always seem obvious, the final decision on where to host a Grand Prix is not based solely on the quality of the track itself—though producing an ultimate test of man and machine is always important. Other issues, such as proximity to major conurbations and ease of access for spectators are taken into consideration. And it's also important to appeal to the world's glitterati, the stars and jet-setters who provide F1 with its allure, as well as to the racing teams themselves and their cash-rich sponsors. Advertising and promotional activities became integral aspects of F1 as it in turn became increasingly commercialized,

which is why it's now just as important to look after those enjoying corporate hospitality as it is to cater for the traditional fans in the grandstands and on the bankings.

Every Grand Prix has its pecking order, with the lavish corporate hospitality of the F1 Paddock Club at its zenith. But few of those who follow F1 begrudge the better seats to those who can afford them because for everyone who attends a Grand Prix weekend the most important part is being there—and being a part of the greatest spectacle on Earth.

But while it's the undoubted responsibility of the governing bodies to ensure that all the

LEFT: *An aerial view of the Silverstone circuit before the 2006 British Grand Prix.*

ABOVE: *Geoffrey Crossley (Alta GP) passes the retiring Prince Bira (Maserati 4CLT/48) during the first race of the first official World Championship at Silverstone in 1950.*

circuits involved in the F1 circus provide that heady mix of excitement, accessibility, and visibility, that doesn't mean they will always be able to please everyone.

In Great Britain, for example, there has been a strong motorsport heritage stretching back more than 100 years when the world's first purpose-built track opened at Brooklands in 1907. Later, Silverstone, set between the towns of Northampton and Oxford, billed itself 'The Home of British Motorsport', yet there are many who criticize the fact that it's based on a former World War Two airfield and so its setting is in the middle of a wide expanses of featureless open fields. No matter how much redevelopment has taken place, with new grandstands and spectator banking, its essential character has not really changed.

Similarly, criticism has been directed at Magny-Cours, where the French Grand Prix is held. Not only is it remote and difficult to get to, but it also lacks the geographical features such as a natural 'viewing bowl' that might add either interest or improve the lot of the spectators.

On the other hand, there are some of the most scenic places on the planet at Spa-Francorchamps in Belgium or the Nürburgring in the Eiffel mountains of Germany. And the city-based circuits of Monaco, Shanghai, Singapore, and even Long Beach offer stunning urban views as well as plenty of viewing angles and camera shots.

Though it is undoubtedly true that money talks in Formula One, the opinions of the racing drivers themselves can also make or break a venue. A classic example is the Nordschleife Nürburgring in Germany. Following a fatal accident in 1970 involving Piers Courage, the drivers threatened to boycott the circuit unless substantial changes were made. Some changes were introduced but it was not enough. In 1976, after Niki Lauda was badly burned in an accident, the drivers decided that the circuit was simply too dangerous and that year's Grand Prix was the last to be held on the original Nordschleife circuit. Ever since then, the Grand Prix Drivers' Association (GPDA) has been able to influence the design of motor racing venues.

The very first Chairman of the GPDA was Britain's ace driver Stirling Moss, in 1961. Though many drivers have forcefully made their views felt over the years, one of the most active and effective was Jackie Stewart during his reign as

World Champion. But it was not until 1994 and the tragic deaths of first up-and-coming Austrian driver Roland Ratzenberger and then the late, great Brazilian Ayrton Senna—both killed during the San Marino Grand Prix—that the drivers gained greater influence. Ironically, a few short hours before his fatal accident, Senna had been elected President of the GPDA. As a result of the deaths, and of the demands of the drivers, the Autodromo Enzo e Dino Ferrari circuit was revised to reduce the risk of further high-speed accidents.

Bernie Ecclestone, as the Chief Executive Officer of both Formula One Management and Formula One Administration, is regarded popularly as the sport's 'Supremo'. But despite controlling all the financial strings within F1, safety is a perennial concern of his, too. When he acquired the ownership of the former Paul Ricard racing circuit at Le Castellet, near Marseille, France, in 1999, he decided to explore the potential for creating the world's ultimate racing circuit. It is notable for its multi-surface, safety run-off areas—in blue and red—and also its advanced Tecpro barrier system. Many of the improvements that he has been able to incorporate, at what is known as the Paul Ricard High Tech Test Track (HTTT), have been incorporated at several of the other new Formula One venues that have been added to the calendar in recent times.

And racing drivers, too, have increasingly become involved in the development of new circuits in recent years, with seven-times World Champion Michael Schumacher being well known for his close ties with the German circuit designer Hermann Tilke. Some have criticized his designs as dull and unexciting but his clean-sheet approaches have always been highly respected by those most closely involved—the drivers.

But while common safety standards are the aspiration of all involved in F1, it is the sheer range of different styles and characters of the many different circuits around the world that makes Formula One so exciting. Some circuits make massive architectural statements; some make national statements; others are surrounded by natural beauty; others still are overlooked by the skyscrapers of a 21st century economy.

New circuits are being built all the time because F1 offers not just a massive financial and commercial boost to those who can afford to become one of its partner venues. It also offers instant, global recognition, so that it has the ability to put places like Dubai and Singapore almost literally on the map.

The following chapter contains information on all the circuits used for the official World Championship since the first race at Silverstone in 1950. Maps of the 2008 season circuits are shown with the relevant entries.

ABOVE: *An aerial view of the Bahrain International Formula One Circuit a month before it hosted its first race in 2004.*

Argentine Grand Prix

Autódromo Oscar Alfredo Gálvez

Type: purpose-built
Location: Buenos Aires
Circuit Length: 3.61 miles (5.81 km)
Lap Record: 1:27.981 (G Berger/Benetton-Renault 1997)

The Autódromo Oscar Alfredo Gálvez in Buenos Aires has not been used for the Argentine Grand Prix since 1998 despite its fine facilities. Instead, it is now used both for national motor racing meetings and for hosting major outdoor events.

The track was first developed in 1952 by Argentine President Juan Péron, who wanted to attract the world's attention to the achievements of the country's best known and most successful racing driver, Juan Manuel Fangio. The circuit was duly constructed on what had been marshland just outside Buenos Aires but instead of being named for Fangio, it was called the Autódromo 17 de Octubre to celebrate the date that Péron was released from prison— after which, he went on to win the forthcoming election and rule the country. Following Péron's overthrow, however, the circuit was named for Oscar Gálvez, another Argentine driver, though one who only started a single Grand Prix.

When it was first opened, the circuit consisted of a newly-built inner circuit combined with some existing local roads, creating a 3.6-mile (5.75 km) track with 15 turns. After being extended to include a lakeside section with two fast straights (Recto del Longo and Recto del Lago) it became the first truly international racing circuit in South America, though it has since lost that pre-eminent position to the Brazilian Grand Prix at Interlagos.

Unsurprisingly, Fangio himself was the most successful driver at the Argentine Grand Prix, clocking up four wins at Buenos Aires. Stirling Moss, in his Cooper-Climax, also recorded the first ever victory for a rear-engined racing car at the circuit. In the very last Formula One race held at the circuit, in 1998, David Coulthard took pole position though the race itself was won by Michael Schumacher. After that, financial problems made it impossible for further races to be held in Buenos Aires.

BELOW: *Giuseppe Farina (Ferrari 625/555) leads Karl Kling (Mercedes-Benz W196) during the 1955 Argentine Grand Prix.*

Australian Grand Prix

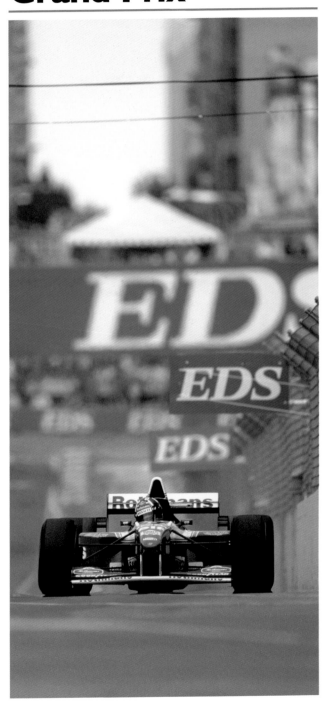

ABOVE: *Damon Hill (Williams FW17B Renault) on his way to victory in the 1995 Australian Grand Prix at Adelaide.*

Australia's first ever Grand Prix was held in 1985, though surprisingly it was not located in the capital Canberra, but instead on a circuit comprised mainly of public roads in Adelaide. The Adelaide Street Circuit was never expected to become a permanent venue though for 11 years the track was created annually in a large city car park and its adjoining public park right next to a horse-racing track and overlooked by many private houses.

In total the track was 2.35 miles (3.78 km) long and, as at Monaco and other street race circuits, the grandstands and other buildings were taken down after the Grand Prix weekend to allow the area to revert to its normal state. For the duration of the race, however, the streets were given race-related names, celebrating Australian stars in the Brock Straight, Brabham Straight, and Jones Straight, and international stars too, as in the Senna Chicane.

The circuit at Adelaide with its 16 turns was very fast, though overtaking was never easy. Perhaps that is why so many overtaking attempts ended in controversy, such as the clashes between Michael Schumacher and Damon Hill as each battled to become World Champion in 1994. It was also here in 1986 that Nigel Mansell suffered a blow-out on the Brabham Straight, putting paid to his Formula One title hopes despite the amazing car control he displayed at the time.

Despite increasing pressure from environmentalists to stop the racing at Adelaide, it was not their lobbying, but Mika Hakkinen's terrifying high-speed accident in 1995 that resulted in the eventual closure of the Adelaide venue. It was a shame, because the Australian Grand Prix at Adelaide was always very popular, with as many as 500,000 Formula One fans flocking to the venue during a typical Grand Prix weekend. It was also popular with those more directly involved in Formula One, as the party atmosphere of Adelaide cemented its reputation as the leading 'fun' circuit on the Grand Prix circus.

Adelaide Street Circuit

Type: city park
Location: Melbourne, Australia
Circuit Length: 3.29 miles (5.29 km)
Lap Record: 1:24.125 (M Schumacher/Ferrari 2004)

Australian Grand Prix

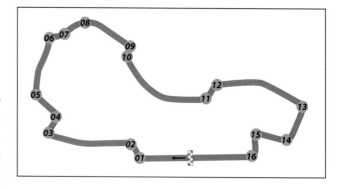

Following safety concerns after a high-speed accident in free practice in Adelaide in 1995, the Australian Grand Prix moved to Albert Park in Melbourne. At the time, officials in Australia were negotiating to bring the Pacific Grand Prix to the country, which, with their own Australian Grand Prix, would have given them two races. Melbourne was originally intended for the Pacific Grand Prix but, when it became clear that the Australian Grand Prix could not remain at Adelaide, the circuit was rapidly upgraded for the 1996 season and Melbourne has hosted the Australian Grand Prix ever since.

Situated only around a mile from the skyscrapers of the Central Business District, the Melbourne Grand Prix's 3.29 mile (5.29 km) circuit backdrop consists of public roads. Despite its 16 corners, it is one of the fastest street circuits in the world, with top speeds of over 185 mph (300 kph), and average lap times of around 140 mph (225 kph). Because the track consists of conventional road tarmac, traction in the early stages of the Grand Prix weekend is always an issue until a 'racing line' is laid down over the course of the race weekend. It's also a tough track for both men and machinery since as many as 3,500 gear-changes are made during the race and full-throttle is used for three-quarters of an average lap. Further difficulties are caused by the fact the track is bumpy and has very limited run-off areas, so a sound chassis is essential for success and to avoid making high-speed contact with the walls.

Like Adelaide before it, however, the Melbourne Grand Prix is always eagerly looked forward to. Not only is the weather usually magnificent, but the typical Australian hospitality and welcome ensures that the first race on the Grand Prix calendar is always one of the most popular.

Albert Park

Type: city park
Location: Melbourne, Australia
Circuit Length: 3.29 miles (5.29 km)
Lap Record: 1:24.125 (M Schumacher/Ferrari 2004)

PREVIOUS SPREAD: *Kimi Räikkönen—who went on to win the race in his Ferrari F2007—leads the field on the opening lap of the 2007 Australian Grand Prix at Albert Park.*

BELOW: *Lewis Hamilton, (McLaren MP4-23 Mercedes) leads as Felipe Massa (Ferrari F2008) gets out of control during the 2008 Australian Grand Prix at Albert Park.*

ABOVE: *Michael Schumacher (Ferrari F2003 GA) punches the air to celebrate his race win during the 2003 Austrian Grand Prix at A1-Ring*

Austrian Grand Prix

With the Alps creating a backbone for much of Austria, it comes as no surprise to discover that the A1-Ring, near Spielberg, is far from flat. In fact, it was developed using part of the winding and very fast Österreichring, which was renowned for its hilly nature.

The A1-Ring is a very fast circuit with only ten corners during its 2.68 miles (4.31 km) lap. It also boasts four straights, and even though two of them have slight kinks, the circuit sees drivers revving right up to the red line and reaching speeds of up to 190 mph (304 kph) before going hard on the brakes for a succession of epic corners, including the Remus, Gösser, Niki Lauda, Jochen Rindt, and Castrol Kurves. But as well as the engine and brakes coming under extreme pressure, the A1-Ring is a severe test of the suspension, too, thanks to its many bumps and the extremely high G-forces generated in the quicker bends.

Formula One first came to the A1-Ring in 1997 after Hermann Tilke thoroughly revised the circuit, though concerns

A1-Ring

Type: purpose-built
Location: Spielberg, Austria
Circuit Length: 2.68 miles (4.31 km)
Lap Record: 1:08.337 (M Schumacher/Ferrari 2003)

about safety resulted in it later losing its place on the F1 calendar in 2003. The circuit also suffered financial problems, and when the final Formula One race lost money the facilities fell into the hands of the local authority which demolished the pit lane and other circuit infrastructure. The circuit itself is now owned by Dietrick Mateschitz, owner of the Red Bull energy drink and the Formula One teams named for it. However, attempts to bring Formula One back to the A1-Ring have failed despite repeated efforts by Mateschitz to attract top level racing back.

Meanwhile, Michael Schumacher remains the lap record holder, achieving a time of 1 minute 08.337 seconds in his Ferrari in the final race in 2003.

Austrian Grand Prix

Österreichring

Type: purpose-built
Location: Spielberg, Austria
Circuit Length: 3.68 miles (5.92 km)
Lap Record: 1:28.318 (N. Mansell/Williams-Honda 1987)

While the first Austrian Grand Prix was held at the Zeltweg Airfield circuit near Knittelfeld, some 45 miles (72 km) north of Graz, the Österreichring was a very different track, built in the hills near Spielberg in the region of Styria. It first hosted a Grand Prix in 1970, when Austria's national Formula One hero was Team Lotus driver Jochen Rindt. Sadly, Rindt failed to win that inaugural event and was killed during the very next Grand Prix in Monza, Italy. Since he had already won five of that year's ten Grands Prix, he became the first posthumous World

Champion and one of the Österreichring's corners was named for him.

The original circuit was 3.68 miles (5.92 km) long and despite extreme changes in elevation as it went up and down the hills, it was a very fast circuit consisting of only nine bends and a chicane at the end of a start/finish straight. It was not only around 60 percent longer than the A1-Ring that it later developed into but it was also one of Europe's most picturesque venues thanks to its Alpine surroundings. Unfortunately, it was also the scene of some terrible high-speed accidents, compounded by its lack of run-off safety areas. Following the death of American driver Mark Donohue, Alain Prost—who then represented the Formula One drivers and was the circuit's most successful driver, having won three times—suggested that rather than making wholesale changes to the circuit all that was needed was to create more run-off areas.

Regrettably, the authorities decided otherwise and the last Formula One race was held at the Österreichring in 1987 before it was converted to become the shorter A1-Ring. In 2006 another Austrian driver, Alexander Wurz, tried to buy the circuit with the intention of returning it to its former glory but sadly nothing came of the attempt.

BELOW: *Österreichring, Austria, 1982: With the two Alfa Romeo 182's of De Cesaris and Giacomelli causing chaos at the start, Rupert Keegan (March 821 Ford) clips the pitwall in the startline melée damaging a steering arm.*

Austrian Grand Prix

In the early 1960s, a group of Austrian motor racing enthusiasts whose ambition it was to establish an Austrian Grand Prix, traveled to Silverstone in England, a racing circuit that had been created on a former aerodrome. The Austrians were looking for inspiration to turn the former airbase at Zeltweg into a venue for the Grand Prix and, after seeing how the Silverstone track had been created, they duly submitted plans to the Styrian local government authorities to develop the Zeltweg Airfield along similar lines.

Because it was a military airfield that was not in operational use for very much of the time, it was a relatively straightforward job converting it into a circuit. However, the result was an unimaginative and uninspiring track that was created with the help of little more than bales of hay and some bollards marking out a circuit on the main runway. It consisted of a rather basic L-shaped design incorporating a long start/finish straight followed by the right-hand Flatschacher-Curve, then another shorter straight leading to the 90-degree Hangar-Curve. Another short straight led to the left-handed Inner-Curve, joined by another featureless straight to the Südenburg-Curve, which led back to the start/finish straight at the end of a lap that was only 1.98 miles (3.19 km) long.

The track was first opened in 1959 for national motor racing events. Even then competitors complained about the surface of the concrete runways which caused wear and tear problems for many of the competing cars, the tires and suspension systems of which were nowhere near as advanced as they are today. Eventually, the track did manage to attract the Grand Prix circus, though in the event only one race was ever held there, in August 1964 when Lorenzo Bandini took the checkered flag in his Ferrari. After that it was decided that Zeltweg really wasn't a suitable venue and so the Austrian Grand Prix was switched to the nearby Österreichring.

ABOVE: *Jack Brabham (Brabham BT11 Climax) passes the crashed car of Trevor Taylor (BRP 1 BRM) during the 1964 Austrian Grand Prix at Zeltweg.*

Zeltweg Airfield

Type: airfield
Location: Knittelfeld, Austria
Circuit Length: 1.98 miles (3.19 km)
Lap Record: 1:10.560 (D Gurney/Brabham-Climax 1964)

Bahrain Grand Prix

The Bahrain International Circuit was the worthy recipient of the inaugural FIA Institute Center of Excellence Trophy in 2007. First opened in 2004 following an investment of some $150 million, it's a state-of-the-art motorsport circuit built in the desert around 20 miles (32 km) south of Bahrain's capital Manama. The inspiration for the new track came from Bahrain's Crown Prince Shaikh Salman bin Hamad who saw Formula One as a means of boosting the international profile of his small Middle Eastern country.

It wasn't Bahrain's first foray into international motorsport as it had already hosted a series of rallying and desert raid events but the Formula One project was on an altogether different scale. The circuit was designed by Hermann Tilke while the CEO of the project was Martin Whitaker, the former head of Ford's Motorsport division. From the very outset it was decided that the brand new facility would be the world's most eco-friendly motorsport complex.

The 3.36 miles (5.41 km) lap of the Grand Prix track consists of 15 corners and four straights, the longest of which is 1,192 yards (1,090 meter) from start to finish. There's plenty of variation, as the track rises and falls nearly 20 yards (18 meters) and varies in width from 15 to 24 yards (14 to 22 meters). Building the track was a massive operation, not least because the schedule for completion was brought forward by six months. Created from scratch out in the desert, construction involved excavating 34 million square feet

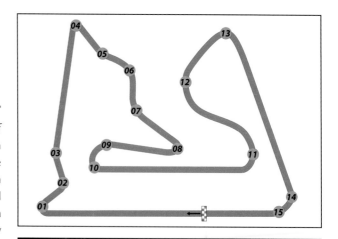

Bahrain International Circuit

Type: purpose-built
Location: Manama, Bahrain
Circuit Length: 3.36 miles (5.41 km)
Lap Record: 1:32.408 (Nico Rosberg/Williams-Cosworth 2006)

(968,459 cubic meters) of rock; laying 132,000 tonnes (120,000 metric tons) of asphalt and 18.5 million gallons (70,000 cubic meters) of concrete; erecting 13,000 yards (12,000 meters) of guard rails and 5,500 yards (5,000 meters) of FIA safety fencing; placing 82,000 tires, and even laying 6,000 square yards (5,000 square meters) of grass carpet.

When it hosted the 2004 race, Bahrain was the very first Grand Prix to be held in the Middle East. That first race was won by Michael Schumacher in his Ferrari.

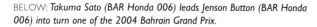

BELOW: Takuma Sato (BAR Honda 006) leads Jenson Button (BAR Honda 006) into turn one of the 2004 Bahrain Grand Prix.

ABOVE: *Didier Pironi (Ligier JS11/15-Ford Cosworth) leads the field at the start of the 1980 Belgian Grand Prix at Zolder.*

Belgian Grand Prix

The Belgian purpose-built Circuit Zolder was opened in 1963, to replace a street racing circuit called the 'Omloop van Terlaemen' in the Eastern, Flemish-speaking part of the country, which had operated for the previous ten years. The Zolder circuit quickly earned a high reputation, partly because it was undoubtedly a high-quality track, partly because of the friendly welcome, and partly also perhaps because of the waffles and fries that were served to racers and racegoers alike.

It wasn't until 1973 that the first Formula One race was held at the track, following the installment of additional chicanes and crash barriers both to increase the challenge but also to increase safety levels at the venue. The Belgian Grand Prix was held at Zolder for ten years, but after the tragic death of the ever-popular Canadian Ferrari driver, Gilles Villeneuve in qualifying for the 1982 event, only one more Formula One race was ever held there. After that, the Belgian Grand Prix was moved to Spa-Franchorchamps in the Ardennes region.

That was unfortunate because Zolder was well-liked by drivers. The circuit had a 2.49 miles (4 km) lap length in a challenging undulating woodland track comprising ten corners, four chicanes (to bring speeds down and reduce lap times) and three straights, including the start/finish alongside the main paddock area that is repeated on its opposite side. As well as the Grands Prix meetings, Zolder regularly hosts motorcycle races and was the first overseas venue to host a round of the British Formula Ford Championship. It also regularly features in the German Touring Car Championship, the Renault World Championship series, and even truck racing events.

Despite losing the Grand Prix, the Zolder circuit continues to be upgraded and a number of important circuit safety measures were incorporated in 2006. Zolder is still a busy and significant circuit, used regularly both for testing and for corporate entertainment purposes.

Circuit Zolder

Type: purpose-built parkland
Location: Zolder, Belgium
Circuit Length: 2.49 miles (4 km)
Lap Record: 1:19.294 (R. Arnoux/Ferrari 1984)

Belgian Grand Prix

Nivelles-Baulers Circuit

Type: purpose-built
Location: Nivelles, Belgium
Circuit Length: 2.314 miles (3.72 km)
Lap Record: 1:11.31 (D Hulme/McLaren-Cosworth 1974)

Because only two Formula One races were held at the Nivelles-Baulers Circuit, in 1972 and 1974, it is often forgotten despite being a highly significant and historically important part of Belgium's rich motorsport heritage. The track was located some 25 miles (40 km) from Brussels, the capital of Belgium, in the heart of the Walloon Region.

The Nivelles-Baulers track was 2.31 miles (3.72 km) long, starting with a lengthy start/finish straight, followed by a fast right-hand corner leading onto another short straight, and then a double-apex right-hand corner. The next section consisted of a quick burst into a long right-hander, then sharp left to a short straight that had an extended chicane at the beginning and the end. This then left another short straight and then a hairpin bend back onto the start/finish line. Unlike most circuits, none of the corners were named and this apparent lack of interest by the circuit's authorities seems to have been reflected in the response of the drivers who found it dull and uninteresting compared to tracks such as the Nürburgring. Certainly, it was rather flat and featureless but it was also modern and safe, with large run-off areas.

Opened in 1971, the track ran into financial difficulties after the withdrawal of Formula One in 1974 and was closed. After the original Francorchamps circuit was deemed too dangerous for racing the Belgian Grand Prix moved to Zolder in 1971 and the intention was that it should thereafter alternate with Nivelles-Baulers. Sadly, it was not to be. The area is now Les Portes de l'Europe industrial park, and parts of the old track are used as access roads. The outline of the circuit can still be seen from the air.

Brazilian driver Emerson Fittipaldi won both of the Formula One races held at Nivelles-Baulers, in a Lotus 72D Ford in 1972 and in a McLaren M23 Ford in 1974.

BELOW: *Emerson Fittipaldi (Lotus 72D Ford) on his way to first position in the 1972 Belgian Grand Prix at Nivelles-Baulers.*

ABOVE: *Michael Schumacher (Ferrari F310) makes his way through Eau Rouge at Spa-Francorchamps during the 1996 Belgian Grand Prix.*

Belgian Grand Prix

Spa-Francorchamps is located in Belgium's beautiful Ardennes Forest region, close to the German border. It is one of the most spectacular racing circuits in the whole of the Grand Prix calendar, greatly enjoyed by the drivers for its undoubted challenges and supported by thousands of enthusiastic spectators who create a noisy party atmosphere in and around its many camp sites. In many ways, Spa-Francorchamps is a reminder of the original Nürburgring Circuit in Germany, in that it is long, challenging and set in wonderful natural scenery.

It now boasts the longest lap of any Grand Prix circuit at 4.34 miles (6.98 km), which incorporates part of a local main road that is understandably closed to traffic during the race weekend. From the start/finish line, drivers accelerate first to La Source hairpin, often the scene of first-lap incidents, before speeding through the steep downhill section leading to the Raidillon chicane. Next comes a long, steep uphill climb along the Kemmel Straight and through Les Combs, a complex succession of right-left-right bends that require a perfectly balanced suspension and nerves of steel from the driver. Next comes a further fast downhill section to the Rivage hairpin, followed by a left into the short Malmedy straight, another left through Pouhon and then a further series of bends. The driver then reaches the fast Curve Paul Frere and then onto the public road to Blanchmont, the fastest point of the circuit. It's then hard on the brakes for the chicane which replaced the

Spa-Francorchamps

Type: purpose-built parkland
Location: Spa, Belgium
Circuit Length: 4.34 miles (6.98 km)
Lap Record: 1:45.108 (K Raikkonen/McLaren-Mercedes 2004)

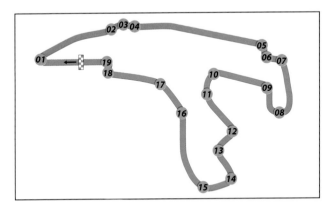

famous 'Bus-stop', and then back onto the start/finish straight.

The full Grand Prix distance is 191.5 miles (308.2 km), which is tough on both cars and drivers because of the number of corners, the inclines and also the very high speeds that are reached—up to 186 mph (300 kph), with Kimi Raikkonen's lap record averaging just over 109 mph (176 kph). Along with the Suzuka circuit in Japan, Spa-Francorchamps is generally considered to be one of the world's most challenging circuits.

Brazilian Grand Prix

Autódromo Internacional Nelson Piquet, Jacarepaguá

Type: purpose-built
Location: Rio de Janiero, Brazil
Circuit Length: 3.126 miles (5.03 km)
Lap Record: 1:32.507 (R Patrese/Williams-Renault 1989)

Rio de Janeiro has a long motorsport heritage, dating back to the 1930s when the very first Brazilian Grand Prix was held in the streets of the city on an 8 miles (12.8 km) circuit that remained in use until 1952. In more modern times the Brazilian Grand Prix joined the Formula One calendar in 1973, when it was won, fittingly, by Brazil's own Emerson Fittipaldi at Interlagos. The Grand Prix switched to Rio in 1978 and was held there again from 1981 to 1989. Originally known as the Autódromo de Jacarepaguá, this circuit opened in 1966 and was then redesigned to comply with FIA specifications in 1978. Later still it was renamed in honor of one of Brazil's most famous Formula One champions, Nelson Piquet.

The circuit, developed in an area of reclaimed marshland, is generally flat and lacks any outstanding features apart from the stunning views of the mountains overlooking Rio. The track consists of two main straights and a complex infield section, making up a total length of 3.12 miles (5.03 km). Nelson Piquet won the Brazilian Grand Prix twice during his career, and both times it was here rather than at the alternative Brazilian Grand Prix venue of Interlagos.

When Rio de Janeiro bid for the 2005 Pan American Games, it was proposed to reduce the length of the circuit to make room for a sports complex and later, when the city bid for the 2016 Olympic Games, it was planned to create an Olympic Training Center at the venue. In fact, another shorter track, known as the Emerson Fittipaldi Speedway, was built and this hosted the American CART (Championship Auto Racing Team) series from 1996 to 2000 on its 1.87 mile (3.01 km) oval track. The Brazilian Motorcycle Grand Prix was also held here between 1995 and 2004. Elements of both tracks still exist in a present-day circuit that is 2.07 miles (3.33 km) in length that mainly hosts national race series.

ABOVE: *Nigel Mansell (Ferrari 640) on the way to winning his debut race for Ferrari at the 1989 Brazilian Grand Prix at Jacarepaguá.*

ABOVE: *Carlos Pace (Brabham BT44B Ford) during the 1975 Brazilian Grand Prix at Interlagos: this was to be his first and only Grand Prix win.*

NEXT SPREAD: *Felipe Massa (Ferrari F2008) in first position at the start of the 2008 Brazilian Grand Prix at Interlagos.*

Brazilian Grand Prix

The current home of the Brazilian round of the World Formula One Championship—always an exciting event because it's normally the last event of the year where the Drivers or Constructors Championships are often decided—is the Autódromo José Carlos Pace, Interlagos. It is located in the suburbs 11 miles (17.7 km) south of the city of São Paolo.

Before 1980, the Interlagos Grand Prix circuit was longer and faster than it is today, and got its name as it's located between two large lakes. It fell out of favor, however, because of its close proximity to extensive favelas—slums—which were not felt to reflect Formula One's glamorous values so the race was switched to Rio de Janeiro until 1990, after which the Grand Prix circus returned to a remodeled Interlagos. By now the track was 2.667 miles (4.29 km) long but it remained extremely challenging both because of its hilly nature and because of its bumpy track.

The start/finish straight leads into a tricky downhill series of bends that have ended many drivers' races on lap one, as they all jostle for the single optimum fast line through the sequence. Next up is the Curva do Sol, then a fast straight into the Curva do Lago, followed by a gentler left-hander that leads into another difficult series of six bends that test the mettle of both the driver and the car. Unusually in Formula One, the Interlagos circuit runs counter-clockwise which can cause difficulties for drivers more used to clockwise circuits. Car set-up is crucial for success at this challenging circuit as engineers have to try to

balance power with downforce and aerodynamic efficiency. To make matters even more difficult, the circuit is tough on cars, too, because of its abrasive surface; because São Paolo is set at nearly 2,500 feet (760 meters) the thinner air reduces power output by 8 percent. However, this is one of the rare Formula One circuits where overtaking opportunities are plentiful.

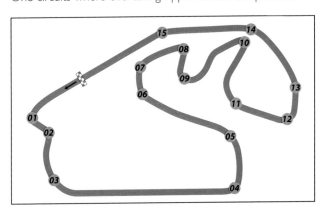

Autódromo José Carlos Pace, Interlagos

Type: purpose-built
Location: Interlagos, São Paolo, Brazil
Circuit Length: 2.667 miles (4.29 km)
Lap Record: 1:11.473 (JP Montoya/Williams-BMW 2004)

British Grand Prix

Aintree

Type: purpose-built equestrian
Location: Liverpool, England
Circuit Length: 3.00 miles (4.83 km)
Lap Record: 1:55.000 (J Clark/Lotus-Climax 1962)

Aintree is best known in the UK as the home to the Grand National, the annual horse race over large jumps that is one of the country's most popular sporting events. Earlier, it was also the venue for the British Grand Prix. Aintree is situated close to the west coast port of Liverpool, and its 3 mile (4.83 km) long circuit hosted the Grand Prix five times between 1955 and 1962. Unusually, the motor racing circuit shared the main grandstand and other ancillary buildings of the horse racing track, with the result that its facilities were actually far superior to those at Silverstone, with which it alternated the Grand Prix at that time.

First built in 1954, the Aintree track was often called 'The Goodwood Of The North', mainly because like Goodwood, Aintree was both a motor racing and a horse racing venue. The first Aintree Grand Prix was held in 1955, when Stirling Moss in his Mercedes W196 pipped Juan Manuel Fangio not only to win the inaugural Aintree race, but also to record the first ever British Grand Prix win by a British driver. Moss clocked up another first at the 1957 European Grand Prix at

Aintree when he shared victory with Tony Brooks in a Vanwall and thus secured the first Formula One British Grand Prix victory by a British driver in a British car. Moss won yet again in the 1959 Grand Prix at the fast Aintree circuit. The very last Grand Prix held there was in 1962 during which the fastest ever lap time was set by the eventual winner, Jim Clark in a Lotus-Climax. Interestingly, the first six places in that race all went to British cars.

Although the former Grand Prix track is now disused, there is still motor racing at Aintree. Thanks to the efforts of local enthusiasts and car club members, a Sprint Circuit has been devised that incorporates part of the east end of the original track, together with a new infield section. A number of club racing meetings are held throughout the year.

BELOW: *Juan Manuel Fangio (Maserati 250F) at the 1957 British Grand Prix at Aintree.*

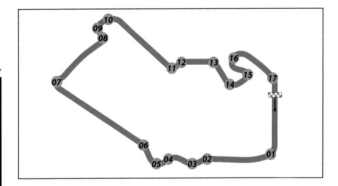

ABOVE: *Jean Alesi (Benetton B196 Renault) leads Mika Häkkinen (McLaren MP4/11 Mercedes) and Michael Schumacher (Ferrari F310) during the 1996 British Grand Prix at Silverstone.*

British Grand Prix

Silverstone Circuit

Type: purpose-built airfield
Location: Silverstone, England
Circuit Length: 3.18 miles (5.12 km)
Lap Record: 1:18.739 (M Schumacher/Ferrari 2004)

There is a large sign outside the gates of Silverstone that proudly declares that this is 'The Home of British Motorsport.' During World War II numerous new airfields had been built in the English countryside which were surplus to requirements once peace had been established. So when the Royal Automobile Club started looking for a venue where motor racing activities could be restarted, Silverstone on the Northamptonshire/Buckinghamshire border looked ideal. Farmer James Wilson Brown was growing crops in the infield and the RAC employed him to turn the perimeter roads into a circuit. Incredibly, he finished the task in just two months so the first RAC Grand Prix could be held there in October 1948.

The original track was 3.67 miles (5.9 km) long although its layout, which used the former main runway, was very different to today's circuit. In one of many alterations that have been made at Silverstone since, it switched to the full airfield perimeter road circuit in 1950. A chicane was added in 1975

to slow drivers before the notorious Woodcote Corner and changes were made at Bridge in 1987. In 1990/91, a major redesign resulted in the creation of the new Luffield Complex and introduced some elevation to other parts of the track.

Despite the changes, Silverstone remains one of the fastest of all Grand Prix circuits, and during the Grand Prix weekend its main runway becomes Britain's busiest airport and heliport. From the start opposite the pits there's a fast right-hander at Copse which is followed by Maggotts, Becketts, and Chapel curves. Then it's into the extremely fast Hangar Straight, at the end of which is Stowe Corner, followed by the dip into Vale and a very challenging 90-degree left and the gradually unwinding right of Club Corner. After Abbey Curve, there's the short Farm Straight, then under Bridge for first Priory, followed by Luffield and finally Woodcote, and back on to the start/finish straight. The circuit is being altered radically for 2010 and it has been announced that from 2010 the British Grand Prix will be moved away from Silverstone, to Donington in the East Midlands.

British Grand Prix and European Grand Prix

Brands Hatch, in Kent, in the southeast of England is one of the truly great British motor racing venues. It was first used as a dirt circuit for motorbikes then a 1 mile (1.6 km) counter-clockwise Indy Circuit loop was paved in 1950. A few years later, in 1954, the Druids section was added and at that time it was decided to run the circuit clockwise instead. Planning permission was granted in the early 1960s to extend the circuit length to meet Grand Prix demands and it now wound through a heavily wooded area east of the existing track where it incorporated several testing bends and changes of altitude. By now, the track had grown to 2.6 miles (4.18 km), and had become an extremely challenging track for drivers and one of the best tracks of all for spectators. Its location, 20 miles (32 km) southeast of London, was a perfect spectator draw.

At the end of the start/finish straight is the blind Paddock Hill Bend right-hander which falls away sharply, before rising up Hailwood Hill to Druids Bend. Then it's downhill again to Graham Hill Bend, and along the short Cooper Straight behind the main paddock area, before the track goes sharply uphill and left at Surtees before the dip at Pilgrim's, Hawthorn Bend, and the Derek Minter Straight. The right-handed Westfield leads into yet another dip at Dingle Dell, followed by Sheene Curve and then Stirling's Bend, and on down to Clearways, Clark Curve, and finally back on to the Brabham Straight for the finish.

Between 1964 and 1986, the circuit hosted 12 British Grand Prix as well as the European Grand Prix in 1983 and 1985. Though no Grands Prix have been held at Brands Hatch since, it remains the home of numerous top class international racing events. The track is now owned by former Grand Prix driver, doctor, and entrepreneur, Jonathan Palmer, who also controls Snetterton in Norfolk, Cadwell Park in Lincolnshire, and Oulton Park in Cheshire, in addition to the corporate driving center of Bedford Autodrome.

BELOW: *Riccardo Patrese (Brabham BT52B BMW) leads the field through Paddock Hill Bend at the start of the 1983 British and European Grand Prix at Brands Hatch.*

Brands Hatch

Type: purpose-built parkland
Location: Brands Hatch, England
Circuit Length: 2.60 miles (4.18 km)
Lap Record: 1:09.593 (N Mansell/Williams-Honda 1986)

ABOVE: *Ayrton Senna raises his fist to celebrate achieving first position in the 1993 European Grand Prix at Donington Park.*

British Grand Prix and European Grand Prix

The very first race to be held at Donington Park in the East Midlands was on Whit Monday 1931. Although Brooklands was both Britain's and the world's first purpose-built track, Donington claims to be the first parkland racing circuit to be built in the UK. Motorcycle racer Fred Craner—who gave his name to the Craner Curves—persuaded the owners of the Donington Hall Estate to let him build a 2.18 miles (4.5 km) racetrack using existing estate roads.

The first race was such a success that within two years a new track had been created and the first Donington Park Trophy Race was held. The circuit in the early 1930s was very similar to the current layout, though without the recently built 'new' Melbourne Loop. Within a very short time the circuit was

hosting the top teams in the world, most notably in 1937 and 1938, when Donington reveled to the sound of the mighty Auto Union 'Silver Arrows', which, with Bernd Rosemeyer and Tazio Nuvolari at the wheel, blew away the opposition both those years.

During World War II Donington became a military vehicle store. Leicestershire businessman and car enthusiast Tom Wheatcroft bought the site in 1970 and opened a motor museum to display his own cars in 1973. He also invested in the circuit, making revisions in 1977 and adding the new Melbourne Loop in 1985 to extend the total lap length to 2.5 miles (4.02 km) of smooth, flowing tarmac that provides the real challenge of contrasting elevations and 11 different corners. After the start/finish straight the lap starts with the double-apex Redgate, then there's the downhill dip of the Craner Curves, followed by the Old Hairpin which is actually now a relatively gentle left-handed bend. From there, the track wends uphill, past Starkeys Bridge, to the fast right-handed McLean's, followed by a steeper uphill to the blind double-apex right-hander of Coppice, which leads on to Starkey's Straight. A left-right at the Esses takes the driver into the Melbourne Loop and down to the Melbourne Hairpin, which is followed by a dash up the hill to the hairpin at Goddards, and back onto the start/finish straight.

That was the lap completed by Ayrton Senna as he claimed victory in the pouring rain of the 1993 European Grand Prix. The circuit currently holds a contract to host the British Grand Prix from 2010 for 10 years and is being extensively revised.

Donington Park

Type: purpose-built parkland
Location: Castle Donington, England
Circuit Length: 2.5 miles (4.02 km)
Lap Record: 1:18.029 (A Senna/McLaren-Ford 1993)

Caesar's Palace Grand Prix

Money and Formula One go together like the proverbial horse and carriage, which was why the Grand Prix circus headed to Las Vegas after the contract to run the United States Grand Prix at Watkins Glen had expired. Incredibly, the whole of the race was on a circuit created in the car park of the Caesar's Palace Resort and was supported by the City of Las Vegas as a means of drumming up tourism business, and by the hotel as a means of encouraging people to visit the gambling capital of the world.

From scratch, a 2.26 mile (3.64 km) circuit running in a counter-clockwise direction was built in the car park and yet there was so much space available that most drivers said that despite the debilitating effect of the desert sun, they enjoyed the venue because it left them plenty of space for overtaking. More astonishing still was that the temporary track comprised 14 very different corners together with two good length straights that were obtained by doubling the track layout back on itself twice. For safety's sake generous sand-filled run-off areas were provided to slow down cars unfortunate enough to slide off the mirror-like road surface. In fact, there was so little grip that watching the drivers battle with their sliding cars added considerably to the thrill of the event. And since spectators could get very close to the action, it was an unrivaled opportunity to catch the excitement of Grand Prix racing at close quarters.

This being the land of the car, access to the venue was good and a number of steeply banked stands were built around the track to ensure everyone got a good view of the action. Despite this, only two Formula One Championship races were held at Las Vegas, in 1981 and 1982, though two further non-championship events were held in 1983 and 1984. After that, Las Vegas returned to its roots as America's leading vacation and gambling resort.

Caesar's Palace

Type: city center car park
Location: Las Vegas, United States
Circuit Length: 2.26 miles (3.64 km)
Lap Record: 1:19.639 (M Alboreto/Tyrrell-Cosworth 1982)

BELOW: *Alan Jones (Williams FW07C Ford) leads going into Turn 1 on the first lap of the 1981 Caesar's Palace Grand Prix.*

ABOVE: *Jean Alesi (Ferrari 412T2) on the way to his maiden Grand Prix win at the 1995 Canadian Grand Prix at the Circuit Gilles Villeneuve.*

Canadian Grand Prix

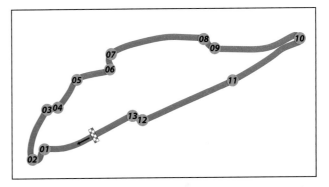

It's not every major city of the world that welcomes the Grand Prix circus, yet Circuit Gilles Villeneuve most certainly does. It's named for the French-Canadian superstar who was tragically killed in an accident while qualifying his Ferrari at the Zolder Circuit in Belgium. It is held on a man-made island in the St Lawrence River, on the site originally constructed for the 1976 Montreal Olympics.

The Parc Jean-Drapeau on the Ile de Notre Dame hosted its first Canadian Grand Prix in 1978, when Villeneuve was just starting to make a major international name for himself. If there had been any doubt before about the wisdom of holding a Grand Prix in the city center, it quickly evaporated as local boy Villeneuve claimed a maiden victory on home turf. The Canadian Grand Prix has been held in the city of Montreal ever since, with the single exception of the 1987 event, which was canceled after an unseemly sponsorship row between the rival Molson and Labatts beer companies.

Despite the fact that the circuit was purpose-designed, in many ways it has the atmosphere of a street circuit, partly because of its limited run-off areas and partly due to the majestic backdrop of the skyscrapers of downtown Montreal. However, Circuit Gilles Villeneuve is faster than any other street circuit and its 2.71 mile (4.36 km) lap is a constant challenge to the teams and their drivers and a thrilling

Circuit Gilles Villeneuve

Type: purpose-built city
Location: Montreal, Canada
Circuit Length: 2.71 miles (4.36 km)
Lap Record: 1:13.622 (R Barrichello/Ferrari 2004)

spectacle for the spectators—there is seating for almost 100,000 spectators around the venue.

There are 15 corners in total, of which six are chicane-type complexes. There is also a long and very fast straight running from the Virage Du Casino to the start/finish area, which provides one of the most enthralling hard braking and tight turn-in sections, at its pit-lane entrance end. Here, drivers 'kiss the wall' at the exit, getting as close as possible to the unyielding concrete that bears the legend 'Bienvenue au Quebec'.

Canadian Grand Prix

Circuit Mont-Tremblant

Type: purpose-built
Location: St Jovite, Canada
Circuit Length: 2.64 miles (4.25 km)
Lap Record: 1:32.2 (C Regazzoni/Ferrari 1970)

The Circuit Mont-Tremblant, which is located in the beautiful Laurentian Mountains north of Montreal in Canada, was reckoned by former World Champion Sir Jackie Stewart to be second only to Monaco for the scale of the challenge is presented to teams and drivers.

The circuit's design followed the natural hilly topography of the region, resulting in numerous elevation changes along its 2.64 mile (4.25 km) length. For spectators, it is perfect, with surrounding hillsides providing great viewing around the circuit. Since the ski resort of Mont-Tremblant is nearby, visitors can sample high-class cuisine and there is plenty of hotel accommodation available in the immediate area. The only drawback is that because of the climate conditions in the mountains, the actual racing season is always quite short.

The first race was held at Mont-Tremblant in 1964, on the 12 turn, 1.5 mile (2.41 km) North Circuit. Local Canadian driver Ludwig Heimrath won in his Cooper-Ford. Then in 1965, the circuit was extended to its current 2.64 mile (4.25 km) length. Yet despite the track's striking beauty and the undoubted driving challenge it presents, the Canadian Grand Prix was only ever held there twice, in 1968 and 1970, though the circuit remains in constant use as one of the world's most attractive racing venues.

The pit lane and start/finish straight runs alongside Lake Moore on the North Loop of the circuit, and leads into a fast right-hand corner at the end of the paddock area; then after Turn 3, it's into the Esses Complex. A short straight follows, then there's the fast left Turn 6, followed by the medium-fast Turn 7, a short straight and then the tight double-apex Turn 8. By now the track has joined the South Loop, with a fast Turn 9 followed by the slower Turn 10 which leads into The Gulch. The driver turns left to Bridge and uphill again toward the Kink, the hairpin at Turn 14, which is followed by a quick left-handed bend back on to the start/finish area.

BELOW: *Johnny Servoz-Gavin (Matra MS10-Ford) leads Piers Courage (BRM P126) during the 1968 Canadian Grand Prix at Mont-Tremblant.*

ABOVE: *Jackie Stewart (Tyrrell 003 Ford) during the 1971 Canadian Grand Prix at Mosport Park: Stewart went on to win the race.*

Canadian Grand Prix

The Mosport International Raceway, which is by far Canada's largest motorsports complex covering some 750 acres (3 square km) and offering a wide variety of different tracks, is located just north of Bowmanville in Ontario, within easy reach of the large population of the whole of the Greater Toronto Area (GTA).

After World War II, Canada had seen plenty of motorsport on circuits constructed on disused airfields but in 1961, the Mosport complex was opened, consisting of a purpose-built 2.48 mile (3.94 km) road course, a half-mile (800 meters) oval called the Mosport Speedway, a 1.5 mile (2.4 km) driver training facility, a quarter mile (400 meters) skid control pan, and also a 0.86 mile (1.38 km) kart track known as the Mosport Kart Complex.

This incredible facility played host to the Canadian Grand Prix on eight occasions between 1967 and 1977. The track consists of 10 corners and at first glance it appears easy to drive thanks to its generous run-off areas and apparently open and straightforward bends. Yet it provided a true challenge even to the best of drivers, because finding the optimum line

through every one of the corners was never easy.

From the start/finish straight the circuit runs into the medium-fast right-handed Corner 1 followed by a straight that leads into the quick left-handed Corner 2. Once out of that corner, the tricky double-apex Corner 3 comes up very quickly and it is followed by the fast left-handed Corner 4, then into the heavy braking area on the approach to the right-handed Corner 5. There is then Moss Corner, and the interconnected Corners 6, 7, and 8. There's another hard braking area on the approach to the left-handed Corner 9, which is immediately followed by the right-handed White Corner that completes the lap.

Mosport International Raceway

Type: purpose-built
Location: Bowmanville, Ontario, Canada
Circuit Length: 2.45 miles (3.94 km)
Lap Record: 1:13.299 (M Andretti/Lotus-Cosworth 1977)

Chinese Grand Prix

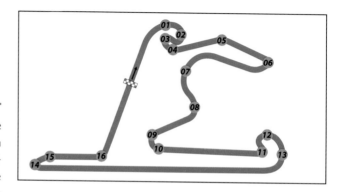

Claimed to be the most advanced Grand Prix track in the world, the Shanghai International Circuit was built from scratch on reclaimed swampland and completed in May 2004 at a cost of some $450 million. Over 3,000 engineers were involved in its construction. The design was entrusted to the celebrated German architect Hermann Tilke, who has no less than 17 international circuits to his name, and bears Tilke's trademark combination of long straights and tight hairpin bends. The inspiration for the layout came from the Chinese character for 'Shang'—the first part of 'Shang-hai'.

The circuit lies adjacent to Shanghai International Automobile City (SIAC), some 18.5 miles (30 km) away from the city center and 12.5 miles (20 km) away from Shanghai Hongqiao Airport. A light rail link connects the complex with downtown Shanghai and the 2010 Expo venue. The circuit itself can accommodate up to 200,000 people and is characterized by its distinctive main buildings, which bridge the track at either end of the start/finish area and give diners in the splendid Sky Restaurant a unique view of the racing below.

The challenging 3.37 mile (5.42 km) circuit has 16 turns, interspersed by two long straights that give drivers ample

Shanghai International Circuit

Type: purpose-built
Location: Shanghai, China
Circuit Length: 3.37 miles (5.42 km)
Lap Record: 1:32.238 (M Schumacher/Ferrari 2004)

opportunity to test their cars' straight-line performance to the limit. The first three turns occur in quick succession after the start/finish area, followed by a fourth that opens out into a faster stretch punctuated by the gentle kink of Turn 5. After the extended hairpin of Turn 6, the track opens out again briefly for the gentler Turns 7 and 8. Then it closes up again for Turns 9 and 10, before the short straight that precedes the slower, more difficult Turns 11, 12, and 13. This complex is followed by one of the longest straights in Formula One, culminating in the tortuous right hairpin of Turn 14, another kink right and then the 90-degree left-hand turn into the start/finish area. Demanding in the extreme, the Shanghai International Circuit has quickly become a favorite with drivers and spectators.

PREVIOUS SPREAD: *Lewis Hamilton (McLaren MP4-23 Mercedes) leads the field at the start of the 2008 Chinese Grand Prix.*

BELOW: *Lewis Hamilton (McLaren MP4-23 Mercedes)—finished first—leads Kimi Räikkönen (Ferrari F2008)—finished third—and Felipe Massa (Ferrari F2008)—finished second—during the 2008 Chinese Grand Prix.*

ABOVE: *Keke Rosberg (Williams FW09 Honda) takes the checkered flag for the win at the 1984 United States Grand Prix at Fair Park, Dallas.*

Dallas Grand Prix

Staging races in urban areas has traditionally been motorsport's way of getting closer to the people. But in the case of the one-off Dallas Grand Prix, held in the city's Fair Park district in April 1984, it was by no means an unqualified success. Sweltering in the unseasonably hot Texas sun, a row erupted after officials failed to recognize the passes of various team members. Without a chance to practice and with no prior history to fall back on, the teams could only guess at what tires to use. And the track itself, part of which was concrete, showed signs of breaking up after a race meeting the previous day.

The tight, unforgiving circuit ran counter-clockwise and took in 21 turns, as well as chicanes, along its 2.41 mile (3.87 km) lap length. The start led into a fast right-hander behind the Cotton Bowl stadium, followed by a sequence of two kinks and a 90-degree left turn onto Grand Avenue. Then came a short straight culminating in a 90-degree right, followed by a kink left and a hairpin complex that involved turning northeast onto Second Avenue before doubling back. The second of the two chicanes on this stretch demanded care before drivers turned left into Pennsylvania Avenue and entered a straight with a small kink two-thirds of the way along. Then it was sharp left into Washington Street, followed by the three-turn complex that led back to the start/finish zone.

Despite the inauspicious start, which took place in a blaze of publicity courtesy of Larry 'J.R. Ewing' Hagman of Dallas fame, the race presented an exciting spectacle and was eventually won by Keke Rosberg in a Honda. Afterward several drivers complained that it was the roughest circuit they had ever raced on—including Britain's Nigel Mansell, who led the race from the start, but broke a driveshaft after hitting a wall on the last corner. Mansell attempted to push his car over the finish line before collapsing with heat exhaustion.

Fair Park

Type: city center park
Location: Dallas, Texas, United States
Circuit Length: 2.41 miles (3.87 km)
Lap Record: 1:45.353 (N Lauda/McLaren-Porsche 1984)

Detroit Grand Prix

Another American foray into the world of urban Grand Prix racing, the Detroit Street Circuit made its unofficial debut in 1982, during which year no fewer than three Grand Prix events were held in North America. The following year, the removal of a tortuous loop between Woodbridge Street and Congress saw Ayrton Senna shave 10 seconds off Alain Prost's previous lap record and the circuit went on to host a further five Grands Prix between 1984 and 1988—for many, a classic period in motor racing.

The Circuit had something of the appeal of Monaco, thanks to the two tunnel sections and 18 turns along its 2.49 mile (4.01 km) length—although, as with all urban tracks, there were limits to how well each corner could be set up for racing. The waterfront start was followed almost immediately by two sharp left-hand handers that doubled back onto Altwater Street, before a 90-degree right turn into Saint Antoine Street. After another right turn into East Jefferson Street, came a series of three progressively tighter left-hand turns into Congress Street East, which curved right, then left,

Detroit Street Circuit

Type: city center street
Location: Detroit, Michigan, United States
Circuit Length: 2.49 miles (4.01 km)
Lap Record: 1:40.464 (A Senna/Lotus-Honda 1987)

before a 90-degree left turn into Beaubien Street. One block later, the circuit turned right into Larned Street and through the smaller of two tunnels along a modest straight that culminated in a left turn into Woodward Avenue, followed by a right onto West Jefferson Avenue. At Washington Boulevard, it was left over the Expressway and into the four bends of Kodak Camera Corner before heading back toward the waterfront and left into the Goodyear Tunnel. Another two bends in Altwater Street presented drivers with a tricky Esses at Ford Corner, before the final dash through a chicane to complete the lap.

During its brief Formula One career, the narrow confines of Detroit Street Circuit acquired something of a reputation for carnage, with around half the field failing to finish each race. The situation was not helped by the patchy quality of the surface, and by the smaller-than-usual run-off areas, which saw a lot of drivers fall victim to punctures.

BELOW: *Chico Serra (Fittipaldi F8D-Ford Cosworth) leads Keke Rosberg and Derek Daly (both Williams FW08-Ford Cosworth) at the 1982 Detroit Grand Prix.*

ABOVE: *Alain Prost and Rene Arnoux (both Renault RE30Bs), lead Didier Pironi and Patrick Tambay (both Ferrari 126C2s) at the start of the 1982 Dutch Grand Prix.*

Dutch Grand Prix

The spectacular dune-peppered Circuit Park Zandvoort, traditional home of the Dutch Grand Prix, upholds the long-held belief in motor racing circles that rural racing circuits should not only follow the contours of the land but also embrace natural hazards. Certainly, there were times at Zandvoort when the occasional sandstorm made life more difficult for drivers, but such freak occurrences could do nothing to dampen the enthusiasm of the spectators who lined the undulating 2.63 mile (4.23 km) track. A Grand Prix was held there almost every year from 1952 until the last Formula One race in 1985 (the only gaps being 1955–57 and 1972). It was much missed by drivers.

There had been some form of road racing circuit on the dunes at Zandvoort since 1927 and races took place there until the outbreak of World War II. During the hostilities of 1940, advancing German troops unwittingly did the local Dutch populace a favor by laying access roads across the dunes to the north of the neighboring seaside resort. After the war this road system led to the first incarnation of the race circuit, where motor racing recommenced in 1948 with a series of non-championship races.

Zandvoort has many good vantage points; and the highest dune in the center of the track offers an almost clear view of every turn. Some of these bends carry names that long ago found their way into motor racing history, including Scheivlak Corner and the Tarzan Hairpin at the end of the pit straight. Just as interesting for the spectator was the exceptionally fast back stretch, which was later ruined by the installation of a chicane. The circuit includes a total of 14 bends of varying severity, a lightly wooded section, and, of course, the dunes themselves. It remains open, and rounds of various European motorsport championships are held there to this day.

Circuit Park Zandvoort

Type: purpose-built seaside
Location: 15 miles (24 km) west of Amsterdam, Netherlands
Circuit Length: 2.63 miles (4.23 km)
Lap Record: 1:16.538 (A Prost/McLaren-TAG 1985)

European Grand Prix

In 2006, it was announced that the German Nürburgring circuit, former home of the European Grand Prix, would henceforth host the German Grand Prix in alternate years with its sister circuit, Hochenheim. A search was hurriedly launched for an alternative venue for the former race, and in 2008 the inaugural race was held at the Street Circuit in Valencia, Spain—the first of a scheduled seven.

The 3.36 mile (5.41 km) Hermann Tilke-designed circuit

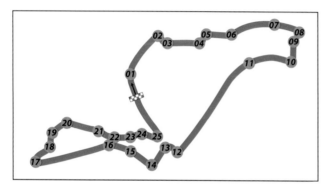

Valencia Street Circuit

Type: street circuit around docks
Location: Port of Valencia, Spain
Circuit Length: 3.36 miles (5.41 km)
Lap Record: 1:38.708 (F Massa/Ferrari 2008)

offers some uniquely appealing features for drivers and spectators alike, including 25 corners that range from taxing chicanes to tricky esses and fast, heart-in-the-mouth open bends. The straight containing the pits is balanced by a long back straight with a fast entry where drivers can easily achieve speeds in excess of 190 mph (300 kph) before braking hard for the right-hander at the end. Another feature of the track is the 450 feet (137 meters) long swing-bridge that allows vessels access to the marina.

The circuit is divided into four zones, the principal being the 'red' zone where the former port warehouses have been turned into pit-lane garages along the start-finish straight. Next is the 'green' Malvarossa zone, which is the least costly for spectators, and the 'blue' Nazaret zone, which offers a grandstand view of the hairpin after the swing-bridge. There is more seating in the 'yellow' Grao zone located behind the paddock. And, just as at Monaco, the marina at Valencia has been opened to visiting boats, making it the second motor racing venue to have direct access from the Mediterranean.

Street circuits tend to be narrow and twisty, which limits both outright speed and also the possibilities for overtaking—although the guarantee of action at close quarters seldom fails to excite spectators. The Valencia circuit largely overcomes these drawbacks by being unusually wide at an average of around 45 feet (14 meters), with several overtaking points and safe run-offs. As such, it offers a clear pointer as to how other street circuits might be designed in the future.

BELOW: *Felipe Massa (Ferrari F2008) crossing the trademark bridge of the Valencia Street Circuit during his winning race at the 2008 European Grand Prix.*

French Grand Prix

Bugatti Circuit

Type: permanent circuit
Location: close to town of Le Mans, France
Circuit Length: 2.75 miles (4.42 km)
Lap Record: 1:36.7 (G Hill/Lotus-Ford Cosworth 1967)

ABOVE: *Chris Amon (Ferrari 312) leads Denny Hulme (Brabham BT24 Repco) during the 1967 French Grand Prix at the Bugatti Circuit.*

In the land where motor racing began, one circuit has remained synonymous with the sport throughout its history—Le Mans. To date, only one French Grand Prix has taken place there—the first, in 1906. But in addition to hosting the famous 24-hour sports car and motorcycle endurance races, Le Mans is the permanent home of many less high-profile motorsport events, including single-seater and classic races, touring car competitions, and track days. Rumors continue to circulate that Formula One racing will one day return there—especially following the demise of the French Grand Prix at Magny-Cours.

In fact, there are two circuits at Le Mans. The 24-hour races use the full 8.5 mile (13.68 km) long Circuit de la Sarthe, which is extended by using public roads. Lying within this is the 2.75 mile (4.42 km) fully enclosed Bugatti Circuit—named for Ettore Bugatti, the French-domiciled Italian whose splendid blue-painted road and racing cars became one of motoring's most iconic marques during the 1920s and 30s. The company's success at Le Mans culminated in two victories in the 24 Hours for driver Jean-Pierre Wimille (in 1937 with Robert Benoist and in 1939 with Pierre Veyron).

The Bugatti circuit sets out in a clockwise direction from the permanent Le Mans start/finish line for a fast entry into Dunlop Curve before hitting another short straight. At this point the extended circuit continues straight while the Bugatti Circuit turns into the La Chapelle right-hand hairpin. From there, another short straight takes drivers up to the left-handed Museum Curve, which pitches the cars back toward another tight right-hander known as Garage Vert. This hairpin is followed by a medium-length straight to the left-right Esses at Chemin aux Boeufs, and then the double apex right-hander of Garage Bleu. The drive is completed by a medium-fast left-hand turn into the double right-hand bend of Raccordement, at which point the cars re-enter the La Sarthe Circuit and end the lap.

French Grand Prix

Circuit Charade

Type: permanent circuit
Location: close to the town of Clermont-Ferrand, France
Circuit Length: 5.00 miles (8.05 km)
Lap Record: 2:53.9 (C Amon/Matra 1972)

The Circuit de Charade, also known as the Circuit Louis Rosier, was home to the French Grand Prix in 1965, 1969, 1970, and 1972. Located in the heart of France's volcanic Massif Central region, close to city of Clermont-Ferrand—the headquarters of the Michelin tire company—the circuit is built around the edge of an extinct volcano and has motor sporting connections that date back to 1958, when motorcycle racing began there.

While the Charade circuit's picturesque hillside location undoubtedly heightened its appeal, it also presented

problems for top-class racers. Drivers of the period reported that it resembled a shorter, twistier Nürburgring. And although the track was cleaned for Formula One racing, several drivers were struck by loose stones that found their way onto the surface—including the Austrian Helmut Marko, whose career was ended in 1972 when he was hit in the eye. Although Marko's injury spelled the end of Formula One racing at the venue, a smaller circuit of just 2.4 miles (3.86 km) was developed in the early 1990s to host local and national race series.

The Grand Prix circuit involved numerous changes in direction, but only 14 named bends. The start/finish line was short, culminating in a tight left-hander that opened out into a medium-length straight leading to Manson Curve. Then came a fast downhill section which ran to the left at Golf, followed by a series of bends leading to the right-hand hairpin of Belvedere. The circuit continued to thread its way toward Le Jumeaux before arriving at Gravenoire and another sequence of bends. From here, a second fast downhill stretch took competitors toward Champreaux and a series of esses, followed by a narrow section of track leading to the left-hand hairpin at Petit Pont. After that came more bends and another right-hand hairpin, followed by the faster and memorably challenging left-hander at Tredes. A left-handed sweep into Rosier, followed by another right-hand hairpin into the start/finish area, completed the lap.

BELOW: *Jochen Rindt (Lotus 49B-Ford Cosworth) on his way to taking first place in the 1969 French Grand Prix at Circuit Charade.*

ABOVE: *Mauricio Gugelmin (March CG891 Judd) is involved in a huge crash at the start of the 1989 French Grand Prix at Circuit Paul Ricard.*

French Grand Prix

The Circuit Paul Ricard was founded in 1969 by the French drinks magnate of the same name. A long-time fan of motor racing, Ricard chose a site high in the hills 25 miles (40 km) north of the Mediterranean port of Marseille for his new circuit, which was built from the outset to accommodate various different formulae. The original track was 3.6 miles (5.79 km) in length and was generally felt to be one of the safest in the world until the popular Italian driver Elio de Angelis was killed there after a crash during practice for the 1986 French Grand Prix. This led to a number of safety modifications, including a shortening of Europe's longest straight, the Mistral, and the last five Grand Prixs to be held at the Paul Ricard (between 1986 and 1990) took place over the shortened 2.36 miles (3.8 km) circuit.

The Paul Ricard track ran in a clockwise direction, starting with the start/finish straight running alongside the pit lane, followed by a fast left-right kink at Verrière. A short straight ended in a right-left-right chicane followed by a further short straight before the double-apex right-hand bend at Saint Beaurne. Next came the challenging left-hand bend at L'école and the start of the Mistral Straight, which was punctuated by a chicane partway along its length. The track continued through the sweeping right-hander at Signes, followed by another short straight that ended in the tightening right-hand curve of Beausset. Then came a final complex of four bends— Bendor, Village, Tour, and the hairpin Virage du Pont—which lead back to the fast finishing straight.

The basic layout of the circuit remains as it was, and is now owned by Excellis, a company owned by Formula One supremo Bernie Ecclestone. He has added a luxury hotel and invested heavily in upgrading all aspects of the track and its facilities. It is now known as the Paul Ricard High-Tech Test Track. The popular Provence circuit now includes a track-drenching facility and state-of-the art run-off areas.

Circuit Paul Ricard

Type: permanent circuit
Location: Le Castellet, France
Circuit Length: 3.6 miles (5.79 km) up to 1985;
2.36 miles (3.8 km) 1986–90
Lap Record: 1:39.914 (K Rosberg/Williams-Honda 1985)

French Grand Prix

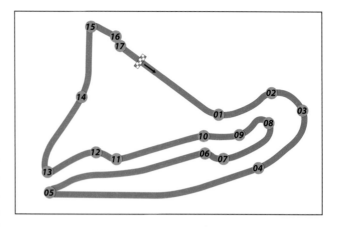

For a nation so closely associated with the history of Grand Prix motor racing, it could be argued that the French Grand Prix should be regarded as the high point of the Formula One season. It is therefore ironic that the Circuit de Nevers Magny-Cours, the track that has hosted the race more times than any other, remains one of the most controversial choices of venue in the calendar—not least because it is heartily disliked by most competitors and spectators.

The 2009 season marks the circuit's 50th anniversary. It began life in 1959 as a kart track, built on land owned by the mayor of Magny-Cours, Jean Bernigaud. By 1961, it had grown into the 1.5 mile (2.41 km) long circuit and had been given the name of the Jean Behra track. Ten years later it was again extended and by then was 2.4 miles (3.86 km) in length. In 1988, the facilities were once again significantly extended in order to attract the Formula One circus and the new complex, which also included a technology park, was subsequently opened by French president, François Mitterand. The French Grand Prix duly moved to Magny-Cours in 1991. Subsequent improvements to the circuit included a slight extension in 1992 and further extensions in 2003, mainly to improve safety run-off areas, after which it remained largely unchanged until 2008.

Magny-Cours was always a very quick track, with a typical lap starting on the wide start/finish straight leading into the fast left-handed Grande Courbe. After another short straight, a slight left led up to the medium-speed Estoril right-hand bend; then on to the back straight, which featured the fast kink right at Golf half way. The highly challenging Adelaide Hairpin was the scene of countless indiscretions as drivers

Magny-Cours Circuit

Type: permanent circuit
Location: 10 miles (16 km) south of Nevers, France
Circuit Length: 2.4 miles (3.86 km) 1971–91;
2.63 (4.23 km) 1992–2002; 2.73 miles (4.39 km) 2003–08
Lap Record: 1:15.377 (M Schumacher/Ferrari 2004)

struggled under hard braking to find the best line through the bend to the right. The next section comprised the fast Nürburgring right hand bend, followed by an equally fast left-hand curve to the turn known as '180' with its difficult tightening exit. Then came the Imola Complex of right and left hand bends, followed by the tight-right Chateau d'Eaubend, a straight leading to another right-handed bend at Lycée then through the chicane at the start of the pit straight.

PREVIOUS SPREAD: *The 2007 French Grand Prix at Magny-Cours, Nevers: Vitantonio Liuzzi (Toro Rosso STR02-Ferrari) and Anthony Davidson (Super Aguri SA07-Honda) collide and end their races early on.*

BELOW: *Nelson Piquet Jr. (Renault R28) leads Lewis Hamilton (McLaren MP4-23 Mercedes) during the 2008 French Grand Prix at Magny-Cours.*

ABOVE: *Juan Manuel Fangio (Alfa Romeo 159, number 4), Giuseppe Farina (Alfa Romeo 159, number 2), and Alberto Ascari (Ferrari 375, number 12) on the front row of the 1951 French Grand Prix at Reims-Gueux.*

French Grand Prix

The main road circuit of Reims-Gueux lies just to the west of the city of Reims—capital of France's champagne-producing region and a highly appropriate place to stage Formula One victory celebrations. The first French Grand Prix was held there in 1950, the very first year that the Formula One championship was contested, and the circuit hosted a further 11 races until the last one in 1966, which was won by Jack Brabham in his Brabham/Repco.

A triangular-shaped track was first established between the villages of Thillois and Virage de Gueux in 1926, at a time when it was quite permissible to chop down trees or even demolish any building that got in the way of the creation of the fastest possible circuit. In essence, a lap of Reims consisted of a fast long road between the two villages, together with a section along the RN31 to Garenne to create the corners at the end of each of the circuit's triangular sections. This became the scene of many epic speed battles, as drivers fought to take advantage of each other's slipstreams. Later, the original route

Reims-Gueux

Type: road circuit
Location: 10 miles (16 km) west of Reims, France
Circuit Length: 5.1 miles (8.21 km)
Lap Record: 2:11.3 (L Bandini/Ferrari 1966)

was extended to create a more challenging Grand Prix circuit by taking in the corners of Virage de la Hovette, Brettelle Nord, and Virage de Muizon before returning toward Garenne.

Reims-Gueux was still in regular use until 1972, when operating problems and shortage of money forced the historically important circuit to close. More recently, in 1997, an attempt was made to stage a commemorative event there; local by-laws prohibited this so the event never happened. The original pit-lane buildings can still be seen beside the public road, though they have fallen into sad disrepair. In 2002 much of the original racetrack was destroyed, encouraging the formation of a non-profit organization known as 'Les Amis du Circuit de Gueux' whose aim is to keep memories of the Reims circuit alive. It has been successful in preserving some of the original track.

French Grand Prix

The road-based Rouen-Les-Essarts circuit hosted its first Formula One event in 1951 and the French Grand Prix was held there the following year. Further stagings of the event took place in 1957, 1962, 1964, and 1968, when a fatal crash by promising French driver Jo Schlesser in his new Honda Formula One car effectively put an end to the circuit's Grand Prix aspirations.

Originally developed by the Automobile Club of Normandy, Rouen-Les-Essarts was laid out on public roads in the undulating countryside to the west of Rouen and featured a blisteringly quick downhill stretch through a series of fast bends to a cobbled hairpin, before returning uphill through a densely wooded area. The circuit was extended in 1962, adding just over a mile to its original length of 3.16 miles (5.08 km).

The hazardous nature of the layout was due in no small part to the fact that many of its 13 main corners occurred on hilly stretches that rendered them completely blind to drivers. Following Schlesser's death, top Scots driver Gerry Birrell was killed at the same spot in 1973. Two years later, two rising

BELOW: *Tony Maggs (Cooper T60-Climax) leads Masten Gregory (Lotus 24-BRM) during the 1962 French Grand Prix at Rouen-les-Essarts.*

Rouen-Les-Essarts

Type: road circuit
Location: 3 miles (5 km) south of Rouen, France
Circuit Length: 4.06 miles (8.14 km)
Lap Record: 2:11.4 (J Brabham/Brabham-Climax 1964)

young French Formula Three stars—Denis Dayan and Jean-Luc Salomon—both died in crashes, the second of which also saw veteran French driver Bob Wollek seriously injured when his car plunged into trees.

Following these unfortunate incidents, chicanes were built to keep speeds in check and the circuit underwent further alterations when a new motorway was carried across it. In this new, improved guise, Rouen went on to become one of the biggest events in the Formula Two calendar, with victories there going to such household names as Eddie Cheever, Emerson Fittipaldi, Bruno Giacomelli , Ronnie Peterson, and Frenchman Jean-Pierre Jarier. In 1978, the circuit also became the home of the French Formula Three series, which was run there until 1993. But as speeds rose in more modern cars, the undulating Rouen-Les-Essarts track was deemed too dangerous, even for less powerful racing cars.

ABOVE: *Gilles Villeneuve (Ferrari 312T4) leads Rene Arnoux (Renault RS10) at the finish after an epic battle during the 1979 French Grand Prix at Dijon-Prenois. They finished in second and third positions respectively.*

French Grand Prix and Swiss Grand Prix

Popularly known as the 'Mexican Hat', due to its sombrero shape, the Circuit de Dijon-Prenois not only played host to the French Grand Prix in 1974, 1977, 1979, 1981, and 1984, but also to the Swiss Grand Prix of 1982. The circuit was also the scene of the first victory by a turbocharged Grand Prix racing car—the Renault of Jean-Pierre Jabouille in 1979.

Perched above the city of Dijon, the hilltop circuit's original 1972 layout and one-minute lap times proved to be too short, leading to severe overcrowding problems as back markers too

Dijon-Prenois

Type: permanent circuit
Location: 7 miles (11 km) west of Dijon, France
Circuit Length: 2.36 miles (3.8 km)
Lap Record: 1:05.257 (A Prost/McLaren-TAG 1984)

quickly became caught up with the race leaders. Consequently, in 1975, the track was extended to incorporate the Parabolique hairpin, which increased its length to 2.36 miles (3.8 km), as well as providing the circuit with its new nickname. With hindsight, it seems remarkable that the first French Grand Prix was held there at all, given that there was as much overcrowding off the track as there was on it. The eight slowest qualifying teams from the previous Grand Prix were obliged to vacate the paddock altogether and only 22 cars were permitted to start the race—a decision which mystified some and greatly annoyed others.

The long straight incorporating the start/finish area ends with the accurately named right turn known as the Double-Droite de Villeroy, before rising to the 'S' des Sabeliers. Drivers then negotiate the fast left-hand sweeper at Gauche da la Bretelle, before reaching the surprisingly fast Parabolique to the right. After another short, undulating straight comes the left-handed Double-Gauche de la Bretelle, followed by a brief uphill run to the fast right-hand sweeper at Virage de la Combe. Then the route dives downhill again to the Courbe de Pouas right-hander and the Ligne Droite de la Fouine that signifies the end of the lap.

German Grand Prix

AVUS

Type: city circuit
Location: suburbs of Berlin, Germany
Circuit Length: 5.15 miles (8.29 km)
Lap Record: 2:04.5 (Tony Brooks/Ferrari 246 1959)

The tight oval of the AVUS street circuit, which threads its way through the Grünewald district of southwest Berlin, seems an unlikely venue for a Grand Prix race—and in fact, only one has taken place there since World War II. The name 'AVUS' is derived from Automobil Verkehrs und Ubung Strasse, which means 'road for automobile driving and exercises'. The circuit which was originally built in 1921 was 12.14 miles (19.54 km) long and was little more than a pair of long motorway straights linked by turns at each end—the Nordschleife to the north and the Südschleife to the south. After the war the circuit was reduced to 5.15 miles (8.29 km), with the 13.5 yards (12.35 meters) radius Südschleife terminating close to the border of the newly established Russian sector. At the same time the Nordschleife was banked and made wider, with a radius of 54 yards (49.38 meters), to make it an even faster part of the circuit, as well as the only purpose-built section.

As well as the single Formula One race, the AVUS has been used for the German Touring Car Championship, the International Touring Car Championship, and for Formula Three races. Because of its rather bland layout, the only way to overtake was to dive out of the slipstream of another car and brake heavily into one of the turns. This made the circuit a serious challenge for the drivers and their cars and many argued it was an unsuitable circuit for Formula One.

Despite this, the German Grand Prix went ahead there in 1959 and was won by Englishman Tony Brooks. Unfortunately, during the same weekend, the famous French driver Jean Behra was killed when his Porsche flew off the unprotected north banking during a sports car race. The banking was dismantled in 1967. More recently, chicanes were installed in an attempt to slow down the competing cars and to introduce an additional element of challenge on the long straights. Yet in 1995 the circuit's dangerous reputation was underlined when British touring driver, Keith Odor, died following a collision at the Nordschleife. The circuit ceased being used for racing in 1998.

ABOVE: *Tony Brooks (Ferrari Dino 246) leads Stirling Moss (Cooper T51 Climax) on the banked Nordschleife turn during the 1959 German Grand Prix at AVUS.*

German Grand Prix

Although it has been through several major transformations since it first began to be used for Formula One racing back in 1970, the Hockenheimring is a superb venue for both drivers and spectators alike. The circuit was first opened as a motorsport center in 1932 and served as a test track for both Mercedes and Auto Union before the original triangular layout was altered to something closer to its present form in 1938. It has always been notoriously fast, claiming the lives of Jim Clark in a Formula Two race in 1968 and Formula One driver Patrick Depailler in 1980. New chicanes were later added at the locations of both fatal crashes in an effort to cut speeds and make the circuit safer for the drivers.

When Grand Prix racing began at the Hochenheimring, the circuit was heavily wooded at its eastern end which prevented spectators from viewing the action. But in 2001, $60 million (62 million Euros) was invested to reduce the length of the circuit from around 4.23 miles (6.81 km) to 2.83 miles (4.55 km). At the same time, spectator facilities were greatly improved and the run-off areas were upgraded to make them among the safest in the world. The building of an arena just before the start/finish area made it possible to accommodate non-sporting events, such as rock concerts. However, Hockenheim remains first and foremost a multi-discipline motorsports circuit, and during an average season plays host

NEXT SPREAD: *First corner action at the start of the 2006 German Grand Prix at Hockenheim.*

BELOW: *Rene Arnoux and Alain Prost (both Renault RE30Bs) lead the field away at the start of the 1982 German Grand Prix at Hockenheim.*

to everything from single-seat formulae, classic, sports, and touring car racing to drifting championships and drag racing.

From the start/finish area near the pits, drivers first of all have to contend with the fast right Nordkurve and a short straight before reaching the tight right-hander and extended fast left that leads to the sweeping Parabolika curve. Following this, a right-hand hairpin leads to a short back straight, after which a right-left-right series of corners leads to another short straight. The track then turns right at the Mobil 1 curve into the stadium complex, which incorporates the famous Sachs hairpin. One last left-right-right series of bends before the Südkurve completes the lap.

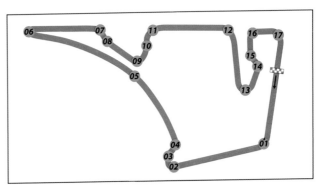

Hockenheimring

Type: permanent circuit
Location: 15 miles (24 km) west of Heidelberg, Germany
Circuit Length: 2.83 miles (4.55 km)
Lap Record: 1:13.780 (K Raikkonen/McLaren-Mercedes 2004)

German Grand Prix, European Grand Prix and Luxembourg Grand Prix

Few Grand Prix venues in the motor racing world possess more charisma than the Nürburgring, located amid the spectacular scenery of the Eifel Mountains in western Germany. The original 14.16 mile (22.79 km) long Nordschleife circuit was built in 1927 as the authorities became increasingly concerned about the safety aspects of racing on public roads. It is still used today as a racing circuit and, unusually, it's also open to the public who can pay by the lap to drive their own cars on the famous track. However, since 1984 Formula One racing has taken place on a shorter circuit of 3.2 miles (5.15 km), which is more accommodating to the TV cameras, as well as being far safer for the drivers.

Capable of both attracting and accommodating vast crowds of spectators, this circuit, too, has been modified at regular intervals, with new chicanes, improved run-off areas, and even greater driver challenges. It has hosted the German and European Grands Prix from time to time and also the Luxembourg Grand Prix in 1997 and 98 as well as many other sporting events including single-seater formulae, motorcycle and 24-hour endurance racing, sports car and saloon racing, and even truck racing.

The Nürburgring is also used by the world's leading car makers as a proving ground for their performance cars, and several manufacturers maintain permanent technical facilities nearby, not least because there is enormous competition surrounding the fastest lap time by a production car.

While the original Nordschleife circuit contains some of the most famous-name bends in motor racing history—the Flugplatz, Karusell, Hohe Acht, and Pflanzgarten—even the shortened Grand Prix circuit contains some of the fastest and most difficult bends in the current Formula One calendar. The only real overtaking opportunities are at the highly-demanding Castrol S-Bend at the end of the start/finish straight and the Michael Schumacher-designed Veedol-Schikane which comes on the run down from the Bit-Kurve on one of the fastest downhill sections in the world.

Nürburgring

Type: permanent circuit
Location: Village of Nürburg, west of Bonn, Germany
Circuit Length: 3.20 miles (5.15 km)
Lap Record: 1:29.468 (M Schumacher/Ferrari 2004)

BELOW: *Mike Hawthorn (Lancia-Ferrari D50) leads Juan Manuel Fangio (Maserati 250F) in the closing laps of the 1957 Grand Prix at Nürburgring. Fangio later passed Hawthorn to win his greatest race.*

ABOVE: *Heikki Kovalainen (McLaren MP4-23 Mercedes)—who won the race—leads Nico Rosberg (Williams FW30 Toyota) during the 2008 Hungarian Grand Prix.*

Hungarian Grand Prix

The Hungaroring at Mogyoród near Budapest made its debut as a Grand Prix circuit in 1986. It was altered in 2002/03 by extending the start/finish straight and some of the faster back stretches, resulting in its present length of 2.72 miles (4.38 km). Known locally as the 'Shallow Plate', its location in a valley surrounded by rolling countryside creates a natural viewing bowl for spectators and it means that the vast majority of the action can be seen from any one point around the circuit.

The circuit has become a popular venue for racegoers from all over central Europe and also attracts a high proportion of Finnish fans, who drive there via the Baltic states and Poland.

With 16 bends ranging in radius from around 20 yards (18 meters) to 400 yards (370 meters), the Hungaroring presents plenty of overtaking opportunities for drivers—made all the more exciting by the opportunities to view the action from above. At almost exactly 1 km (0.62 miles) in length, the start/finish straight is also long enough for most Formula One cars to reach speeds of around 200 mph (320 kph), before going hard on the brakes for the following hairpin bend which offers excellent overtaking opportunities.

Thereafter, drivers progress through another fast stretch with a right kink toward a sharp left turn that doubles back into a right-left-right hairpin and the first of two back straights. A kink to the right at the end is followed abruptly by a turn to the left and a sweeping right-hander leading to the right-left hairpin of turns eight and nine. Sharp left and right turns break

Hungaroring

Type: permanent circuit
Location: 12.5 miles (20 km) northeast of Budapest, Hungary
Circuit Length: 2.72 miles (4.38 km)
Lap Record: 1:19.071 (M Schumacher/Ferrari 2004)

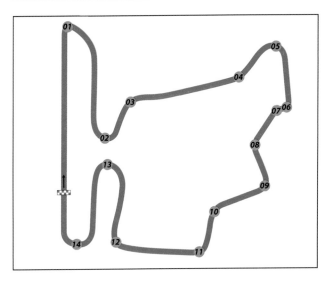

up the otherwise fast back section, which ends in a 90-degree right-hander that precedes the second straight. Then comes a loop, crowned by a fairly tight 180-degree left-hand turn, before the slightly quicker right-hander that returns the driver to the flat-out start/finish straight.

Indianapolis 500 and United States Grand Prix

North America may possess its fair share of conventional road circuits, but it is oval tracks that predominate. But only one oval has become a by-word for American motorsport—the Indianapolis Motor Speedway, usually referred to as just 'Indy' or 'The Brickyard'. It's called that because the start/finish line was marked by a line of bricks that remain there to this day.

When Formula One started in 1950, Indianapolis was the only race held outside Europe and it was very different for both cars and drivers. Despite this, the Indy Speedway hosted 11 Grands Prix between 1950 and 1960. At first, many European drivers did not cross the Atlantic to compete and most races were won by local drivers, in Offenhauser-powered cars. Having said that, Jim Clark won the 1965 Indy 500 in his Lotus-Ford Formula One car and the following year Graham Hill took the checkered flag in his Lola-Ford, which just went to prove that Indy was not the exclusive preserve of American cars and drivers.

While the Indy 500 today is still held on the oval track, the modern Indianapolis Grand Prix circuit combines an extensive infield area with much of the original south curve and the west straight. It also runs in a clockwise direction in contrast to the oval circuit. It has played host to the United States Grand Prix eight times between 2000 and 2007, despite its reputation for being an extremely tough track.

In 2006, 10 cars went out following collisions on the track but there was an even worse result in 2005, when only six cars took to the grid. Following several tire failures during practice, which were blamed on the newly resurfaced track, Michelin advised the teams that used its tyres not to take part on safety grounds. This left only the Bridgestone-shod Ferrari, Jordan, and Minardi teams to contest the race. Michael Schumacher eventually won, but it was a completely hollow victory: the controversy surrounding the event greatly tarnished the reputation of Formula One in the United States and represents one of the sport's most inglorious moments.

Indianapolis Motor Speedway

Type: permanent circuit
Location: Indianapolis, United States
Circuit Length: 2.60 miles (4.18 km)
Lap Record: 1:10.399 (R Barrichello/Ferrari 2004)

BELOW: *The cars and teams on the grid before the start of the 2007 United States Grand Prix at Indianapolis.*

Italian Grand Prix

Autodromo Nazionale Monza

Type: permanent circuit
Location: 9.3 miles (15 km) northeast of Milan, Italy
Circuit Length: 3.59 miles (5.78 km)
Lap Record: 1:21.046 (R Barrichello/Ferrari 2004)

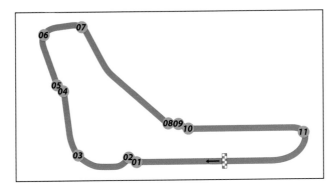

The Autodromo Nazionale di Monza, located within a park to the north of the city of the same name, is the most famous motor racing circuit in Italy and one of the best-known in the world. It was built in 1922 by the Milan Automobile Club on the club's 25th anniversary and had the backing of Fiat, Alfa Romeo, and other Italian car manufacturers, who were looking for somewhere to test their latest vehicles with an eye toward the export market. The new circuit was designed from the outset to host the Italian Grand Prix which had formerly been held at Montichiari near Brescia, a track that was exciting and quick but lacked facilities.

Monza's circuit was always a high-speed layout that incorporated both a 3.4 mile (5.5 km) road track and a 2.8 mile (4.5 km) oval with banked sections that boosted top speeds without unduly compromising safety. The original Grand Prix road track has remained largely unaltered for most of its existence, although concerns about its high speed and consequent safety, have seen the addition of speed-reducing chicanes and improved run-off areas from time to time. Notable exceptions were some of the Grands Prix in the 1950s and 1960s for which the circuit was extended—a crossover created an elongated figure-of-eight layout with a total length of 6.2 miles (10 km) that included the banked section of the oval track.

In common with other famous motor racing venues, Monza's corners have become famous throughout the world. They include the Variante del Rettifilo, the tight chicane that's the first hazard the drivers meet after the start of the race. This is followed by the fast Curva Grande and yet another chicane at Variante della Roggia. A short straight is then followed by the challenging double right-handed Curve di Lesmo, which in turn leads onto the equally challenging Curva del Serraglio. From here, there's a short straight under the original banked oval and into the fast Variante Ascari chicane. This is followed by another short straight and finally into the long right-handed 180-degree Curva Parabolica that leads back to the start/finish straight.

BELOW: *Michael Schumacher (Ferrari 248F1) leads Robert Kubica (Sauber F1.06-BMW) during the 2006 Italian Grand Prix at Monza.*

Japanese Grand Prix

Fuji International Speedway—so-called because the original organizers intended it as a venue for NASCAR racing—was opened in 1965 against the spectacular backdrop of the volcanic Mount Fuji. In the event, NASCAR racing never arrived and the circuit was converted to a 2.7 mile (4.36 km) road racing track. After a series of accidents, the banked section that had been a feature of the original track was eliminated and the circuit was made fractionally longer.

The first Grand Prix to be held there was in 1976, when

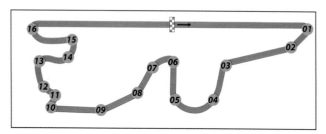

Fuji Speedway

Type: permanent circuit
Location: 40 miles (64 km) west of Yokohama, Japan
Circuit Length: 2.83 miles (4.55 km)
Lap Record: 1:18.426 (F Massa/Ferrari 2008)

James Hunt and Nikki Lauda battled for the World Championship in torrential rain in a race eventually won by Mario Andretti. The following year, French driver Gilles Villeneuve was involved in a horrific crash that saw the deaths of two spectators, causing the circuit to be dropped from the Formula One calendar. Under the ownership of the Toyota Motor Corporation, Fuji was reinstated as a venue for the Japanese Grand Prix for 2007 and 2008. Despite disappointing attendance figures, it has been announced that henceforth the Fuji International Speedway will alternate with the Suzuka Circuit to host the Japanese Grand Prix.

A lap of the circuit begins on the mile-long start/finish straight, which is one of the longest in the current calendar. Drivers then have to brake hard for the right-hand hairpin at the end of the straight before powering through the gently right-curving Second Corner to the fast left-handed Coca-Cola Corner—a blind exit that is unforgiving of those who fail to take the correct line. The track curves gently to the right between Coca-Cola and Fifth Corner, then slows right down for Hair Pin Corner, before opening up again on a right-curving section that is ideal for overtaking. At the end of this section is Dunlop Corner, an extended right then left chicane which precedes a complex of turns that includes the Thirteenth Corner, Netz Corner, and, finally, the right-handed Panasonic Corner. Drivers here must strive to maximize their exit speed to make full use of the Main Straight, providing one of the most exciting grandstand views in Formula One.

BELOW: *Fernando Alonso (Renault R28)—on his way to claiming first position—leads Felipe Massa (Ferrari F2008) during the 2008 Japanese Grand Prix at Fuji Speedway.*

ABOVE: *Fernando Alonso (Renault R26) passes Ralf Schumacher (Toyota TF106B) on his way to winning the 2006 Japanese Grand Prix at Suzuka.*

Japanese Grand Prix

Originally designed in 1966 by the distinguished Dutch track-builder John Hugenholtz (1914–1995), Suzuka International Racing Course is one of the few circuits in the world to employ a figure-of-eight crossover layout. At a total length of 3.6 miles (5.80 km), its intricate and highly technical layout offers a considerable challenge for drivers: in particular, the changes in elevation create a number of blind bends where judging the exit can be difficult. Equally, the circuit never fails to provide some thrilling incidents for those watching, given added spice by the fact that the Japanese Grand Prix often determines the outcome of the World Championship.

Now owned by the Honda Car Company, Suzuka is home to a number of world-class motorsport events. In addition, it hosted an unbroken run of 20 Grand Prix races from 1987 until 2006, when it was dropped from the Formula One calendar in favor of Fuji. Reinstated for the 2009 season, it is henceforth scheduled to alternate with Fuji as a venue for the Japanese Grand Prix.

A lap of the track commences one-third of the way up the start/finish straight, which leads into the extended right-handed

Suzuka Circuit

Type: permanent circuit
Location: Suzuka City, Japan
Circuit Length: 3.6 miles (5.80 km)
Lap Record: 1:31.540 (K Räikkönen/McLaren 2005)

hairpin of Turn One—also known as First. After a short straight comes a sequence of five bends, culminating in the fast Dunlop left-hander which leads into the mid-speed right at Degner and a tighter right at Turn Nine. The circuit then ducks under the crossover bridge to the fast right-hander at Turn Ten, followed by the sharply left-handed Hairpin. Drivers continue through another double-apex right-hander and on to the very fast Spoon—an extended left-hander that leads to the Crossover, the fastest stretch of the track. This is followed by the incredibly challenging left-handed 130R, which has undergone extensive modification following serious accidents in 2002 and 2003. Finally, it's into the Casio Triangle, three corners numbered 15, 16, and 17 which effectively meld into one long right hander that opens onto the start of the finishing straight.

Malaysian Grand Prix

Built on the site of a former palm oil plantation, and designed from the ground up by the celebrated German architect Hermann Tilke, the Sepang International Circuit was completed in a record 14 months. The project involved moving nearly 12 million cu yards (9 million cu meters) of earth and planting around 5,000 trees to improve the looks of the new facility. It was opened on March 9, 1999 by the Prime Minister of Malaysia.

The Sepang Circuit is one of the most easily accessible as it's only 2 miles (3 km) from Kuala Lumpur International Airport and is close to motorways and railways. Sepang's astonishing facilities include an enormous three-storey Pit Building which, as well as the 33 pits, contains all the management offices and officials' quarters. Next door is the Welcome Building which boasts shops, restaurants, and an exhibition center. On the other side of the Pit Building, reflecting the organizers' concern with safety, is a Medical Center that can be converted in an emergency into a fully-equipped hospital, complete with operating theaters.

The centrally located main grandstands guarantee fantastic views of the action, and can seat 32,000 people as well as accommodating various corporate entertainment suites. Interestingly, the grandstands are built on an east-west axis to ensure that they are protected from the sun's glare for most of the day. Further grandstands at turns 1 and 7 can seat

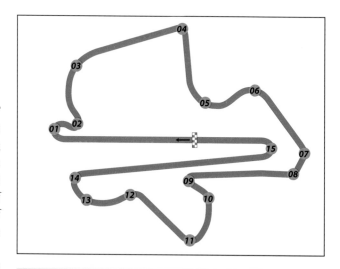

Sepang International Circuit

Type: permanent circuit
Location: Kuala Lumpur, Malaysia
Circuit Length: 3.44 miles (5.54 km)
Lap Record: 1:34.223 (J P Montoya/Williams-BMW 2004)

another 18,500 spectators and, in all, this splendid circuit has a capacity of 150,000.

At just under 3.5 miles (5.54 km) long, the full Sepang Grand Prix circuit contains 15 turns and eight straights, which means some of the highest top speeds in Formula One are seen here. The width of the track also offers plenty of overtaking opportunities. The unique parallel configuration of the start/finish and back straights, with just a single hairpin in between them, allows the track to be divided into North and South circuits for smaller events, such as kart racing.

BELOW: *Felipe Massa (Ferrari F2008) leads the field at the start of the 2008 Malaysian Grand Prix.*

ABOVE: *Jo Siffert (Lotus 49B-Ford Cosworth) follows through The Esses on the opening lap of the 1968 Mexican Grand Prix.*

Mexican Grand Prix

Autódromo Hermanos Rodríguez

Type: permanent circuit
Location: Mexico City, Mexico
Circuit Length: 2.75 miles (4.42 km)
Lap Record: 1:16.788 (N Mansell/Williams-Renault 1991)

The Magdalena Mixhuca Circuit in the heart of Mexico City hosted its first non-Championship Formula One event in 1962, the year of its opening. Despite the fact that local hero Ricardo Rodriguez, one of a pair of driver brothers, was killed in practice, the circuit hosted its first full Mexican Grand Prix the following year. A further 14 races were held there up until 1970, followed by another run from 1986 to 1992. In 1980, the tragic death of the second Rodriguez brother, Pedro, led to the circuit being renamed the Autódromo Hermanos Rodriguez in their honor.

The departure of the Formula One circus after the 1992 season was ascribed to the high altitude which, at 7,380 feet (2,250 meters), took its toll on both drivers and cars. There were also persistent problems with the surface, partly because it was built on a former lake bed that lead to subsidence, and partly because so many different race series were held there that wear was a constant problem. Since then, there have been several rumors that Grand Prix racing will return to the venue, but so far none of them has materialized.

In its heyday the circuit could be configured in a number of ways, even as an oval for stock car racing. The Grand Prix track consisted of a long start/finish straight which lead into an extremely difficult series of bends which exited onto another straight. Drivers were then faced with another awkward complex of 10 bends one after the other that finally ended on part of the oval track, after which they doubled back to the finishing line, about a third of the way down the start/finish straight. The already considerable challenges of the circuit were increased in the early days by indisciplined spectators: there was severe overcrowding at some of the corners, and too often spectators moved onto the track in an effort to gain a better view of the action. Crowd safety was eventually improved, but the venue's other shortcomings remained.

Monaco Grand Prix

By rights, the Grand Prix de Monaco—held on the narrow streets of the tiny Principality—should not exist: at just over 2 miles (3.22 km) in length, the circuit is theoretically too confined for the demands of Formula One. Yet anyone trying to find a word said against this magical venue will struggle, for Monaco truly embraces the spirit of Grand Prix motor racing.

The event predates the formation of the Formula One World Championship by several decades and was the brainchild of Anthony Noghès, president of the Monagasque Car Club. Building on the success of the Monte Carlo Rally, which had been held there since 1911, Noghès persuaded the ruling Grimaldi family to stage an invitation-only Grand Prix in 1929 to enhance the Principality's international profile.

Four years later, the basic layout of the circuit was established, with the start/finish line on the road above the harbor, followed by a tight right at Sainte Devote, then up the hill and left into Casino Square. On the exit of the Square the roads switches downhill to the Mirabeau corner, followed by the ultra-slow Lowe's Hairpin (named for the famous hotel, which later became The Grand). Then it's into the long, slightly right-hand curved tunnel before emerging back into the sunshine for the chicane at the harbor side, followed by the tricky swimming pool section. Finally, it's down to the right-hand final bend at the Gasometer (later to become known as Rascasse) and back into the start/finish straight.

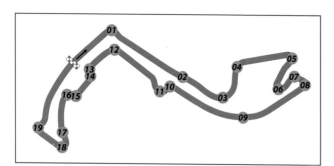

Circuit de Monaco

Type: street circuit
Location: Monte Carlo, Monaco
Circuit Length: 2.07 miles (3.34 km)
Lap Record: 1:14.439 (M Schumacher/Ferrari 2004)

Overtaking opportunities at Monaco are minimal, and the high curbs and roadside walls present a constant threat to drivers who stray off-line. Yet although it's thankfully many years since a car has gone into the harbor, the racing is always eventful at Monaco, and it remains the jewel of the Formula One calendar.

PREVIOUS SPREAD: *Lewis Hamilton (McLaren MP4-23 Mercedes) negotiates the wrecked car of Nico Rosberg (Williams FW30 Toyota) on his way to winning the 2008 Monaco Grand Prix.*

ABOVE: *Fernando Alonso (Renault R26) leads Michael Schumacher (Ferrari 248F1) during the 2006 Monaco Grand Prix. Alonso went on to win the race.*

ABOVE: *Stirling Moss (Vanwall VW5) during his winning drive at the 1958 Moroccan Grand Prix.*

Moroccan Grand Prix

Moroccan interest in motor racing dates back to 1925, when a Grand Prix was held in the Atlantic coastal city of Casablanca during the days when the nation was still a French dependency. In 1930, the event switched venues to the city's newly built Anfa Racecourse, the entry list consisting mainly of French and Monagasque drivers including the great Louis Chiron, who won a touring car race there in 1934—the last year in which the circuit hosted a Grand Prix event.

Formula One motor racing returned to Morocco in 1954 at a sports car circuit in the southern coastal resort of Agadir, where it remained for two years. But in 1957 came the Suez Crisis, which threatened to play havoc with the Grand Prix calendar due to the fuel shortages and transportation difficulties which resulted from the closure of the Suez Canal. Seizing what he perceived as a golden opportunity to supplant one of the big European Grands Prix, Sultan Mohammed V ordered the hasty construction of the Ain-Diab Street Circuit in Casablanca—a project that was completed in just six weeks.

Unfortunately for the Sultan, Europe's difficulties were

Ain-Diab

Type: street circuit
Location: Ain-Diab, Morocco
Circuit Length: 4.75 miles (7.64 km)
Lap Record: 2:22.500 (S Moss/Vanwall 1958)

quickly resolved, and although the first Formula One event to take place at the circuit attracted a world class field, it did not count toward the Championship. The winner was the celebrated French driver Jean Behra in a Maserati.

The following year, an officially sanctioned Grand Prix did take place on the dusty Ain-Diab track and was won by Englishman Stirling Moss driving a Vanwall. Sadly, the event was marred by the horrific crash of Moss's team-mate Stuart Lewis-Evans, whose engine seized (reputedly due to the dust) and sent him plunging into the barriers, his car in flames. Lewis-Evans succumbed to burns injuries back in England six days later. His death cast a shadow over the Grand Prix, which saw the Formula One circus abandon Morocco, never to return.

Pacific Grand Prix

The first races with the title 'Pacific Grand Prix' were held at the Laguna Seca Raceway in Monterey, California, between 1960 and 1963. But although they attracted impressive international fields, these races did not count toward the Championship. However, in 1994 the event was revived by Japanese businessman Haime Tanaka to take place on the Tanaka International Circuit—commonly known as 'TI' or 'Aida'—which he had built four years previously near the city of Mimasaka, Japan, as a private test track for him and his wealthy car-owning friends. Tanaka had opened the circuit in 1990 with an inaugural race of former British Formula One drivers in their historic cars. Thereafter, these drivers gave their names to many of the 13 turns on the 2.31 mile (3.72 km) circuit.

From the start/finish line on the main straight, drivers hit the right-handed double apex of First Corner, followed by the fast, but challenging left-hander at Williams. After a short straight comes the quick left-right-left flick of the Moss Esses and then the double right-handed Attwood Curve. This opens out onto the back straight which ends in a tight right-handed hairpin that leads almost immediately into the left turn at Revolver, followed by a second left-hand turn at Piper. A brief straight leads to the difficult uphill Redman bend, and almost immediately into the double-apex right-handed Hobbs corner. After the right-handed Mike Knight corner cars either flick

right into the pits area or continue to the aptly-named Last Corner and back into the start/finish straight.

Despite its remote location in the countryside in the Kobe region of Japan, the two Grands Prix held in 1994 and 1995 each attracted around 100,000 enthusiastic spectators. Drivers found the narrow circuit less to their liking, due to the lack of overtaking opportunities, and some people dismissed it as a mere rich man's folly. Although it remains open to this day as the Okayama International Circuit, it was dropped from the Formula One calendar after just two races because of its remoteness. The last race, in 1995, was notable for Michael Schumacher's victory which made him then the world's youngest ever World Champion.

Tanaka International Circuit

Type: private circuit
Location: Aida, Kobe, Japan
Circuit Length: 2.31 miles (3.72 km)
Lap Record: 1:14.023 (M Schumacher/Benetton-Ford 1994)

BELOW: *Pacific Grand Prix, 1994: Ayrton Senna (Williams FW16 Renault) and Nicola Larini (Ferrari 412T1) end up in the gravel together at the first corner after Senna had been helped into a spin by Mika Häkkinen that left Larini nowhere to go.*

ABOVE: *Harry Schell (Maserati 250F) takes a corner during the 1957 Pescara Grand Prix. Schell finished the race in third position.*

Pescara Grand Prix

Although Pescara on the Adriatic coast of Italy hosted just a single round of the Formula One World Championship in August 1957, it retains the distinction of being the longest track ever used in an official Grand Prix race. The 15.97 mile (25.7 km) road-based circuit boasted a continuous straight that ran for 4 miles (6.44 km) beside the Adriatic.

More hair-raising by far was the wild ride inland through the hills of Abruzzo, which took in a level crossing, countless loose animals, and a clutch of mountain villages along the way.

Although there were two further straights linking the villages of Capelle and Monte-Silvano with Pescara, the roads were bumpy, and in places exceptionally narrow.

The first race at Pescara was held in 1924, and after that numerous non-championship Formula One events were hosted before it was finally put in the official calendar in 1957. During the 1930s Pescara hosted the famous Coppa Acerbo, named for a local fascist politician, and later, during the 1950s, a popular 12-hour sports car race.

The 1957 Grand Prix's main claim to fame is that it was the longest Formula One race ever run at just under three hours, with a lap record, set by Stirling Moss, at 9 minutes 44.6 seconds. In spite of its popularity, however, it proved a little too hazardous for modern racing. The last race to be held there was a four-hour round of the World Sports Car Championship 1961. After this, the circuit reverted back to public highways on the grounds that, even though the roads were supposedly closed for the duration of races, it was impossible to guarantee the safety of either the drivers or the intensely enthusiastic crowd—up to 200,000 turned out to watch the Grand Prix.

Pescara Circuit

Type: public road circuit
Location: Pescara, Italy
Circuit Length: 15.97 miles (25.7 km)
Lap Record: 9:44.600 (S Moss/Vanwall 1957)

Portuguese Grand Prix

The first Grand Prix event to be held in Portugal was a sports car race that took place in 1951 on the Boavista street circuit in Porto. This was followed in 1954 by a one-off Formula One event in the Montsanto Park in Lisbon, and by the first official Formula One race at Boavista in August 1958. In 1964, the two circuits were joined by the Cascais street circuit, which also ran a sports car Grand Prix, but motorsport enthusiasts in Portugal lobbied for a purpose-built Formula One circuit—and in 1972 their wish was granted.

Built in Estoril, the seaside resort near Lisbon, the new

Autódromo do Estoril soon became a favorite with drivers thanks to its elevation changes and its tight and difficult nature. After hosting many junior formulae and Formula Two European Championship races during the 1970s, a total of 13 Grands Prix were held there between 1984 and 1996. Following the deaths of Ayrton Senna and Austrian driver Roland Ratzenburger at Imola in 1994, the circuit's organizers became increasingly preoccupied with safety. The 2.72 mile (4.38 km) layout was modified to replace the very fast Tanque Corner with a much slower complex of corners known collectively as Gancho, and the Parabolica bend leading on to the start/finish straight was renamed in Senna's honor.

Although Grand Prix racing continued at Estoril for another three seasons, it became clear that even in its modified form, the circuit was simply too dangerous for the latest generation of Formula One cars. It did continue hosting major events including the FAI GT Championships, the DTM series, and more recently a round of the A1 Grand Prix and even the Portuguese Motorcycle Grand Prix. Estoril was suggested as the venue for the 1997 European Grand Prix, but in the end it was decided it could not reach the required safety standards so the idea was dropped.

Autódromo do Estoril

Type: permanent circuit
Location: Estoril, Portugal
Circuit Length: 2.72 miles (4.38 km)
Lap Record: 1:22.446 (D Coulthard/Williams-Renault 1994)

BELOW: *Rubens Barrichello (Jordan 195 Peugeot) leads Mika Häkkinen and Mark Blundell (both McLaren MP4/10B Mercedes) during the 1995 Portuguese Grand Prix at Estoril.*

ABOVE: *Jack Brabham (Cooper T53-Climax)—who won the race—leads the field into the Avenida da Boavista at the start of the 1960 Portuguese Grand Prix at Circuito da Boavista.*

Portuguese Grand Prix

Circuito da Boavista

Type: street circuit
Location: Porto, Portugal
Circuit Length: 4.62 miles (7.43 km)
Lap Record: 2:27.53 (J Surtees/Lotus-Climax 1960)

Only two Portuguese Grands Prix were held at the Circuito da Boavista in Oporto, in 1958 and 1960, although car racing and 'flying kilometer' events had been staged at the track since 1931. During the 1958 event, spectators were treated to the thrilling spectacle of watching English drivers Stirling Moss and Mike Hawthorn battle it out for the world title. Moss won, but sportingly persuaded the stewards not to disqualify Hawthorn for running off the track, enabling the latter to clinch the Championship by a single point. For the 1960 race, the circuit was substantially redesigned in an effort to enhance its international appeal. Australian Jack Brabham claimed his fifth straight win of the year along with his second world title.

The Grand Prix circuit ran counter-clockwise from the harbor-side start/finish line on the Esplanada do Rio De Janeiro, before a pair of left turns onto the fast Avenida da Boavista. Then came another quicker left turn onto the Avenida de Antunes Guimaraes, followed by a short straight and yet another left onto the Rua do Lidador. Here, a fast right-left lead into another left-handed corner, which turned into Estrada da Cucunvalagio, then back to the finish line.

The route not only contained some exceptionally narrow turns, but also portions of cobbled streets and even tram lines that made it unsuitable for Formula One. After a series of accidents and numerous retirements at the 1960 race, Boavista's brief reign as a Grand Prix circuit ended and it fell into disuse for over 40 years.

More recently, however, Portugal's strong interest in the classic car scene prompted an Anglo-Portuguese consortium to resurrect the circuit for a new audience. After protracted negotiations with the city authorities to ensure that the requisite safety measures were in place, the first 'Historic Grand Prix' classic race was held in 2005 and is now confirmed as a regular biennial event. In 2007, the revitalized circuit also hosted a round of the World Touring Car Championship, welcoming such big names as Alessandro Zanardi, Alain Menu, and the local Portuguese favorite, Tiago Monteiro.

Portuguese Grand Prix

Monsanto Park

Type: city park circuit
Location: Lisbon, Portugal
Circuit Length: 3.38 miles (5.44 km)
Lap Record: 2:05.07 (S Moss/Cooper-Climax 1959)

Although the Monsanto Park circuit 3 miles (4.8 km) west of the Portuguese capital of Lisbon hosted a large number of top-class motor races between 1954 and 1959, only one of them—the 1959 Grand Prix—qualified as a Formula One event. Won by English driver Stirling Moss, who started from pole position and also recorded the fastest lap, the race is chiefly memorable for starting late due to the heat of the intense summer sun, which meant that Moss and his Cooper-Climax car finally crossed the finish line as the light was failing.

The narrow, twisty 3.38 mile (5.44 km) route took in several public roads before traversing the city's Monsanto Forest Park, which today is celebrated as a site of great beauty and scientific interest thanks to its collection of rare plant species. The start/finish line straight led to a roundabout that was converted into the Clover Leaf Hairpin, leading onto the A5 motorway for a short section before the track turned right at Riding School Corner and into the park. The circuit then went through the woods and around a small lake to the right-handed Lake Hairpin followed by a short straight and a complex of right, left, and left bends into the right-handed Windmill Bend. There followed the fast sweeping left-handed curve that finished at the Pits Hairpin which exited onto the start/finish straight once again.

With few overtaking areas the circuit could be frustrating for faster drivers, and all drivers had to contend with a wide range of difficult and bumpy surfaces. A number of accidents, including a terrifying somersault from Jack Brabham, encouraged the authorities to deem the circuit unfit for subsequent Formula One racing, though the entry list for the 1959 Grand Prix—which included Moss, Dan Gurney, Carroll Shelby, Tony Brooks, Bruce McLaren, Brabham, Phil Hill, and Graham Hill—suggests the drivers were less intimidated by the shortcomings of the venue than the sport's governing body. The circuit fell into disuse after 1960, after which the parkland section became fully integrated once more within the Forest Park.

ABOVE: *Stirling Moss (Cooper T51 Climax) on his way to winning the 1959 Portuguese Grand Prix at Monsanto Park.*

San Marino Grand Prix and Italian Grand Prix

The Imola circuit, in the foothills of the Apennine Mountains, was opened in 1952, although the nearby parkland had been used for motocross races for some years before. The circuit was close to the Ferrari factory in Modena, and one of the very first uses of the track was when Alberto Ascari and Luigi Villoresi tested Ferrari 340 sports cars there. Motorcycle racing started there in 1953 and the first sports car race was hosted in 1954. But it would not be until 1963 that the first Grand Prix was held at the circuit, a non-Championship event that was won by Scots driver Jim Clark in a Lotus-Climax.

The track was at first named for the Santerno River which runs alongside it, but Imola was officially renamed the Autodromo Enzo e Dino Ferrari after the death of Enzo Ferrari and his son Dino. In 1980, Imola hosted the Italian Grand Prix in preference to Monza, and in 1981 the circuit adopted the name of the neighboring Principality of San Marino—actually some 50 miles (80 km) away—after which the San Marino Grand Prix became a permanent fixture until 2006, much to the delight of Ferrari's enthusiastic tifosi fans.

The circuit has been changed many times over the years, most notably by the addition of three chicanes—the Variante Bassa in 1973, the Variante Alta in 1974, and the Acque Minerale in 1981—to slow cars down. There have also been alterations to the very fast Tamburello corner, the scene of many terrifying accidents over the years, not least the one in 1994 that killed Ayrton Senna. Villeneuve Corner, where Roland Ratzenberger was killed, was also modified after that year's tragic events. This reduced the total circuit length slightly, but it was extended again to its current length of 3.06 miles (4.93 km) following further safety modifications requested by the FIA. The last Formula One race was held at Imola in 2006, and while motor racing continues at the venue, it remains to be seen if Formula One will ever return.

Autodromo Enzo e Dino Ferrari

Type: permanent circuit
Location: Imola, 25 miles (40 km) east of Bologna, Italy
Circuit Length: 3.06 miles (4.93 km)
Lap Record: 1:20.411 (M Schumacher/Ferrari 2004)

ABOVE: *Michael Schumacher (Ferrari 248F1) leads Jenson Button (Honda RA106) early in the 2006 San Marino Grand Prix. Schumacher went on to win the race.*

NEXT SPREAD: *Fernando Alonso (Renault R26) during a pitstop at the 2006 San Marino Grand Prix.*

Singapore Grand Prix

Marina Bay Street Circuit

Type: street circuit
Location: Marina Bay, Singapore
Circuit Length: 3.15 miles (5.07 km)
Lap Record: 1:45.599 (K Raikkonen/Ferrari 2008)

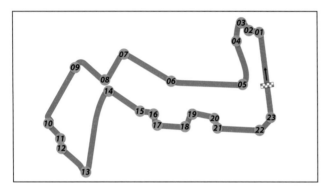

The 'new' Singapore Grand Prix was first held in 2008 on a 3.15 mile (5.07 km) circuit created on public roads in the Marina Bay suburb of the city. Memorable for being held at night, the race took place against a stunning vista of illuminated skyscrapers and provided a thrilling spectacle for all who watched it.

In fact, the first Grand Prix event held in Singapore was the Orient Year Grand Prix, which took place back in 1961 on an older road circuit in the Thompson Road district. The following year, the race was confusingly renamed the Malaysian Grand Prix and in 1965, after Singapore gained its independence, it reverted to the Singapore Grand Prix. The event was finally dropped from the Formula One calendar after the 1973 season following two fatal crashes and complaints about the widespread disruption involved in closing roads.

The 2008 Formula One race was the result of a S$150 million ($103 million) deal signed by the FIA, the Singapore government, and Singapore Telecommunications, and was run in a counter-clockwise direction on a circuit consisting of no less than 10 right-hand and 14 left-hand turns. Lap times came down quickly as drivers got used to the night-time conditions, but the use of hi-tech projectors to illuminate the track ensured that the race ran smoothly—despite a number of collisions against the high curbs at Turn 10.

The event, which was eventually won by Fernando Alonso in a Renault, was also a huge commercial success, with around 110,000 tickets sold and all of the corporate hospitality suites sold out. The Singapore Grand Prix is scheduled to return in 2009 with slight modifications to the circuit. The Malaysian Grand Prix in Kuala Lumpur is staged only 180 miles (290 km) away, but the evident popularity of Formula One in this part of the world suggests that there is room for both to thrive.

BELOW: *Fernando Alonso (Renault R28) on his way to winning the 2008 Singapore Grand Prix.*

ABOVE: *Ayrton Senna (McLaren MP4/8 Ford) leads Michael Schumacher (Benetton B192B Ford) during the 1993 South African Grand Prix at Kyalami.*

South African Grand Prix

The Kyalami Circuit hosted the South African Grand Prix 20 times between 1967 and 1993 and would probably have staged more had it not been for an international boycott during the Apartheid years of 1986 to 1991 and a spat between the sport's governing bodies in 1981 that resulted in that race being classified as a Formula Libre, rather than Formula One, race. It took over as South Africa's premier motorsport venue after the Grand Prix was moved from the East London circuit in 1967.

Kyalami in Zulu, one of South Africa's 11 languages, means 'my home', and since it first opened in 1961 it has welcomed many different race series to Johannesburg. Today's circuit is very different to the original that was in use from 1967 to 1985. Then, it was 2.55 miles (4.1 km) long and one of the fastest circuits on the calendar. It had a long main straight, punctuated by The Kink and then the very challenging Crowthorne Corner and Barbeque Bend. Then another long sweep up to Sunset Bend, a tough left Clubhouse Bend, then left again into The Esses, before the long Leeukop bend back onto the start/finish straight.

In 1985, while the Grand Prix was absent, Kyalami was radically revised, and only a small section of the original track was retained. The new track with its admirably smooth surface offered a variety of fast and slow corners and presented an interesting technical challenge to drivers. By this time it was slightly longer than before, at 2.66 miles (4.28 km).

Despite this, the Grand Prix returned on only two occasions, in 1992 and 1993 before its promoter went bankrupt. Since then, Kyalami has hosted many other races, including the A1 Grand Prix series. The Formula One circus did return in 2000 for testing though there are no immediate prospects of a return to Formula One racing at the likeable South African venue.

Kyalami Circuit

Type: permanent circuit
Location: Johannesburg, South Africa
Circuit Length: 2.66 miles (4.28 km)
Lap Record: 1:17.578 (N Mansell/Williams-Renault 1992)

South African Grand Prix

Grand Prix racing regularly took place at the Prince George Circuit in East London, in the Eastern Cape province, from 1934 until the outbreak of World War II. After a considerable break, the circuit was redeveloped in 1959 and it hosted the revived South African Grand Prix three times in 1962, 1963, and 1965. Each of these was won by a British driver, incidentally, with Jim Clark winning twice and Graham Hill picking up the third win.

The first of those pre-war races was on an enormously long 15 mile (24.15 km) track that was created on the outskirts of East London. It was won by the American Whitney Willard Straight in a Maserati 8CM. The circuit was then reduced to a mere 11 miles (17.7 km) for the remaining pre-war races between 1936 and 1939 (no race was held in 1935).

However, after the war, circuits of that length were considered unsafe. A new 2.44 mile (3.93 km) track was constructed using some short sections of the old track, but the majority was newly built in a natural amphitheater near the coastline. It was triangular in shape with a long start/finish straight leading to the very fast Potters Pass Curve, through Rifle Bend and on to the tight Cocobana Corner. Then it was along Beach Straight to a tricky infield section incorporating Butts Bend, The Esses, Cox's Corner, and The Sweep. The Back Straight and Beacon Bend then finished the lap.

The first race in 1960 was won by Paul Frère in a Cooper-Climax, but that and the following year's race were classified as non-Championship. Therefore, the first 'proper' Formula One South African Grand Prix took place in 1962 when Graham Hill's Lotus-Climax took the honors.

Of the remaining East London races, the 1966 event was again classified non-Championship and that was the last Grand Prix held at the circuit.

BELOW: *Jim Clark (Lotus 25-Climax), Jack Brabham (Brabham BT7-Climax), and Dan Gurney (Brabham BT7-Climax) lead off the front row of the grid at the start of the 1963 South African Grand Prix at Prince George Circuit.*

Prince George Circuit

Type: permanent circuit
Location: East London, South Africa
Circuit Length: 2.44 miles (3.93 km)
Lap Record: 1:27.600 (J Clark/Lotus-Climax 1965)

ABOVE: *Kimi Räikkönen and Felipe Massa (both Ferrari F2008) lead the field at the start of the 2008 Spanish Grand Prix.*

Spanish Grand Prix

Often referred to simply as 'Barcelona' (which has its own circuit, Montjuïc), the Circuito de Catalunya near the town of Montmeló was opened on September 10, 1991 with strong backing of the Catalan Government and the Reial Automòbil Club de Catalunya (RACC). Nineteen days later it hosted the first of a 16-year run of Spanish Grand Prix events, in a race that will always be remembered for the head-to-head dual between Nigel Mansell and Ayrton Senna that lasted the entire length of the start/finish straight.

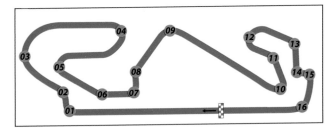

Circuit de Catalunya

Type: permanent circuit
Location: 13 miles (21 km) north of Barcelona, Spain
Circuit Length: 2.91 miles (4.65 km)
Lap Record: 1:21.670 (K Räikkönen/Ferrari 2008)

Catalunya has three different layouts: the Grand Prix track, the National track, and the RACC School track. The 2.91 mile (4.65 km) Grand Prix track is characterized by its exceptionally long starting straight and 16 highly demanding turns. A typical lap starts with a lengthy burst down the starting straight, followed by a right turn at Elf Corner and then a fast left onto the extended Renault right-hander. The track then keeps right into the double-apex Repsol bend, then straightens briefly before the slow Seat Bend. After this it dips to Wurth and climbs up again to the left-handed Campsa, before entering a fast downhill section that ends with the slow uphill left turn at Caixa. Drivers face an even stiffer test as they enter the Bank Sabadell complex of turns before passing through the fast right-hander at New Holland to return to the start/finish straight.

A much commented-on feature of the circuit is the wind, which can abruptly change direction during the day and throw the cars' sensitive aerodynamic set-ups into disarray. Criticism has also been leveled at the circuit's constant use as a test track, the implication being that drivers are over-familiar with it. Such could not be said of Finnish driver Heikki Kovalainen who left the track in 2008 at 150 mph (241 kph) following a wheel collapse. After an agonizing few minutes, during which he lost consciousness, Kovalainen signaled his recovery to the much-relieved crowd by giving a triumphant thumbs-up.

Spanish Grand Prix

Circuito Permanente Del Jarama

Type: permanent circuit
Location: 18.5 miles (30 km) north of Madrid, Spain
Circuit Length: 2.15 miles (3.4 km)
Lap Record: 1:17.818 (A Jones/Williams-Cosworth 1981)

The Spanish Grand Prix was staged nine times between 1968 and 1981 at the Circuito Permanente Del Jarama, north of Madrid. It was conceived in 1967 by the Real Automóvil Club de España (RACE) with the intention of creating a rival to Montjuïc Park circuit in Barcelona. The original plans were drawn up by Dutch track designer John Hugenholz and executed on an expanse of arid scrubland by Italian architect Sandro Rocci.

BELOW: *Mario Andretti leads team-mate Ronnie Peterson (both Lotus 79 Fords) during the 1978 Spanish Grand Prix at Jarama. They finished in first and second positions respectively.*

The Spanish Grand Prix alternated between Montjuïc and Jarama until 1976, when the race moved permanently to Jarama after a crash at the former in 1975 killed four spectators. However, from 1981, the Grand Prix circus left the Madrid venue for good, reappearing briefly at Jerez in 1986 before finding a new home at the Circuito de Catalunya in 1991.

At 2.15 miles (3.4 km) in length, Jarama was a relatively short, narrow circuit with only one short straight, whose complexes of 11 corners made overtaking very difficult—this was one of the official reasons for its abandonment as a Grand Prix venue. If proof of this were needed, it came conclusively during the 1981 race when French driver Gilles Villeneuve (who set the lap record in 1979 which still stands) in a Ferrari successfully clung onto his lead almost from the start against four clearly faster cars. Although Villeneuve drove faultlessly, the authorities concluded that the circuit was no longer suitable for racing at the highest level.

Motorsport events are still held at Jarama, which is also in constant demand as a test track. However, RACE has recently published a feasibility study for a replacement circuit to be built in the same area, adjacent to Madrid's Barajas International Airport. Although the new circuit is ostensibly to be used for testing, it is quite possible that it might lead to an attempt to bring the Spanish Grand Prix back to the Spanish capital.

ABOVE: *Jackie Stewart (Matra MS80-Ford Cosworth) on his way to winning the 1969 Spanish Grand Prix at the Montjuïc Circuit.*

Spanish Grand Prix

Consistently rated as one of the greatest Grand Prix venues of all time, Montjuïc was a street circuit built in the hills overlooking the city of Barcelona. Despite being so highly regarded, it only played host to the Spanish Grand Prix four times, between 1969 and 1975.

Heavily wooded, with stunning views and dramatic changes of elevation, Montjuïc demanded total concentration from drivers and was a thrilling place for spectators as there were several places on the bumpy track at which cars frequently had all four wheels off the ground.

From a slightly downhill start before the sweeping uphill curve of Rasiente, a left-handed hairpin brought the field to the equally tight right-hand hairpin known as Rosaleda. Two left-handers at Font Del Gat and Teatro Griego then lead into an uphill stretch to the challengingly fast right-handed Vias corner. After the right-hand left turn at Guardia Urbana and a short straight, came a demanding section that took in the corners of La Pergola and Pueblo Español. Then came a downhill chicane (constructed to negotiate a roundabout) and

finally a long left turn at Saint Jordi to rejoin the start/finish straight. Unusually, it was a counter-clockwise circuit, half of which was very fast and the other half relatively slow.

Despite the circuit's popularity, major concerns were expressed about its safety prior to the 1975 Grand Prix, prompting two-time winner Emerson Fittipaldi to withdraw. Montjuïc's fate was sealed during the 26th lap of the race itself when the Lola of German driver Rolf Stommelen crashed and caught fire. Worse still, the large aerodynamic spoiler attached to Stommelen's car was detached in the accident and flew into the spectator area, killing four instantly. The race was stopped. It was a sad end for what had briefly been a splendid venue. A commemorative event was held there in 2007.

Montjuïc Circuit

Type: public road circuit
Location: a hill in center of Barcelona, Spain
Circuit Length: 2.35 miles (3.78 km)
Lap Record: 1:23.8 (R Peterson/Lotus-Cosworth 1973)

Spanish Grand Prix

Pedralbes Circuit

Type: street circuit
Location: Barcelona city center, Spain
Circuit Length: 3.94 miles (6.34 km)
Lap Record: 2:16.93 (J M Fangio/Alfa Romeo 1951)

There had been racing on the Penya Rhin circuit in the hills above Stiges, outside Barcelona, for some time before World War II but afterward, it became increasingly clear that it was no longer suitable for Grand Prix cars. As a result, a new circuit was laid out in the streets of the Pedralbes suburb of Barcelona in 1946. At that time it was 2.77 miles (4.46 km) long and consisted of a triangle taking in the Avenida del Generalisimo Franco, Esplugues Street, and Pedralbes Avenue.

For the first Grand Prix that was staged there, in 1951, the circuit was increased to 3.9 miles (6.32 km) and with its main straight extending more than three quarters of a mile (1.3 km) in length, Pedralbes quickly gained a reputation for being the fastest street circuit in the world. It was a tough race for cars and drivers because of the rough surface which included cobbles at some points.

It was extended a little further for the 1954 Grand Prix, to 3.94 miles (6.34 km) which raised top speeds even more. The start was in the middle of the Avenida del Generalisimo Franco straight, at the end of which was a sharp right-handed hairpin that lead on to another fast straight. A gentle curve left and a slower corner right lead on to the Avenida de la Victoria, and then a fast left turn onto the Paseo de Manuel Girona, another fast stretch with just a hint of a kink in the middle. Two right-handers intersected by the Calle de Numancia lead back onto the enormous start/finish straight (which, after the overthrow of Franco was renamed El Diagonal).

Unfortunately for Pedralbes, the massive accident at Le Mans in 1955 resulted in the cancelation of the Spanish Grand Prix that year, and it also lead to a complete re-appraisal of circuit designs—the high speeds that were regularly attained at Pedralbes were no longer considered safe. When the Spanish Grand Prix returned in 1968 it was moved to Jarama.

BELOW: *Juan Manuel Fangio (Alfa Romeo 159) takes the checkered flag to win the 1951 Spanish Grand Prix at Pedralbes Circuit.*

ABOVE: *Nelson Piquet and team-mate Nigel Mansell (both Williams FW11B Hondas) lead Ayrton Senna (Lotus 99T Honda) into Curva Expo at the start of the 1987 Spanish Grand Prix at Jerez.*

Spanish Grand Prix and European Grand Prix

The picturesque circuit at Jerez in the southwest of Spain hosted the Spanish Grand Prix five times from 1986 to 1990, and the European Grand Prix in 1994 and again in 1997. It was first opened at the end of 1985 when it staged a round of the Spanish Touring Car Championships but the big attraction for the Mayor of Jerez, who had supported the construction of the track to publicize the region and its famous Sherry wines, was the Grand Prix.

The track was built in a natural bowl between surrounding hills, and provided good viewing for the 125,000 spectators the venue could accommodate. Nothing like that number turned up to watch one of the most exciting races of the year as Ayrton Senna and Nigel Mansell battled for first place. Mansell had been some five seconds behind Senna but rapidly caught him in the last few laps and pulled out to overtake in site of the checkered flag. The two cars crossed the line side by side though eventually the timers gave the race to Senna, by a margin of only 0.014 seconds, the closest finish in the history of the sport.

Jerez was famous for other incidents at the later 1997 European Grand Prix when Michael Schumacher, battling Jacques Villeneuve for the world title, was judged to have deliberately driven him off the road. Schumacher had all his points that year stripped for his unsporting conduct, Villeneuve was declared Champion and, as a sidenote, Mika Häkkinen won his first Grand Prix.

There was one final controversy in that race: the Jerez Mayor barged onto the podium to make a presentation that should have been made by someone else and the Formula One authorities vowed the race would never be held there again. Jerez remains a very fine facility that is often used for Formula One testing, though to date there is no real sign of it regaining the Spanish Grand Prix.

Circuito Permanente de Jerez

Type: permanent circuit
Location: six miles (9.5 km) from Jerez de la Frontera, Spain
Circuit Length: 2.76 miles (4.44 km)
Lap Record: 1:23.135 (H-H Frentzen/Williams-Renault 1997)

Swedish Grand Prix

The Scandinavian Raceway was built 3 miles (5 km) east of Gislaved in Sweden in 1968, having been designed by Sven Åsberg. It is built on flat, marshy land in the middle of a forest and is an extremely fast circuit owing to its long straights.

A lap starts with a run down to the StartKurvan, a right-hand hairpin that leads into a short straight that finishes at the left-hand hairpin, Opel. The first of the circuit's straights leads to the left-handed Hansen Curve then it's down to the fast and challenging 180-degree right-turn at Karusell. Gislaved marks the end of the Karusell, then there's a short blast to the double-apex Södra which leads on to the longest straight. It's called the Flight Straight, not least because it doubles as a runway. At the end is the difficult right-handed Norra corner that leads to a brief straight and then another right-hander at Läktar that leads back on to the start/finish straight.

Six Formula One races were held at the Scandinavian Raceway between 1973 and 1978, with the first one prominently featuring local hero Ronnie Peterson. He claimed pole position in his Lotus-Climax and for most of the race it looked as if he and team-mate Emerson Fittipaldi would score a 1-2. Eventually, however, Fittipaldi was sidelined with transmission problems and when Peterson's tires started wearing, Denny Hulme passed Peterson on the penultimate lap.

Later on, the Swedish Grand Prix was the scene of two audacious engineering experiments. In 1976, Tyrrell raced with a six-wheeled car which came in triumphantly first and second. Then in 1978, Brabham introduced its 'Fan Car' which added to the ground effects by having a huge fan at the back to increase the airflow under the car. It was a resounding success and gave Niki Lauda an easy victory. The car was passed as legal, but Brabham withdrew it and it never raced again.

The last Swedish Grand Prix at the Raceway was held in 1978, the year in which Swedes Gunnar Nilsson and Ronnie Peterson both died.

Scandinavian Raceway

Type: permanent circuit
Location: Anderstorp, Sweden
Circuit Length: 2.5 miles (4.02 km)
Lap Record: 1:24.836 (N Lauda/Brabham-Alfa Romeo 1978)

ABOVE: *Jody Scheckter leads Patrick Depailler (both Tyrrell P34 Fords) during the 1976 Swedish Grand Prix. They finished in first and second positions respectively, though this was the car's only Grand Prix win.*

Swiss Grand Prix

Circuit Bremgarten

Type: permanent parkland circuit
Location: Bremgarten, Berne, Switzerland
Circuit Length: 4.52 miles (7.27 km)
Lap Record: 2:39.700 (J M Fangio/Mercedes-Benz 1954)

The Circuit Bremgarten, which is beautifully situated in the ancient forest near the city of Berne, hosted the Swiss Grand Prix between 1950 and 1954. The circuit was purpose-built for motor racing and the Grand Prix only stopped being held there following the tragic accident at Le Mans in 1955 which resulted in the authorities banning motor racing on Swiss soil.

Before that, Switzerland had been one of Europe's most enthusiastic motorsport countries, putting on numerous international car and motorcycle races over the years—most notably hosting the 'Grand Prix Bern' on the Bremgarten track from 1934 to 1939 and then again after the War from 1947 to 1954. The first of these, in 1934, saw Hans Stuck in his Auto union victorious, though the most successful drivers at the track were Rudolf Caracciola and Alberto Ascari, who each won three times. Juan Manuel Fangio was not far behind with two wins and he remains the last person to take the checkered flag in Switzerland.

The circuit itself follows an oval shape and, unusually, there are no straights of any length throughout its 4.52 miles (7.27 km). It was a fast circuit and one which could be highly dangerous as it coursed through the trees, because of sudden changes of light and an inconsistent surface that was especially difficult in wet conditions.

The Grand Prix Bern got a new lease of life during the summer of 1998, when for a single day classic motorcyles returned for a parade event on the historic Bremgarten track. Later, in 2004, a similar event for cars was held and it is planned to continue the tradition every three years. An attempt to raise Switzerland's ban on motor racing was made in 2007 but it was not successful.

ABOVE: *Alan Brown (Cooper T20-Bristol) leads Stirling Moss (HWM 52-Alta), Emmanuel de Graffenried (Maserati 4CLT/48-Plate), George Abecassis (HWM 52-Alta), and Peter Collins (HWM 52-Alta) at the 1952 Swiss Grand Prix.*

Turkish Grand Prix

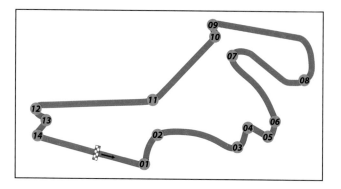

The Istanbul track that hosts the Turkish Grand Prix was designed, as were so many other modern Grand Prix circuits, by Hermann Tilke. The Istanbul Park circuit, which was opened in 2005 close to the Sabiha Gökçen International Airport, was designed to follow the contours of the countryside on the Asian side of the city. As well as having numerous changes of elevation, the track mirrors some of the most famous corners from other tracks around the world but also has one of its own that presents a unique challenge to Grand Prix drivers. It's called simply Turn 8 and it's a massively long left handed bend with four separate apexes during which the cars are pulling up to 5G in cornering force.

This extremely challenging 3.31 mile (5.34 km) sinuous circuit runs counter-clockwise, making it, along with Brazil, the only current Grand Prix circuit to do so. Unlike many Tilke circuits, there are no long straights followed by a tight bend or hairpin to provide overtaking opportunities. Instead, Istanbul's four different gradient changes and successions of technical corners make it easy for a driver under pressure to

Istanbul Park

Type: permanent circuit
Location: Tuzla, Istanbul, Turkey
Circuit Length: 3.31 miles (5.34 km)
Lap Record: 1:24.770 (J Montoya/McLaren 2005)

make mistakes, though the start finish straight at almost half a mile (800 meters) in length permits speed of over 200 mph (322 kph) to be reached. There's plenty of variation in the width of the track, too, ranging from 18.5 to 26.5 yards (17 to 24.25 meters), excluding the safety run-off areas, and in all there are 14 corners, of which six are right turns and eight turns to the left.

As might be expected of a brand new facility, spectators are well looked after with parking for 20,000 cars and a grandstand seating capacity of 130,000.

PREVIOUS SPREAD: *Giancarlo Fisichella (Force India VJM01 Ferrari) slams into the back of Kazuki Nakajima (Williams FW30 Toyota) during the 2008 Turkish Grand Prix.*

BELOW: *Felipe Massa (Ferrari 248F1) leads Michael Schumacher (Ferrari 248F1) through the chaos at the start of the 2006 Turkish Grand Prix.*

ABOVE: *The 1989 United States Grand Prix in Phoenix, Arizona. Ayrton Senna leads Alain Prost (both McLaren MP4/5 Hondas) and Alessandro Nannini (Benetton B188 Ford) at the start.*

United States Grand Prix

The United States Grand Prix was hosted three times on the streets of Phoenix, Arizona, between 1989 and 1991, in yet another attempt in North America to organize a successful city center race. The idea was sound, but in reality Phoenix failed, just as many other temporary Grand Prix venues had.

The biggest problem was faced by the drivers who had to contend with little grip, poor and inconsistent road surfaces, and a dull succession of blind 90-degree corners. Another problem was that the catch fencing required for safety was both ugly and restricted spectators' views. Finally, the first Phoenix Grand Prix was held in the searing heat of summer which not only took its toll on the drivers but also on the spectators, many of whom left early to seek cooling refreshment and shelter from the Arizona sun.

The following two years the event was brought forward to a more sensible springtime date but this was not enough to encourage the crowds to attend in any number. In fact, one year more locals turned out to watch an ostrich race than attended the Grand Prix. Clearly the writing was on the wall

and after the 1991 event Formula One left the United States, not to return until 2000 when a new Grand Prix was inaugurated at the Indianapolis Motor Speedway.

The Phoenix Grand Prix was held downtown, its counter-clockwise circuit starting on Jefferson Street and taking in Monroe Street, Washington Street, 3rd Avenue, Adams Street, and 5th Avenue before a long double left-hand sequence to return to the start/finish straight. For 1991, however, the construction of the state baseball stadium, the Bank One Ballpark, meant the course changed course, to run along Madison Street after the start, with the Monroe Street loop being eliminated.

Phoenix Street Circuit

Type: street circuit
Location: Phoenix, Arizona, United States
Circuit Length: 2.32 miles (3.73 km)
Lap Record: 1:26.758 (J Alesi/Ferrari 1991)

United States Grand Prix

Riverside International Raceway

Type: permanent circuit
Location: San Bernadino, California, United States
Circuit Length: 3.29 miles (5.29 km)
Lap Record: 1:56.300 (J Brabham/Cooper-Climax 1960)

Riverside International Raceway near San Bernadino in California was not North America's first purpose-built permanent race track, but along with two other Californian tracks –Willows Springs near Lancaster and Paramount on the former Paramount movie ranch—it was instrumental in the 1950s in introducing more permanence to the North American racing scene.

Riverside, which could be adapted into numerous different circuit layouts, was enthusiastically received by both spectators and drivers. It was fast, relatively safe with generous run-off areas and required great precision to put in

a great lap. In the United States, oval course specialists would generally not show a great deal of interest in a venue like Riverside, but here they made an exception. Many of them visited and left singing the track's praises thanks to its challengingly technical nature and its sheer driver appeal.

Just one United States Grand Prix was held at Riverside, in 1960. In front of a disappointingly small crowd, it was won by Stirling Moss from his team-mate Innes Ireland in their Lotus-Climaxes, with Bruce McLaren third in his Cooper-Climax. Many in the crowd had turned out to watch local hero Dan Gurney who had qualified third on the grid, but were disappointed when his BRM retired after only 18 laps.

Even if the Grand Prix circus only made one visit to Riverside, the track hosted all sorts of other prestigious events including the NASCAR Winston Cup Series, the CART Series, Indycars, IMSA and many others.

Over the years the track was altered from time to time, mainly to improve safety standards but sadly, in the late 1980s Riverside was closed and turned into a shopping mall and new housing development. After 32 years as one of the leading motorsport venues in the United States, it seemed an ignominious end for Riverside and many in the American motorsport fraternity were deeply saddened by its demise.

BELOW: *Stirling Moss (Lotus 18 Climax) on his way to winning the 1960 United States Grand Prix at Riverside.*

ABOVE: *Stirling Moss, Jack Brabham, and Harry Schell lead away at the start of the 1959 United States Grand Prix at Sebring.*

United States Grand Prix

The Sebring International Raceway, located in the center of Florida, is one of the finest tracks in the whole of the United States and yet it only hosted a Grand Prix once. The track was built after World War II on the site of a former military bomber airbase and in many ways it resembled Silverstone in the UK, as both started out using the airfield perimeter roads for racing.

In 1959, Sebring had the honor of hosting the very first Formula One Grand Prix in the United States other than the Indianapolis 500 which was included in the World Championship but to which very few European competitors

ever bothered to travel. This race was different, with a full turnout of European teams competing. The event was eventually won by Bruce McLaren in a Cooper-Climax from Maurice Trintignant and Tony Brooks after Stirling Moss retired with gearbox problems and Jack Brabham ran out of fuel. Sadly for the locals, United States driver Phil Hill also retired early with clutch problems.

The United States Grand Prix was switched to Riverside in California the following year but Sebring continued to host some of the world's greatest races. The Sebring 12 Hours, part of the prestigious Le Mans Series, attracted the leading drivers during what was perhaps the pinnacle of sports car racing—Ford's GT40 was up against the Ferrari 512 and the Porsche 917, and drivers of the caliber of Mario Andretti, Juan Manuel Fangio, Stirling Moss, Jackie Ickx, Phil Hill, and Mike Hawthorn all raced there.

In the late 1990s financial problems looked likely to cause the closure of the venue but the Panoz Motorsport Group invested heavily to vastly improve the facilities and amend the track to its current 3.7 miles (5.96 km) length. Sebring is now in use year-round, hosting track days, club events, corporate hospitality events as well as racing and automotive testing facilities. Its future now looks assured.

Sebring International Raceway

Type: permanent circuit
Location: Sebring, Central Florida, United States
Circuit Length: 5.24 miles (8.43 km)
Lap Record: 3:05.000 (M Trintignant/Cooper-Climax 1959)

United States Grand Prix

The last time a Grand Prix was held at Watkins Glen in New York State was in 1980, though up to that time it had been one of the most popular of all the United States circuits, hosting the Grand Prix 20 times in all. It was built by Cameron Argetsinger, near Seneca Lake not far from the town of Watkins Glen from which it took its name. The first races were held in 1948 and the track soon gained a well-deserved reputation among both drivers and spectators.

At first the track consisted of a number of different surfaces but by 1956 a permanent circuit had been constructed some 2.3 miles (3.7 km) in length. From then on, the track grew in stature, hosting its first NASCAR stock car race in 1958, its first international Formula Libre meeting in 1958, and its first Grand Prix in 1961.

Watkins Glen attracted huge crowds of very knowledgeable fans and it was extremely popular with the Formula One teams partly because appearance and prize money was far greater than at other events around the world and partly because it was three times awarded a prize for the best organized Grand Prix in the calendar.

BELOW: *Jim Clark (Lotus 43 BRM) takes the checkered flag to win the 1966 United States Grand Prix at Watkins Glen.*

Watkins Glen

Type: permanent circuit
Location: near Watkins Glen, New York, United States
Circuit Length: 2.35 miles (3.78 km)
Lap Record: 1:34.068 (A Jones/Williams-Cosworth 1980)

The Glen became so successful as a venue that before long it was hosting TransAm, CanAm, Formula 5000, the Indy CART series, and even Six-Hour endurance races. As a result, the track was expanded in 1971 to 2.35 miles (3.78 km). However, the decline of Watkins Glen was as rapid as its initial growth. After the last Grand Prix was held there in 1980, the circuit faced serious cash flow problems and although a final CART series meeting was held in 1981, the track fell into bankruptcy.

It was bought by a division of the Corning Enterprises and renovated, after which NASCAR returned in 1986 and Indy Cars in 2005. However, it looks unlikely ever again to host a Grand Prix meeting.

United States Grand Prix West

The street circuit at Long Beach California in the south of the massive, sprawling Los Angeles metropolis, first welcomed the Grand Prix circus in 1976, though it had hosted a Formula 5000 race the year before. It's a very scenic venue and since the race was held in March or April, California's spring sunshine was always a welcome sight. The track followed the palm-tree lined waterfront and the organizers rather hoped the venue would develop a reputation rather like Monaco's, but despite visitor attractions such as the old *Queen Mary* liner and Howard Hughes' *Spruce Goose*—the largest propeller plane ever built—it always lacked the style and heritage that the Monte Carlo circuit offered.

Long Beach was a reasonably challenging circuit because it was both twisting and bumpy and it was substantially more interesting than some other North American tracks laid down on car parks in various cities. At first, the start/finish line was situated on Ocean Boulevard but it was later moved to Shoreline Drive, a long sweeping right-hand bend that was one of the fastest parts of the course. After that it was on the brakes for the Toyota Corner, actually an extended chicane that took the cars into an infield series of corners including the right-hand Michelob Corner. After a succession of left-hand curves came the Seaside Way straight followed by a right turn into the left-handed Indy corner. Very quickly after the exit the Le Gasomet hairpin brought the track back to Shoreline Drive at the end of a 2.04 mile (3.28 km) circuit.

The last United States Grand Prix West, as it was known, was held at Long Beach in 1983, when John Watson's McLaren-Ford took the honors. Since then the circuit continued to stage a number of prestigious events including CART, Indy, Champ Car World Series, GrandAm and TransAm Series, and the very popular Toyota Pro-Celebrity race at which crowds of up to 200,000 are commonplace.

Long Beach Street Circuit

Type: street circuit
Location: Long Beach, California, United States
Circuit Length: 2.04 miles (3.28 km)
Lap Record: 1:28.330 (N Lauda/McLaren-Cosworth 1983)

ABOVE: *Mario Andretti (Lotus 78 Ford) leads Niki Lauda (Ferrari 312T2) during the 1977 United States Grand Prix West at Long Beach.*

THE CONSTRUCTORS

Soon after the motorcar was invented people began to wonder how fast and how far they might be made to go. Reliability trials and actual races were soon commonplace. From that time onward, the standard offering from motor manufacturers would never be good enough, because to race ever faster required more and more specialized machinery.

At the beginning of the 20th century, in the very earliest days of motorsport, it was mainly the motor manufacturers who entered their own cars in races and trials to try to prove that theirs was superior to the opposition. But these competitions did more than show that one car was better than another. They also became an essential part of the vehicle development process and were used to refine and test individual components and even complete vehicles. But as motorsport evolved, the carmakers started being left behind. While some still supplied the chassis and engines onto which a special body might be fitted, increasingly the job of designing, building, and refining racing cars was left to specialist engineers.

These were often privateers, running small operations funded by wealthy racing enthusiasts. Motor racing itself had operated on a loose, ad-hoc basis before World War II, but after peace finally returned in 1945, the French-based Federation Internationale de l'Automobile (FIA) laid down the first formal regulations that would apply to top-level motor racing in Europe. The first set of FIA rules applied from 1946, but the most significant move came in 1950 when the Formula One Championship was launched.

At that time the specialist motor manufacturers—and especially those like Ferrari or Lotus which build sports cars—justified their racing activities because of the motto 'race on Sunday, sell on Monday'. In short, that racing success filtered directly to the showroom and encouraged more sales of road cars. This approach worked especially well in the production categories of motorsport, in which the racing car shared a clear family resemblance with the road cars. But Formula One cars bear no relation with any road cars and so a different approach was needed. Instead, manufacturers tried to draw attention to the mechanical sophistication of their engineering, and suggest —subtly or otherwise—that road cars are improved as a direct result of thecutting edge engineering and design of the Formula One car.

LEFT: *Dan Gurney (Brabham BT7 Climax) in action during his winning race at the 1964 French Grand Prix.*

ABOVE: *Stirling Moss (left, driving a Maserati 250F) and Juan Manuel Fangio (right, driving a Mercedes-Benz W196) compete at the 1954 British Grand Prix.*

But this was by no means an easy task, and as time went on the manufacturers found they were increasingly less successful at the top echelons of motorsport than smaller, specialist firms were. The concept of bringing all elements of racing car construction under a single umbrella—the design, engineering, engine and chassis development, suspension, transmissions, aerodynamics, and even aesthetics—became the norm. And this is what brought the era of the constructor to the fore.

The inaugural Formula One Championship in 1950 (which was for Drivers, as the Constructors Championship would not be introduced until 1958) involved Europe's leading six Grands Prix and the Indianapolis 500 in the United States. Alfa Romeo dominated the first years of Formula One racing with Giuseppe Farina and Juan Manuel Fangio taking the first two titles before Alberto Ascari won the next two in a Ferrari. Needless to say, there were winners and losers in the early years of Formula One, as constructors arrived and then withdrew from racing, while a number of tragic accidents and both driver and spectator fatalities highlighted the dangers of the 'new' sport.

Remarkably, 18 different teams contested Formula One's 1950 debut season, though many dropped out very quickly when they realized the true scale of the costs involved. As a result, there were so few competitive cars for much of the first decade of Formula One that Formula Two cars were admitted to fill the grids. Of all the manufacturer teams, Ferrari is only one that competed in 1950 and has been involved in Formula One continually ever since.

The key to success in Formula One, as in other forms of motorsport, was squeezing the maximum horsepower from the four-stroke engines that powered the cars. Though some specialist constructors designed and built their own engines, others turned to the motor manufacturers for their help and expertise. The manufacturers gained in being part of a success story, but it was also important in the postwar years because national pride was an important issue as countries struggled to re-build their economies. For the major industrial companies in Britain, Italy, France, and Germany, it meant a lot to support what were essentially national teams, still racing in national colors.

But as well as the motor manufacturers, aeronautical companies started being attracted to Formula One, where they could highlight their expertise in specific development areas, such as lightweight chassis construction and the use of lightweight materials.

Lightness is directly related to outright speed, partly because for a given horsepower the speed decreases in direct proportion to the weight, and partly because lighter cars tend to be more nimble and handle better. But achieving a balance between weight and reliability was never easy because cars had to retain enough strength and enough durability to survive the rigors of a Formula One race. As the old racing adage goes: 'To finish first, first you have to finish'.

Colin Chapman was one of the first to take the issue of lightweight construction seriously. When he designed his Lotus cars in the 1950s, his stated aim was to produce the ultimate racing car—and by that, he meant a car that was just durable enough to finish a race, but which carried not an ounce of excess weight. With his innovative designs he walked a knife-edge between dependability and even safety, but they were risks that he and his drivers were prepared to take. Eventually, every team followed in his footsteps.

In the early days of Formula One, there was no such thing as sponsorship. The teams were funded either by themselves or by a parent company and hopefully they would earn enough in winnings to go some way toward covering their costs. Enzo Ferrari—or 'Il Commendatore' as the Ferrari founder was known—was smart enough to realize very early on that it was branding that was crucial to the on-going survival of his racing operation. Every time a Ferrari won on the track, the image of the brand would be enhanced and more cars would be sold both for use on the road or for privateers to take on the track. But in time, even the mighty Ferrari found it needed outside funding and was taken over by Fiat Auto.

Sponsorship was an integral part of American racing long before it became commonplace in Europe. But in time, following the example already set in the various North American racing championships, outside sponsors started getting involved in Formula One. Many, inevitably, had an automotive background, and so lubricating oil companies, tire manufacturers, and spark plug manufacturers tended to be the first to get involved. Some of them, such as Champion Spark Plugs, were already supporting American Stock Car series and used Formula One

as a means of boosting its products in the European markets.

Even in terms of sponsorship, national pride was an issue so it was no surprise to find an Italian petrol company supporting Ferrari or Alfa Romeo, a British components company sponsoring BRM or Lotus, or a French tire company backing Renault or Matra.

By the 1960s, advertising and sponsorship were so much a natural part of Formula One that companies were almost lining up to put their names on racing cars, but once again it was the great innovator Colin Chapman at Lotus who showed the way forward, painting his car in the colors of the Gold Leaf tobacco brand at Monaco in 1968 in place of the traditional British Racing green. From that moment, there was no turning back the commercial tide that was encompassing the sport.

Formula One racing experienced glory days right through to the 1970s, at which time British teams and British engines started to dominate the championship. Virtually very year the shape and design of cars evolved as constructors vied with each other to produce the purest aerodynamic form. At the same time structural changes in the sport were being introduced, with race distances being shortened and tracks improved or dropped from the calendar in the name of safety and also to increase spectator appeal.

As the popularity of Formula One around the world continued to grow over the following two decades an increasing

ABOVE: *Four of the most influential figures in Formula One history in conversation at the 1997 Hungarian Grand Prix: From left to right, Frank Williams, Bernie Ecclestone, Ron Dennis, and Ken Tyrrell.*

number of multinational corporations started taking an interest in the sport. They may have been banks, computer companies or soft drink manufacturers that had no connection with the automotive world but they saw Formula One as a means of spreading their message across the globe. Many millions of pounds, dollars, francs, and marks were injected into the sport, which had two effects. First, it made Formula One an even more competitive business as constructors had more to spend on research and development. But at the same time, it transformed

Formula One into one of the most potentially lucrative businesses in the world. The teams that managed to attract the millions that the tobacco, drinks and other companies had to spend on publicizing their products and brands, became extremely profitable entities.

In the early days, Formula One was all about speed and victory at any cost. Motorsport was dangerous and occasional accidents—even deaths—were seen as unfortunate, but part and parcel of the sport. But after the 1994 season when two drivers

ABOVE: *Felipe Massa (Ferrari F2008) leads during the first lap of the 2008 Brazilian Grand Prix. He went on to win the race.*

died and two others were critically injured, the emphasis changed somewhat. The FIA responded rapidly to the crisis and enforced a series of new rules, which were intended to reduce speeds, improve the safety of the cars and impose new and more stringent circuit safety standards.

This has done nothing to diminish Formula One's appeal as the world's leading global motorsport series, with the biggest television audiences, the largest budgets, and arguably the most prestige and glamor too. The top drivers have become world-renowned superstars and new venues have brought places like Bahrain, Shanghai, and Singapore to the world's attention.

Yet in many ways it is the constructors who remain the single most important part of the jigsaw. Because in the final analysis, it's they who ensure that throughout the season, the cars are there to line up on the grid, ready for the next round of gladiatorial action.

Benetton

Benetton Formula Ltd., which was usually simply called Benetton, competed as a Formula One constructor for 16 years, from 1986 to 2001, although the company had started sponsoring Formula One as early as 1983. The team was taken over by the French vehicle manufacturer, Renault in 2000.

Controlling the team was the Italian Benetton family, whose retail empire encompassed a worldwide chain of 6,200 fashionable clothing stores carrying the family name. After Renault took over the team, the cars remained liveried as Benetton for the 2001 season though for the following year and thereafter, Renault Formula One's colors were emblazoned on the body.

Benetton's first Formula One sponsorship deal was with the British Tyrrell team in 1983, largely because former Tyrrell driver Nani Galli, then supplied woolen products to the Italian fashion giant and, perhaps more importantly, was able to open doors to the potentially valuable American market for the firm. But the following year Benetton turned its allegiance back to Italy and the Alfa Romeo team. In 1985, Benetton sponsored both Alfa Romeo and Toleman and at the end of the year, with the Benetton family seeking more direct control over its motorsport activities, it bought the Toleman and Spirit teams.

Now a constructor, rather than a sponsor, the Benetton team was fairly successful, in the early years though it would only come to full prominence once Michael Schumacher joined as a driver in 1994. The brilliant German, supported by Johnny Herbert, took the team to its first World Constructors Championship in 1995, as Schumacher claimed his second Formula One World Championship. But success was not only down to the drivers. Benetton also enjoyed the services of one of the sport's most charismatic managers, Flavio Briatore. Typically Italian, he was a master of expressive language, expansive gestures, and flamboyant off-track exploits.

He managed the team from 1990 to 1997, though strangely, it raced under an Italian license from 1996, despite its UK base and its headquarters being in Oxfordshire. However, family and politics intervened with the arrival of Rocco Benetton, the youngest son of company founder,

ABOVE: *Team Principal Flavio Briatore (left) celebrates with Michael Schumacher (right) at the 1995 Pacific Grand Prix. Schumacher's victory in the race clinched Benetton's first championship.*

Luciano. Rocco was originally employed as an aerodynamics engineer in 1998 but when the team went through a lean patch he was responsible for the sacking of Briatore and his replacement by Prodrive boss David Richards.

Richards not only ran one of the UK's most successful motorsport operations, but he was also popular, smart, and media savvy. Despite this, he was only at Benetton for a year before he was fired after a dispute about the team's future engine strategy. Rocco Benetton then got the top job and was left unhindered to run the team for three further years until it was sold to Renault. The amount Renault paid for Benetton reflects how desperately keen it was to own its own racing team, as opposed to just acting as an engine supplier: the business changed hands for an astonishing $120million, far more than had ever been paid for an Formula One team before.

The high point of Benetton history was undoubtedly its winning association with Michael Schumacher. The German

ABOVE: *Johnny Herbert (Benetton B195 Renault) in action at the 1995 Spanish Grand Prix. He finished in second position, with team-mate Michael Schumacher winning the race.*

ABOVE: *Fernando Alonso (Renault R25) crosses the line to take victory at the Malaysian Grand Prix during his championship winning season in 2005.*

accounted for 21 of the team's 27 victories and two Drivers titles. When he departed for Ferrari, taking key Benetton personnel such as Ross Brawn, Nigel Stepney, Rory Byrne, and 11 others with him, it left Benetton much weakened.

After Renault bought the team from Benetton, Flavio Briatore returned to the fold, and during the 2001 season drivers Jenson Button and Giancarlo Fisichella continued to race under the Benetton banner. The team was renamed Renault Formula One for 2002 and in 2005 would see Fernando Alonso win the World Championship for drivers, as well as the company taking victory in the Constructors Championship.

Over the years Benetton Formula One drivers included: Michael Schumacher, Ayrton Senna (under Toleman), Jenson Button, Nelson Piquet, Martin Brundle and, Gerhard Berger.

Brabham

Australian racing driver, Jack Brabham, was one of the very first drivers to become a Formula One constructor. He established the team with fellow countryman Ron Tauranac in 1962, and had his first success at Solitude, near Stuttgart. It was a non-championship race but Brabham still became the first owner/operator ever to win a Grand Prix.

ABOVE: *Dan Gurney on the podium at the 1964 French Grand Prix. His victory in the race gave Brabham their first Formula One win.*

Although Brabham had built a run of successful earlier models (from the BT2), by 1964 nine BT8 sports cars had been built, and there were Brabham cars running in Formula One, Formula Two, Formula Three, and at Indianapolis. That year, Dan Gurney gave Brabham its first Formula One victory at the French Grand Prix and followed it up with a second win in Mexico. Brabham himself scored a handful of points-scoring finishes.

Brabham had built nearly 40 racing cars before the decision to start selling Formula One cars as well was taken in 1965. Chassis were sold to customers such as Rob Walker, Bob Anderson, and John Willment and with Jack Brabham himself now much more involved in development work, he drove less often and selected Denny Hulme to drive alongside Gurney.

BELOW: *Denny Hulme (Brabham BT24 Repco) on his way to victory in the 1967 German Grand Prix. That year Hulme and Brabham won the Drivers and Constructors Championship respectively.*

That season Gurney had a number of podium finishes and the team finished a creditable third in the Constructors title.

When new Formula One regulations were imposed in 1966, Brabham persuaded Repco to build an engine to power his new BT19. He paired himself with fellow driver Hulme. The car had its first victory in the International Trophy at Silverstone in May. More victories followed at the French, British, Dutch, and German Grands Prix. By the end of a highly successful season, Jack Brabham was World Champion and Brabham also won the Constructors title.

Meanwhile, in Formula Two, Brabham ran factory cars with Honda engines which completely dominated, with the Brabham chassis winning all but one of that year's races.

Hulme and Brabham were again dominant in 1967 though on this occasion it was Denny who won the world title with Brabham runner-up with the team taking a second consecutive Constructors title. The team enjoyed fewer wins during the 1968 and 1969 seasons, though Brabham was still successful in selling cars for others to run. However, once he decided it was time for him to retire from driving, Brabham sold the team to Bernie Ecclestone's Motor Racing Developments (MRD) in 1972.

In 1973, Ecclestone hired Gordon Murray, a young South African who was a brilliant engineer and designer. He came up with a series of unique innovations including the trapezoid chassis on the BT42/BT44, the integrated radiator/heat exchanger on the arrow shaped BT52, and the infamous BT46B 'Fan Car' that won first time out before being withdrawn. The Brabham team achieved a number of successes in the early 1980s, and lead driver Nelson Piquet won the World Drivers Championship twice, though the Constructors title eluded them.

The BMW-powered BT55 (rather unkindly nicknamed 'The Flounder') marked the beginning of the end for the team. After attempts to sell MRD, Ecclestone withdrew the team entry from the 1988 Formula One Championship.

After the team and the rights to its name were sold to Swiss financier Joachim Luithi, Brabham was back in 1989, but the team was sold again, this time to the Japanese Middlebridge company. Herbie Blash, a long-time Brabham manager, returned to run the business and recruited David Brabham, son of the team's founder, as one of its drivers.

The team was not very successful, though hopes were raised when Blash persuaded Yamaha to supply its V12 engines in 1991 and Martin Brundle and Mark Blundell were recruited to drive. Between them they won only three points in the BT59Y and at the end of the season Yamaha switched allegiance to the Jordan team, leaving Brabham with uncompetitive Judd engines, old cars, and little money.

ABOVE: *Nelson Piquet (Brabham BT52B BMW) in action during his winning race at the 1983 Italian Grand Prix.*

NEXT SPREAD: *Mario Andretti (Lotus 79 Ford) leads Niki Lauda (Brabham BT46B Alfa Romeo) and the rest of the field at the start of the 1978 Swedish Grand Prix. Lauda went on to win the race for Brabham.*

Landhurst Leasing provided some capital and Brabham started the 1992 season with Eric van de Poele and female racer Giovanna Amati as drivers. Giovanna was later replaced by Damon Hill but the uncompetitive Brabham only qualified in three races and the team was forced to quit Formula One.

Ferrari

Although it is always possible that its tally can one day be beaten, it will take a prodigious effort over many years for any team to top Ferrari's unrivaled record as the most successful Formula One team of all time.

The facts are truly astonishing: Ferrari is the only team that has competed every year since Formula One began, starting 780 Grands Prix by early 2009 and clocking up 209 race victories. As well as winning more than one in four races in which it competed, the bright red Ferrari cars—every one of which is powered only by Ferrari's own engines—have also claimed 203 pole positions. And in total, Ferrari drivers have stood on the podium more than 620 times. Ferrari took its first Formula One title at Monaco in the year the championship started in 1950; and won its first constructor points at Argentina in 1958, again, the first year that championship was inaugurated.

As long ago as 1979, Ferrari became the first team ever to amass more than 100 points in one season. And although Ferrari can't claim the outright record for the most wins in a season (it has to share that honor with McLaren as both have managed 15), no other constructor has ever managed 29 podiums and 262 points in just one year.

Sadly, Ferrari's record also includes one statistic that overshadows its successes. More drivers have been killed in a Ferrari than in any other Formula One car, though the seven sad deaths are more a reflection of the number of races started by Ferrari, than any suggestion that its cars are inherently more dangerous than others.

The team was first founded in 1929 by Enzo Ferrari, universally known as 'Il Commendatore'. A racing driver himself in his youth, he started competing in Grand Prix racing using Lancia cars. Ferrari's famous 'prancing horse' logo was actually first used on those Lancias, before Ferrari started building the cars that bore his own name.

Ferrari is not just the most successful Formula One team in the world, it is also the team that has the most ardent following. It's a passion that has been developed over many years and is now so strong that its fans even have their own name, the tifosi, who turn out in their thousands for every Grand Prix around the world.

Like all teams, Ferrari has had its period in the doldrums and it struggled during the 1980s and early 1990s. During that period of famine, Ferrari was blighted by engine failures, political and economic controversies, and allegations of in-fighting among its team members. But when Michael Schumacher joined the Ferrari team, for a reputed $45 million, the winning combination had a spectacular effect, giving Ferrari one of its most productive periods and also creating massive worldwide interest and additional spectators to the Formula One arena. Ferrari won five consecutive double titles (Drivers and Constructors Championships) from the years 2000 to 2004, something no other team has ever got close to emulating.

The team had benefitted from astute leadership under Enzo Ferrari, and although the team lost direction after the

RIGHT: *Team Principal Jean Todt and Michael Schumacher celebrate another Ferrari victory. This time at the 2006 Italian Grand Prix.*

great man died, by the turn of the millennium, Jean Todt, the highly successful former leader of Peugeot's Rally team, reestablished Ferrari as a stable and formidable unit.

The drivers' list reads like a 'Who's-Who of Formula One', and includes Alberto Ascari, Juan Manuel Fangio, Mike Hawthorn, Phil Hill, John Surtees, Niki Lauda, Jody Scheckter, Michael Schumacher, and Kimi Räikkönen, all of whom secured the title of World Champion. The rest were no less than outstanding either. Alain Prost, Nigel Mansell, Gilles Villeneuve, Eddie Irvine, and Rene Arnoux have all been Ferrari drivers. Yet, Ferrari has seldom been without capable rivals: Clark-Lotus, Mansell-Williams, and Senna/Prost-McLaren dominations proved that and helped keep the sport exciting. Even so, Ferrari personnel have been able to construct a formidable supremacy in the ranks of Grand Prix. And there is assuredly more to come from the foremost constructor.

ABOVE: *Ferrari team boss Enzo Ferrari (right) talks in the pits with race winner John Surtees (left) at the 1964 Italian Grand Prix.*

ABOVE: *The Ferrari team cheers Michael Schumacher (Ferrari F2004) across the line as he takes victory in the 2004 Japanese Grand Prix.*

Lotus

Ferrari might be described as the most charismatic constructor in Formula One, but the British Lotus outfit is not far behind.

The company was founded by Colin Chapman, a brilliant engineer with a truly imaginative turn of mind whose mantra was always to seek improvements in performance through simplicity of design and saving weight wherever possible. His first car was a modified Austin 7 which he built and raced himself. Other specials followed and he set up Lotus Engineering in 1952. While Chapman was its well-known figurehead, Lotus was far from a one-man band, however. Over the years its successes have come about thanks to great teamwork.

In 1957, Lotus moved into Formula Two with the Lotus 11. Chapman himself drove, alongside Cliff Allison and Reg Bricknell and although Chapman won one race at Brands Hatch, the car was no real match for the Cooper Formula Two car of Roy Salvadori. For 1958, the Lotus 12 appeared, powered by a 2.2-

ABOVE: *The 1992 Monaco Grand Prix: Mika Häkkinen (Lotus 107 Ford) left the race when his failing clutch caused the gearbox to break.*

liter Coventry Climax engine and Lotus moved into Formula One, entering two cars for Graham Hill and Allison at the Monaco Grand Prix. But even after the engines were later bored out to 2.5-liters, Chapman's front-engined racing car remained uncompetitive, so he took the decision to create an

BELOW: *During the 1963 Italian Grand Prix Jim Clark (Lotus 25 Climax) gives team boss Colin Chapman a lift, as they celebrate finishing in first position and clinching the Drivers and Constructors Championship titles.*

ABOVE: *Emerson Fittipaldi (Lotus 72D Ford) on his way to victory at the 1972 Spanish Grand Prix.*

all-new rear-engined design in 1960—the Lotus 18.

Rob Walker's private Lotus entry provided the first victory for a Lotus Grand Prix car, in the Monaco Grand Prix with Stirling Moss at the wheel. Then Team Lotus clocked up its first win in 1961 when Innes Ireland took the checkered flag at the United States Grand Prix.

By this time, the Lotus road car business was also thriving. Mainly due to Lotus's racing success, the Lotus Seven Elite, Lotus Elan, and Ford Lotus Cortina all sold in encouraging volumes.

But the real breakthrough for Lotus came in 1963 after Jim Clark had joined the team to drive the innovative, lightweight monocoque Lotus 25. He was second in the Championship in 1962 but his seven victories in 1963 gave the team its first Constructors Championship and him his first Drivers title. Ferrari came out on top in 1964 but Clark and Lotus gained their second titles in 1965. A 3.0-liter Grand Prix formula was introduced in 1966. Initially Chapman chose unreliable BRM engines, but after switching to the Cosworth DFV in 1967, Graham Hill lifted the title in 1968 in the Lotus 49.

Two years later the highly aerodynamic Lotus 72 took Jochen Rindt to a sadly posthumous World Championship in 1970 and in 1972 Emerson Fittipaldi in a revised version of the same car, gave Lotus yet another World Championship.

Ground-effect technology on the Lotus 79, another of Chapman's brilliant innovations, helped Mario Andretti to win the Drivers title in 1978, and another Constructors title for Lotus. Unfortunately, Chapman's death in 1982 meant the loss of a guiding hand for the team.

Peter Warr took over the team management, but the Lotus-Renault 93T was unsuccessful. Ayrton Senna arrived in 1984 and drove the Lotus-Renault 97T to victory in Portugal and Belgium while team-mate Elio de Angelis won at Imola. In 1986, Senna was on pole eight times, though he only won in Spain and Detroit, but his talents were instrumental in getting Honda to agree an engine supply contract. With Honda power, the active-suspension Lotus 99T powered Senna to victory at Monaco and Detroit in 1987 and he ended the season third in the Drivers Championship.

Senna moved to McLaren in 1988 to be replaced by Nelson Piquet in the Lotus-Honda 100T. In 1989, turbocharged engines were banned and Lotus first used the Judd V8, then, in 1990, the Lamborghini V12 engine. Peter Collins and Peter Wright launched the new Team Lotus with Mika Häkkinen and Julian Bailey driving for 1991, but the team only achieved fifth in the Constructors title. Results didn't improve and, in October 1994, the team was sold to David Hunt, brother of James. The following year a merger with Pacific Grand Prix saw the name Team Lotus finally disappear.

McLaren

With eight Formula One Constructors titles under its belt, McLaren's run of successes is second only to that of Ferrari. It remains a well-funded and fascinatingly advanced constructor and it's unlikely that it will not add to its roll of honor before much longer.

Team McLaren was launched by former racer Bruce McLaren. Its first car was the M1, basically a CanAm sports car chassis with an Oldsmobile engine. After Robin Herd was recruited as designer he produced the M2B, whose Serenissima 3.0-liter engine was underpowered although McLaren was able to make it onto the podium at the British Grand Prix in 1966. From 1968, the Cosworth DFV engine became available and Herd built an all-new car, the M7, which won four races in Formula One. Tragically, Bruce McLaren was killed testing the 1970 M8 car at Goodwood, so management of the team passed to Teddy Mayer. Formula One successes in 1971 and 1972 were few and far between, though McLaren dominated CanAm at that time.

Then in 1973, Gordon Coppuck was brought in to develop the M23 and this was to be the car that would turn round McLaren's fortunes, winning the British and Canadian Grands Prix. There was more to come in the following season in 1974.

ABOVE: *Dan Gurney leads Denny Hulme (both McLaren M7A Ford) at the 1968 Canadian Grand Prix. Hulme went on to win the race.*

BELOW: *Robin Herd, Chief Designer, talks with owner Bruce McLaren and Teddy Mayer at the Team McLaren factory in 1968.*

ABOVE: *Ayrton Senna leads team-mate Gerhard Berger (both McLaren MP4/5B Honda's) with Alain Prost (Ferrari 641) following behind during the 1990 Italian Grand Prix. Senna went on to win the race.*

Teddy Mayer managed the Formula One Marlboro Texaco team with Denny Hulme and Emerson Fittipaldi driving, while the Yardley McLaren team was separately managed by Phil Kerr with Mike Hailwood driving.

Though Hailwood suffered a major accident and was replaced by Jochen Mass, the big story was the success of Emerson Fittipaldi, who won three times and took four other podium places to win his second Drivers title. More importantly for McLaren, he also provided the team with its first Constructors title.

The next year Fittipaldi had another good season with two wins and another four podium finishes, then left to join his brother's Copersucar-funded team, so McLaren contracted James Hunt. Driving a revised M23, Hunt won the 1976 world title after a nail-biting end to the season.

The 1977 season started poorly because of reliability problems with the M26 but Hunt went on to win three races and pick up enough points to finish the season respectably. 1978 was a disastrous season and the following few seasons were also dismal for McLaren. However, a new chapter was started in 1980 when Project Four Racing, the Formula Two team run by Ron Dennis, teamed up with McLaren with sponsorship from Marlboro. John Barnard was appointed technical director and he set about designing the new MP4/1. McLaren came second in that year's Constructors Championship with John Watson also second in the Drivers title.

McLaren then agreed a partnership with the TAG Group and switched to turbocharged engines built by Porsche. At first there were reliability problems but in Barnard's latest MP4/2 chassis, Niki Lauda and Alain Prost won 12 races between them, with Lauda clinching the Drivers title from Prost by just half a point. McLaren, meanwhile, was the runaway winner of the Constructors title. They won again in 1985 and Prost won the Drivers title in 1985 and 1986.

By 1987 it was clear that McLaren was no longer competitive. A deal was struck with Honda to supply engines for 1988 and Brazilian Ayrton Senna joined Prost in the driver line-up. Between them they won an astonishing 15 races, with Senna just winning the title. Next year they won 10 races between them though this time it was Prost who won the Drivers title as McLaren picked up yet another Constructors title.

1990 saw McLaren's third consecutive world title as Senna won yet again and a fourth Constructors Championship came in 1991 as Senna won the Drivers title once more.

It would be another seven years before McLaren won the Constructors title again, in 1998 when Mika Häkkinen also won the Drivers title. In the meantime, Marlboro had withdrawn its sponsorship and Mercedes-Benz was now the engine supplier and had acquired a 40 percent shareholding in McLaren. Ferrari dominated Formula One for a period of years, but McLaren started a comeback in 2007, and in 2008 saw its young British driver Lewis Hamilton lift the Drivers title.

Renault

Renault is not just one of the oldest motor manufacturers in the world, it is also one of the very first to get involved with motorsport.

Founder brothers Louis and Marcel Renault both raced regularly until Marcel was killed during the Paris to Madrid race of 1903. Renault also has the distinction of winning the very first Grand Prix in 1906 when Ferenc Szisz took the honors in his Renault AK 90 CV.

More recently, Renault returned to the Formula One fold in 1976 when it set up Renault Sport. The first few seasons were frustrating as its first and second generation cars were uncompetitive and unreliable and it took another two years before J-P Jabouille scored Renault's first Formula One points with fourth place at Watkins Glen. However, Renault does have the distinction of being the first manufacturer to introduce a turbocharged engine into Formula One when its RS01 car debuted at the British Grand Prix in 1977. Renault may have struggled with the technology at first, but very soon all the other engine manufacturers followed Renault's lead.

Two cars were entered for the 1979 season, driven by Jabouille and his new team-mate Rene Arnoux. Jabouille won the home French Grand Prix that year to clock up the team's first ever Formula One victory and a further smattering of race victories buoyed spirits over the next couple of years. Then, in 1981, Alain Prost joined the team alongside Arnoux and won three times, taking Renault to third place in the Constructors title. Another third place came in 1982 after Prost and Arnoux each won twice. The 1983 and 1984 seasons were not what the team had hoped for, especially when Prost won four times in 1983 and that still was not enough to beat Nelson Piquet to the Drivers title.

At this time Renault started to supply engines to other teams, including Lotus and Ligier at first, but also Tyrrell, in 1985.

After Prost left, Renault signed Derek Warwick and Patrick Tambay but they failed to win any races—and at first the teams to whom Renault had supplied engines did no better. However, in 1985 Lotus managed three wins from its drivers Ayrton Senna and Elio de Angelis.

At the end of 1986, after Lotus had again made progress but the Renault, Ligier and Tyrrell teams had made none,

ABOVE: *The 1978 United States Grand Prix: Jean-Pierre Jabouille (Renault RS01) on his way to fourth place to claim Renault's first points in Formula One.*

Renault pulled out of Formula One. However, work had already started on the development of a new V10 engine and Renault returned to Formula One two years later as an engine supplier to Williams and Benetton.

Both enjoyed such success that in 2000 Renault decided it was time for a full return to Formula One and bought the Benetton team. For the 2001 season, Flavio Briatore was appointed as manager, and Mike Gascoyne as engineering director. At first, the team struggled to stay on the pace, perhaps because the V10 was no longer as competitive as it had been earlier, but in 2003 victory finally came, when Fernando Alonso won in Hungary. Next season his team-mate Jarno Trulli won in Monaco but Renault's real hopes were pinned on the 2005 season, when Alonso was joined by Giancarlo Fisichella.

Sure enough, Alonso drove brilliantly, putting together a

series of victories that were more than enough to land him the Drivers title and Renault the one prize that had eluded them for so long—its first Constructors title.

Alonso was again the dominant force in Formula One in 2006 and once more he and Renault lifted the main titles. However, he then announced a move to McLaren so Heikki Kovalainen was recruited to join Fisichella. It was not a huge success as the Renault car proved difficult to set up with the new Bridgestone tires they were required to use. However, when McLaren was stripped of all its points, Renault inherited third place in the Constructors title.

Then, Renault was accused of obtaining McLaren secrets in a near copy of the Ferrari-McLaren debacle. Strangely, Renault escaped punishment. Alonso returned for 2008 alongside Nelson Piquet junior, the son of the former World Champion, but results have been hard to come by since then.

ABOVE: *Jarno Trulli (Renault R24) leads Ralf Schumacher (BMW Williams FW26) at the 2004 Monaco Grand Prix. Trulli went on to win the race for Renault.*

ABOVE: *Giancarlo Fisichella (Renault R26) leads Jenson Button (Honda RA106) on his way to victory in the 2006 Malaysian Grand Prix.*

NEXT SPREAD: *2005 San Marino Grand Prix: The Renault team celebrates as Fernando Alonso (Renault R25) crosses the line to take victory with Michael Schumacher (Ferrari F2005) close behind.*

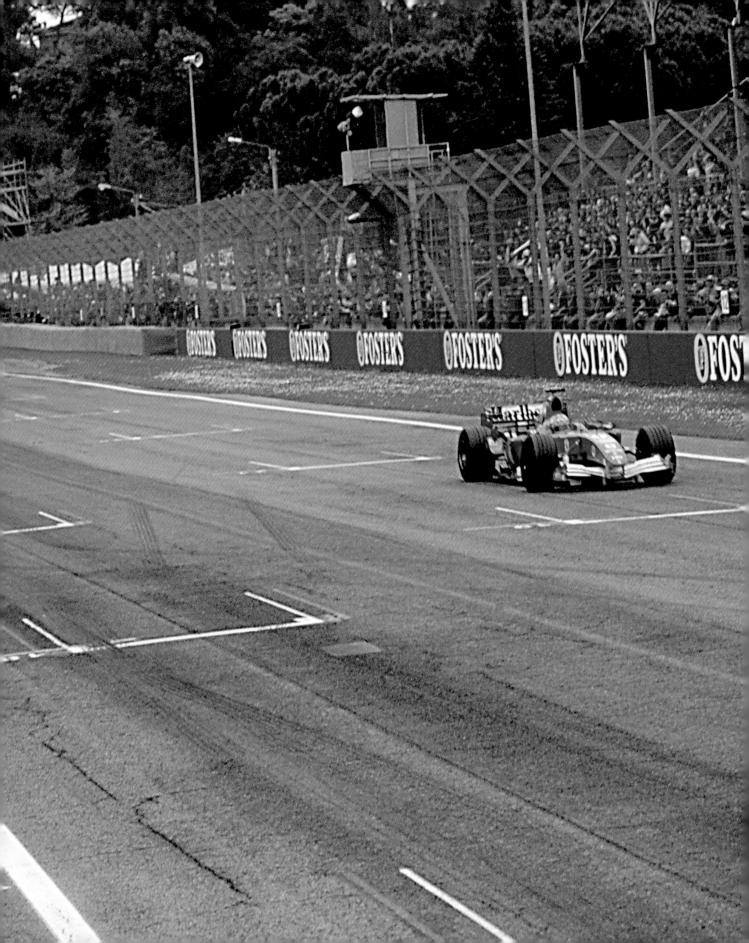

Tyrrell

Ken Tyrrell, the founder of the team that bore his name, was an old-fashioned motorsport enthusiast. His unmistakable lanky figure striding around the Formula One paddock became an integral part of the Formula One scene over many years.

Funding was always a problem for a small independent team but Ken was always happy to assist other teams when he could, and also to nurture a succession of young drivers, who might never have got a chance to drive in Formula One otherwise.

Tyrrell was an independently wealthy man who first came into motorsport as a highly successful driver in Formula Three cars throughout the 1950s. In 1958, he set up a team to contest in Formula Two with Henry Taylor in the driving seat. Then in 1960, he set up his Tyrrell Racing Organisation to manage the factory Cooper team in Formula Junior, and the following year the factory Mini Coopers in the Touring Car Series.

Tyrrell continued in Formula Three all this time and for the 1964 season recruited Jackie Stewart and Warwick Banks to

drive for him. Tyrrell's car and Stewart's innate ability proved a winning combination as the Scotsman won the British Formula Three Championship hands down. The bad news was that Stewart was then poached by BRM to drive in Formula One, but in those more relaxed days Stewart still found time to drive Tyrrell's Cooper in Formula Two in the same season.

Then, following a serious road accident, John Cooper had to hand over management of the Cooper Formula One team to Tyrrell. He started using a Matra chassis in Formula Two and then in 1968 this chassis, mated to a Cosworth DFV engine, became the basis for a Formula One entry, racing under the Matra International banner. Jackie Stewart returned to Tyrrell to drive and won three times during that first season.

Yet more progress was made over the next couple of years, culminating in Stewart lifting his first Formula One Championship title in 1969. At this time, Matra pulled out of Formula One so Tyrrell sought a replacement chassis. He switched to a March chassis, while working behind closed doors on his own Tyrrell 001 chassis.

The Tyrrell proudly debuted in 1970 when Stewart made an immediate impression by taking pole position at the Canadian Grand Prix. Further development saw the introduction of the Tyrrell 003 in 1971, in which Stewart won

ABOVE: *Jean Alesi (Tyrrell 018 Ford) in action during the 1990 United States Grand Prix. He finished the race in second place.*

practice accident, Stewart retired from Grand Prix racing.

The next few years saw mixed successes for Tyrrell, which revealed its innovative thinking with a revolutionary six-wheeled car in 1976. After that, money became short so Tyrrell signed a succession of young, inexpensive but also inexperienced drivers. The loss of long-standing sponsor Elf also made the team's position increasingly tenuous in the Formula One scene.

However, things looked up in 1983 when the Italian fashion company Benetton joined Tyrrell as a major sponsor. Sadly for the team, Benetton switched allegiance the following year though Tyrrell did manage to secure an engine supply deal with Renault Sport.

Tyrrell struggled through the next few years but continued to develop its cars until 1989 when, with Jean Alesi driving, the Tyrrell 018 started producing results. Alesi's success inspired the team, and the 1990 car, the 019, was even better.

Alesi moved to Ferrari in 1991 at which time Tyrrell contracted to use Honda engines. Generally, results were not forthcoming and, in 1997, the Tyrrell family accepted a $30 million payment from British American Racing and handed over its once proud business to the BAR management.

ABOVE: *Team boss Ken Tyrrell (left) on the podium with race winner Jackie Stewart (right) at the 1973 German Grand Prix.*

ABOVE: *Jackie Stewart (Tyrrell 003 Ford) on his way to victory in the German Grand Prix during Tyrrell's only championship winning season in 1971.*

Williams

Although Frank Williams' racing team started in much the same way as any number of other similar operations, there is a gritty determination within the business operation that is not only fed by a passion for winning, but also for making money from what is, after all, a professional sport.

Other teams have come and gone, some promising new marketing gimmicks, while others have charismatic front men, Williams has always managed to build a remarkably strong business first, with racing employed as its means to reach the

ABOVE: *Williams team boss Frank Williams talks with his driver Alan Jones at the 1980 Austrian Grand Prix.*

market. No less than nine Constructors Championship victories have come its way, starting in 1980 and continuing through 1981, then 1986 and 1987, followed by a short break until 1992 and a run of three titles to 1994, culminating in wins in 1996 and 1997. However, despite its professionalism, the company expressed concerns about survival up to the end of 2008 without another team victory.

Frank actually started as a driver, but ran out of cash to run himself and turned to car preparation for other people instead, starting with his friend Piers Courage in 1967. Max Mosley also joined the team as a paying driver. For 1969, Williams ran Courage in Formula Two again, but acquired an ex-works Brabham F1 car for selected races. The season began well and Williams ran up to four cars in Formula Two, with a variety of good drivers. In 1970, Williams and Alessandro de Tomaso partnered and ran Courage in a Dallara-designed de Tomaso-Ford. Tragically, Courage was killed at Zolder. March was chosen by Williams for its 1971 entry, but results were slim.

Although armed with major development funds from sponsor Politoys, 1972 was to be a year best forgotten by Williams. The cars were late in arriving, the prototype was destroyed in the British Grand Prix, and the remaining Marches suffered similar

ABOVE: *Argentine Grand Prix: Alan Jones (Williams FW07-Ford Cosworth) on his way to victory in the first race of his and Williams championship winning season of 1980.*

ABOVE: *Nigel Mansell (Williams FW11B Honda) takes the checkered flag to win the 1987 French Grand Prix.*

fates. Iso-Rivolta came to the rescue for 1973 with Marlboro money and Nanni Galli driving initially. The team struggled financially, but created the first car to bear the Williams name. Forced to enter a partnership with Walter Wolf Racing to settle his debts, Williams ran Hesketh chassis and obtained backing from Marlboro. By 1977, having decided that he had enough, Williams left the team, but not before he managed to convince several of his old team members to join him and, together with designer Patrick Head, Williams Grand Prix Engineering was established in Didcot. A new car for the 1978 season gave Williams the chance to seek new drivers and Alan Jones would drive the Williams FW06, which was great car. More sponsorship funds were generated and Head designed the new FW07, while Clay Reggazoni and Jones drove for the team in 1979.

In 1980, with an updated FW07, the team swept all before it. Jones won in Argentina, France, Britain, Canada, and the United States. Reutemann won in Monaco. Williams won the Constructors' title, Jones was World Champion, and Reutemann came in third. Williams repeated its feat in 1981. Meanwhile, the FW08 of 1982 gave Keke Rosberg a race win and end of season reliability made him the World Champion. A new

Honda-powered, turbocharged FW09 appeared at the final race of 1983. While 1984 was a dud year, Mansell signed for 1985 and secured some race wins. However, before the end of the year, Williams was seriously injured in a car crash near the Paul Ricard circuit and was left paralysed. On the other hand, the team secured two successive constructors' titles in 1986 and 1987.

Engine supply issues dogged the company for the next four seasons and victories were thin on the ground, though the title chase proved successful for the next three seasons from 1992 to 1994. Sadly, the win was marred by Senna's death following an accident at the San Marino Grand Prix. Hill became the team's number one driver and David Coulthard stepped up from his role as test driver. In 1996 and 1997, Williams took two further constructors' titles.

Williams failed to win in 1998 and remained uncompetitive in 1999. While things looked up in 2001 and 2002, Ferrari was stronger and for 2003 the team embarked on a new aerodynamic envelope. Unreliability has remained the greatest problem to Williams since then, which means that it is relying on its business acumen at the moment. The rule changes for 2009 may see a change in its fortunes.

ABOVE: *Alberto Ascari (Ferrari 125, number 40) passes the multi-car accident at the start of the 1950 Monaco Grand Prix.*

places on the podium, with Farina the first-ever winner of a race in the new championship.

Ferrari and Maserati joined the championship in Monaco for the second race, but—after a pile-up at the start chopped the field in half—Fangio finished a clear lap ahead to claim the team's second win, with Ascari second in the Ferrari.

The Indianapolis race was only part of the championship because of its status as one of the world's great races, but none of the European teams turned up and American Johnny Parsons took a victory for Wynn's Kurtis that secured him sixth in the championship.

Back in Europe, Alfa men Fangio and Farina traded victories well ahead of the chasing pack. Farina won in Switzerland and Fangio in Belgium and France, but in a dramatic final race at Monza, a gearbox failure for Fangio gave Farina the win and the title by three points.

1951

Ferrari were driving forward, but Alfa still set the early pace in 1951, with Fangio winning in rainy Switzerland. The second race of the season was at Indianapolis and, once again, the European teams chose not to compete in the United States.

model with more development potential than their rivals. Ascari and Gonzalez scored a 1-2 for Ferrari at Monza, setting up a thrilling title decider.

The final race was on the Pedrables street circuit in Spain, which was also destined to be the last race for Alfa before they quit the sport. Thanks to the talent of Fangio and tire problems that beset his title rival Ascari's Ferrari, it was a happy ending for Alfa. The Argentine won, and took the title.

1952

New 'Formula Two' regulations for Formula One posed no problems for Ferrari and, with Alfa gone, they were now the dominant force in Formula One. Farina joined Ascari and Luigi Villoresi in their lead line-up while Fangio moved to Maserati, but sadly he broke his neck and had to sit out the season.

The open rules allowed many new teams to join Italians Ferrari and Maserati, with the British Cooper-Bristol in the hands of Mike Hawthorn, and French Gordini machines the best of the rest. But they would never be close enough to challenge the establishment.

Ascari missed the first race of the season, in Switzerland, having decided to give the Indy 500 a try, but his replacement—Piero Taruffi—won the race for Ferrari.

Having failed to win at Indianapoils, with victory there going to Troy Ruttman in his Kurtis-Kraft, Ascari returned for round three, in Belgium, and dominated the rest of the season with an amazing run of six consecutive race victories, with the fastest lap in every one.

He mastered the wet in Spa then led a Ferrari 1-2-3 in France and a 1-2 in Britain (where Hawthorn claimed an impressive third in front of his home crowd). Ascari then led a 1-2-3-4 in Germany, where a late pit stop forced him to catch and pass Farina, proving that he firmly had the upper hand over his rivals. Victories in Holland and Italy finished off a remarkable run of dominance and, with only the best four results counting, he notched up a perfect score.

Lee Wallard took victory at Indianapolis for Belanger, but back in the 'real' Formula One, Alfa continued their strong form with Farina taking the flag at Spa-Francorchamps in Belgium and Fagioli sharing his car with Fangio to win in France.

The first victory for Ferrari finally came at Silverstone when Froilán González capitalized on a mistake by fellow Argentine Fangio. Later, Ascari claimed his first win, becuase the long straights of the Nürburgring, a new addition to the calendar, suited his Ferrari.

In fact, Ferrari dominated that race, with five cars in the top six, because they benefitted from a more fuel efficient and newer

1953

Ascari was the man to beat again in 1953, despite the arrival of highly rated Briton Mike Hawthorn at Ferrari, but the return of Juan Manuel Fangio with Maserati saw the Italian teams' rivalry strengthen as the season progressed.

The championship expanded into new territory, going to South America for the first time with a race in Argentina, but on Fangio's home ground Ascari claimed pole, fastest lap, and race victory.

The new Maserati proved fast but fragile and, as it repeatedly broke down, Ascari extended his run of consecutive victories

ABOVE: *Mike Hawthorn (Cooper T20-Bristol) leads Giuseppe Farina (Ferrari 500) during the 1952 Dutch Grand Prix.*

(discounting Indianapolis, which continued to be ignored by the European teams) to nine before Hawthorn finally ended it in France after a titanic battle with Fangio's Maserati.

Ascari won again in Britain and probably would have taken victory in Germany had his wheel not fallen off, handing victory to Farina. However, Ascari secured the title in style at the last but one race in Switzerland, when an unscheduled stop forced him to fight through the field, past Farina and Hawthorn, to claim victory.

In the final race of the year, in Italy, a spectacular slipstreaming battle saw Ascari assume the lead, but he made a mistake on the last lap and spun, taking out team-mate Farina in the process, and letting Fangio through to take Maserati's debut win.

1954

A new 2.5-liter formula was announced for 1954 and opened the door for Mercedes-Benz to make its Formula One debut. The uniquely attractive 'streamliner' machines drew Fangio away from Maserati while Ascari was tempted by the promise of new arrival Lancia. The Argentine would prove to be the one who made the right move.

Fangio's new Mercedes was not ready for the start of the season, in Argentina, so he raced a Maserati to victory. The Indy 500, still counting in the championship, but not contested by the main Formula One field, went to Bill Vukovich. Back in Europe, it was all Fangio.

Fangio won again in Belgium then switched to his Mercedes for France, where the German team dominated on their debut. Fangio led Karl Kling in a dramatic 1-2.

The fairytale start wasn't to be continued at the next race, in Britain. The Mercedes struggled at Silverstone, leaving Gonzalez to claim victory for Ferrari. Sadly, Formula One was again hit by tragedy at the following race in Germany, when Argentine Maserati driver Onofre Marimón became the first driver to die at a Formula One event.

Fangio fought back the tears for his countryman and raced to victory, then went from strength to strength, winning in Switzerland and Italy; the latter victory being handed to him when the Maserati of leader Stirling Moss failed nine laps from the end, leaving the Briton to push it over the line in 11th.

All this time, reigning champion Ascari had been forced to sit on the sidelines while his Lancia team fought to finish his new machine. When it was finally ready, for the season's last race in Spain, he led 10 laps before retiring to hand Hawthorn and Ferrari the final win.

1955

The 1955 season is remembered for tragedy rather than triumph. World motorsport was rocked by the deaths of more than 80 people at Le Mans as well as the loss of former champion Ascari, who crashed testing a sports car mid season, and multiple Indy 500 winner American Bill Vukovich, who died in a crash at Indianapolis.

But the racing went on with Fangio firm favorite for Mercedes, Ascari persisting with Lancia, Jean Behra joining Ferrari to replace Merecedes-bound Moss, and Hawthorn deciding to race for Britain and swapping *scuderia* red for the racing green of Vanwall—though he was to return to Ferrari mid season.

Mercedes started strongly with victory for Fangio in a sweltering January race in Argentina, but both Mercedes cars retired from the second race in Monaco where Frenchman Maurice Trintignant won for Ferrari after Ascari crashed into the harbor. Just four days later, yet another crash claimed the Italian's life.

Fangio and Moss took a 1-2 for Mercedes in Belgium and though the next weekend saw the tragedy at Le Mans, Formula One raced on, with Mercedes dominating to claim a 1-2 in Holland, a 1-2-3-4 in Britain—with Moss claiming his maiden win on home soil—and closing the season off with a 1-2 on the circuit of Monza, handing Fangio his second consecutive title.

1956

This year brought a huge shock to the sport as Mercedes pulled out at the end of their second title-winning season, leaving Fangio fleeing to former enemy Ferrari, who decided to use the Lancia chassis. Meanwhile, Moss made a move to Maserati and Hawthorn had another stab at fighting the British corner by moving to BRM.

Fangio won for Ferrari in Argentina after retiring his car and jumping in his new team-mate Luigi Musso's machine, but his old team-mate Moss claimed victory for Maserati in Monaco with the Argentine coming home in second after again having to borrow a team-mate's car to get to the finish.

American Pat Flaherty won the Indianapolis 500, which continued to have little relevance to the Formula One championship, while in Europe Briton Peter Collins took his first win for Ferrari in Belgium and followed it with victory in France.

Fangio was back in front in Britain, overcoming some strong early race form from local team BRM to lead home a Ferrari 1-2. He then struck a blow to Collins' title hopes with victory in Germany, leaving the Briton and consistent Maserati man Behra in the distance, though still with a slim chance of title success.

The final round, at Monza, saw a unique finish to the championship when Fangio retired with a broken steering arm. Behra also dropped out and Collins, who could have won the title, pulled into the pits and gave the car over to Fangio to hand the Argentine another world championship crown.

1957

It seemed Fangio could never settle with one team. After winning with Mercedes and then with Ferrari, he moved to Maserati to try to claim a consecutive hat-trick of titles, driving in three different manufacturers' cars. The equally indecisive Hawthorn joined Ferrari for a third time while Moss went British with Vanwall.

Argentine Fangio made it four wins in a row at home with victory in Buenos Aires as Maserati finished 1-2-3-4 and Ferrari faltered with mechanical problems. Moss put his Vanwall second on the grid at the next race, in Monaco, but Fangio raced to victory from pole while Moss collided with Collins and created

ABOVE: *Jose Froilán Gonzaléz (Ferrari 625) leads Juan Manuel Fangio (Mercedes-Benz W196) and Stirling Moss (Maserati 250F) at the start of the 1954 German Grand Prix.*

ABOVE: *The field taking the curve after the Raidillon de l'eau Rouge in the 1956 Belgian Grand Prix.*

a multi-car pile-up.

Across the Atlantic, the Indy 500 was won by Sam Hanks in his Epperly machine while, back in Europe, the circus moved on to France for another dominant Fangio victory, though the two Vanwall drivers, Moss and Tony Brooks, were notably missing from the grid.

They returned in Britain and it was a different story, with Moss the star of the day. After building up a lead, Moss was forced to retire his car and took over Brooks' machine, lying in sixth, and raced through the field to claim a memorable victory.

A rattled Fangio put on his best ever display at the next race, in Germany, and secured his fifth and final title when he was second to Moss in the penultimate race at Pescara. The pair then finished the season in style, with Moss taking the win after a spectacular battle at Monza.

1958

It was the end of an era when both Fangio and Maserati retired from Formula One in 1958. But triumph and tragedy were in store and Ferrari looked set to capitalize with their new Dino 246 machine.

In the longest Formula One season so far, with 11 races, Vanwall seemed to be Ferrari's only rivals, but in the opening race they failed to turn up and it was a rear-engined Cooper-Climax 43 (as opposed to the then-standard front-engined design) that claimed victory with Moss at the wheel.

Trintignant took a second win for Cooper in Monaco, then Moss, who had now returned to Vanwall, won in Holland and Brooks made it four out of four for the British teams with a Vanwall win in Belgium. For the record, though with little championship relevance, Jimmy Bryan won the Indy 500 in the States.

It was not going to plan for Ferrari and, though they won in France, with Hawthorn taking his only victory of the year, tragedy struck as Musso was killed. Briton Collins won for Ferrari at Silverstone but, just two weeks later, he was also killed, becoming the second Ferrari driver to lose his life in a month.

Brooks had taken a hollow victory for Vanwall in that tragic German race—Collins having gone off the road in an effort to catch him—and when Moss gave Vanwall another win in Portugal he set up a tense finale in Casablanca, where Moss won but Hawthorn did enough to take the title. Sadly, after retiring in glory, Hawthorn died in a road accident early the following year.

1959

The end of the decade marked a true phase shift in Formula One as the rear-engined Cooper-Climax, with a new 2.5-liter engine, came to the fore. Vanwall had quit and Brooks had joined Ferrari, along with Behra and American Phil Hill, but their front-engined machine failed to perform and a new grid order was created.

The Argentinean Grand Prix was cancelled and at Monaco—now the season opener—the Cooper's superior handling enabled Jack Brabham to win after Behra's Ferrari and Moss' Cooper had retired. Roger Ward won a tragedy-struck Indianapolis 500, after two fatalities in qualifying, then BRM claimed their first victory, with Jo Bonnier winning in Holland.

Ferrari scored a 1-2 in France, with a dominant Brooks leading Hill home after the Italian team sent five works cars to chase victory. They failed to turn up to the next race in Britain, where Brabham scored a second win for Cooper, but were back on top in Germany as Brooks triumphed again.

Moss put himself into contention for the title with wins in Portugal and Italy, but, when the season ended at the first-ever United States Grand Prix three months later, he was forced to retire and Brabham was crowned champion.

ABOVE: *The 1958 Monaco Grand Prix: Maurice Trintignant receives the winning trophy from HRH Prince Rainier and Princess Grace.*

Juan Manuel Fangio

Fangio was one of the sport's all-time greats, a popular and fearless champion of diminutive stature, but a giant presence. He let his racing do the talking, winning in all manner of machinery, and is the only man to ever win Formula One world titles with four different manufacturers.

An Argentine of Italian descent, Fangio was in Formula One from the start and raced on until 1958, winning five titles—for Italian trio Alfa Romeo, Maserati, and Ferrari, as well as German giants Mereedes—taking 29 poles and 35 podiums. With 24 victories from 51 starts, he almost averaged a win every other race.

EARLY YEARS

Born just south of Buenos Aires in 1911, Fangio was a keen runner and a football fan before discovering motorsport as a mechanic at the relatively mature age of 23. He competed for national honors driving Chevrolet cars and took the Argentine title in 1940 and 1941 before the World War II ended his fun.

After showing a real talent when some of the top overseas racers of the day came to Argentina, he was sent to race in Europe for two years by the Argentine Automobile Club in 1948. He won the San Remo race in a Maserati, then took five further wins to secure himself a place with top team Alfa Romeo when Formula One was formed in 1950.

MAKING A MARK

Fangio faced tough competition from the older Giuseppe Farina in Formula One's debut year and, though he won three of the six Europe-based races, including Monaco, his retirements from the other three cost him the crown. It went his way the following year though, with three wins and two second places proving enough to take the title as Ferrari and Ascari became his main contenders.

When Alfa Romeo pulled out, Fangio began what would later become a career-defining tactic, as he picked the best team on the grid and joined them. In 1952, that was Ferrari, but a crash at Monza saw him miss the season with a broken neck while Ascari led the team in a dominant 1-2-3-4 championship success.

With no space at Ferrari in 1953, Fangio made a welcome return to Maserati, but three retirements in the first three races were crucial as Ascari led Ferrari to victory again. Maserati's form improved, with three seconds and a victory in the final five

ABOVE: *Juan Manuel Fangio pictured in his Lancia-Ferrari D50 at the 1956 British Grand Prix at Silverstone.*

races but two wins in the opening two races of 1954 were not enough to keep the Argentine at the team when Mercedes showed their mettle.

END OF AN ERA

He jumped ship to join a team that was clearly going to dominate and took the next two titles with ease, winning eight of the next 11 Europe-based races during his 1954 and 1955 title-winning seasons. When Mercedes pulled out, Fangio chose runners-up Ferrari as his new team and led them to victory, with three wins and two seconds in the five races that counted toward his title-winning margin over former team-mate Stirling Moss in the Maserati.

Fangio saw Maserati's season-ending pace and decided they would be the team to beat in 1957, so he moved in as Moss moved out. Sure enough, in the season's seven Europe-based

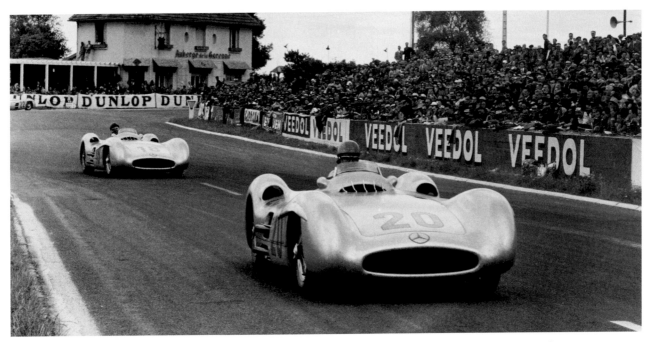

ABOVE: *Fangio trails his team-mate Karl Kling (both Mercedes-Benz W196) during the 1954 French Grand Prix: Fangio went on to win the race.*

ABOVE: *Fangio on his way to winning the 1957 German Grand Prix in a Maserati 250F.*

NEXT SPREAD: *Fangio (Maserati 250F) leads Mike Hawthorn (Ferrari 625) during his victorious race at the 1954 Belgian Grand Prix.*

races he took four wins and two seconds with one retirement. A fifth title was his, but it was the end of an era as Maserati pulled out after a couple of disappointing runs in privateer cars. Fangio retired in 1958.

A survivor from an era that saw many fatalities, Fangio lived on to the age of 84, and died on July 17, 1994, just a couple of months after the man who had come to be the greatest threat to his record of success, Ayrton Senna, lost his life at the racetrack, and a little under four months before the man who eventually would re-write the record books, Michael Schumacher, took his first world title.

Alberto Ascari

The fun-loving son of a legend, Ascari, fueled by the memory of his father's early death would take the fight to Fangio and Farina in the early years of Formula One. His superstitious nature seemed beyond reason, but, tragically he was taken away in his prime in a strangely familiar family fashion.

Ascari was an Italian with a racing pedigree: a father who turned from car dealer to racing star in the 1920s. The first second-generation driver, Ascari competed in 32 races over the opening six-year period of Formula One, taking 14 pole positions, 13 race wins, and two titles in a short but exciting career.

ABOVE: *Alberto Ascari following his victory in the 1952 British Grand Prix at Silverstone.*

EARLY YEARS

Born in Milan in 1918, Ascari was initially a motorcycle racer during his teens and began racing in cars at the age of 22 when he competed in the Mille Miglia in a car owned by his late father's former team-mate Enzo Ferrari. But then the war intervened,

and he would not return to the track until he was nearly 30.

In another link to the past, he joined his father's old Alfa Romeo team in 1948 and, under the watching eye of team-mate Gigi Villoresi, won in San Remo, Italy. He moved to Maserati the following year, but followed Villoresi to Ferrari in

BELOW: *Ascari driving his 4.5 Ferrari 375F1 V12 to victory in the 1951 Italian Grand Prix at Monza.*

ABOVE: *Ascari on his way to winning the 1953 British Grand Prix at Silverstone in his Ferrari 500.*

1949, winning three more races ahead of the start of the new Formula One World Championship.

MAKING A MARK

Unfortunately for Ascari, Ferrari was the wrong team to be with in 1950. Instead, it was rival Italian squad Alfa Romeo who dominated the championship as Giuseppe Farina, Juan Manuel Fangio, and Luigi Fagioli took the top three spots. Ascari failed to register a win and finished fifth.

It was a similar story in 1951, with Alfa winning the first three European races, but Ferrari began a resurgence in Britain when Ascari declined the chance to take over team-mate José Froilán González's car and the Argentine took victory. Ascari won the next two and moved to second in the championship as Ferrari's form gave a hint of what would happen in the years ahead.

With Alfa gone from the championship in 1952 and Fangio, who was due to be Ascari's new team-mate at Ferrari, sidelined through injury, Ascari won six of the seven races and took the title with ease. His dominance continued the following year, with wins in five of the eight Europe-based races securing a second consecutive title as the returning Fangio, unable to find a space at Ferrari, was left defeated and deflated.

END OF AN ERA

Ascari was lured away from Ferrari by the promise of great things to come from the new Lancia team in 1954, but it proved to be the beginning of the end for the two-time champion. The new car was not ready until the final race of the year and, when it did arrive, it broke down after just 10 laps.

The frustrated Italian had picked up drives for Maserati and Ferrari during his disastrous season, but all four had ended in retirement and when Lancia got it together for 1955 he retired twice more, crashing out of the lead spectacularly in Monaco, his final Formula One race, when he went straight on at the chicane and plunged into the harbor. He was unharmed, but the superstitions ran rife and Ascari admitted to rival Fangio that he felt something was going wrong.

Four days later, he lost his life. The fateful day came at Monza where Ascari was watching his friend Eugenio Castellotti test a Ferrari sports car. Ascari decided to try it out but, unable to use his 'lucky helmet', he decided to borrow one. After three laps, he lost control, and the car somersaulted and threw him onto the track. Like his father before him, he died at the age of 36, on the 26th of a month, after crashing at the exit of a fast left-hand corner four days after surviving a serious accident.

THE
1960s

This 10-year period saw Formula One go through what could be seen as the most significant technical developments in its history. British teams led the way and the sport began to build its reputation as the place for innovation at the pinnacle of motorsport.

The decade began with Cooper proving the rear-engine design was the way to go but, after a downgrade to 1.5-liter engines, which stuck for the next five years, Ferrari got the jump with a technologically advanced car that dominated the field.

It would not last long, as innovative designers at Lotus moved the team ahead with a unique monocoque design, superseding traditional space frames, then—later in the decade—made the engine part of the car's structure and introduced aerodynamic wings.

New rules for 3-liter normally aspirated or 1.5-liter supercharged engines were introduced toward the end of the decade and the arrival of the British-bred Cosworth DFV powerplant set the championship standard for years to come.

Meanwhile, the arrival of sponsorship put an end to teams racing in national colors and, as the sport headed into the 1970s, the 13-race calendar could now claim to be fully global, with a core in Europe, but races also run in South Africa, Canada, the United States, and Mexico.

1960
The success of Jack Brabham and his Cooper at the end of the 1950s left nobody in any doubt that the front-engined car had had its day. Nevertheless, Ferrari persisted and got nowhere. Instead, Cooper and the new rear-engined Lotus dominated, with Brabham and Bruce McLaren taking on Moss and Innes Ireland.

Argentina was back as the season opener and McLaren—who won the final race of the 1950s—also won the first of the 1960s after Brabham and Stirling Moss both retired their Coopers. Moss switched to Lotus for the Monaco event and took a win there in the wet, then Brabham finally tasted victory in Holland, a race notable for the debut of young Scot Jim Clark.

LEFT: *The cars line up on the grid before the start of the 1966 British Grand Prix.*

Jim Rathmann won the Indy 500, but having failed to attract the European teams and with the success of the new United States Grand Prix introduced in 1959, 1960 would be the last year that race formed part of the Formula One World Championship.

The European field then moved on to Belgium, but it was one of the worst races in history. Moss had a leg-breaking crash; then, as Brabham raced from pole to victory, Chris Bristow and Alan Stacey were both killed, the latter after his helmet was hit by a bird.

Brabham claimed further victories in France, Britain, and Portugal, where he won the title with two races to go. With the championship over, the British teams boycotted the Italian race due to safety concerns, so Phil Hill won for Ferrari while Moss returned to finish off the season with victory at the final round in the United States.

1961

It was all change on the technical front in 1961, and Ferrari had a very successful season after giving up their efforts the previous year and concentrating on creating their 'sharknose' car specifically for the new 1.5-liter formula.

The season opened in Monaco and Moss, in a privateer Lotus, overcame his inferior machinery to take the win. But Ferrari came back strong with a 1-2 for Wolfgang von Trips and Phil Hill in Holland, then finished 1-2-3-4 as Hill took victory in Belgium.

There was a surprise at the next race, in France, when Giancarlo Baghetti won on his Formula One debut in a privateer Ferrari after all the lead contenders dropped out and he overtook the Porsche of Richie Ginther on the last corner of the last lap. Ferrari were back on top in Britain with von Trips leading a 1-2-3 finish, but Moss fought back in Germany to win for Climax.

Then came Monza, and tragedy. Von Trips took pole but collided with Clark's Lotus at the Parabolica and his Ferrari rolled. He was thrown from the car and was killed along with 12 spectators. The race was stopped but, incredibly, it was restarted and Hill put his team-mate's death behind him to win the race and the world title.

The season concluded in the United States, without Ferrari, and Innes Ireland scored his only win, for Lotus, after Moss and the previous season's champion Brabham (who scored just four points all season) were forced to retire from the race.

ABOVE: *Jack Brabham (Cooper T53 Climax) on his way to victory in the 1960 Monaco Grand Prix.*

1962

A tough and emotional end to 1961 saw Ferrari in turmoil and Moss, perhaps the greatest driver never to win a title, deciding to quit after a pre-season crash. It left BRM, with a new engine, and Lotus, with a revolutionary car, as joint favorites and began a long-running England-Scotland driver rivalry.

Englishman Hill took first blood in the battle when he won the season opener for BRM in Holland after Scotsman Clark was sidelined with gearbox problems. McLaren drove his Cooper to victory in Monaco, but Clark claimed his first-ever win—for Lotus—next, in Belgium, after a five-car slipstreaming battle.

Gurney gave Porsche an historic first win in France, inheriting the victory after three leaders dropped out to make the German team the year's fourth different winner. Clark dominated in Britain, then John Surtees threatened to make Lola the fifth winning team in Germany until Hill won for BRM.

Hill was victorious again in Italy, where Clark failed to finish, and though the Scot won in the United States, claiming pole, fastest lap, and race win, Hill came home in second.

South Africa held the final race and Clark looked strong for victory, having led from pole, until his engine failed and handed Hill, and BRM, the championship title. Having won the title the previous year, Ferrari failed to even win a race and scored just 18 points.

1963

There was no doubting Clark's driving talent and, once Lotus found the reliability, it was destined to be a title-winning partnership. This was set to be that year and with Ferrari still in turmoil—reeling from a team split that saw the formation of rival outfit ATS and the defection of Hill and Baghetti—only BRM could possibly stop them.

ABOVE: *Jack Brabham (left, no. 16) and Carel Godin de Beaufort (right, no. 18) take shelter from the rain before the start of the 1962 German Grand Prix.*

ABOVE: *Jackie Stewart (BRM P83) before the start of the 1967 British Grand Prix.*

The season did not start well for Clark, with gearbox problems halting his charge from pole at Monaco, handing victory to Hill and a BRM 1-2. At the next race, in Belgium, he found himself eight on the grid and must have wondered what was going on. But then, his skill emphasized by the wet weather, he raced through to first on the opening lap. His fortunes changed and he claimed his first victory of the year, then followed it with comfortable wins in Holland, France, and Britain.

Surtees became the first motorcycle star to win in Formula One when he escaped the carnage of six crashes during the first five laps in Germany and capitalized on Clark and Richie Ginther's engine troubles to hand Ferrari their first win for two years.

The Italian team took a new car to Monza for their home race, but its engine failed and Clark won to claim his first championship title, three races before the season finished. Hill's BRM finally found some reliability for him to win in the United States, but Clark rounded out the season with victories in Mexico and South Africa.

1964

Clark and Hill carried on where they left off the season before, but reliability problems for Lotus and BRM coupled with a late resurgence from Ferrari—who had looked out of the fight early in the season—saw the title go right down to the wire.

Hill started the season with victory in Monaco as Clark suffered an engine failure. But the Scot was soon back, winning in Holland, then inheriting victory in Belgium after Gurney, Hill, and McLaren had all dropped out of the lead with fuel problems in the final two laps.

Gurney took Brabham's first win when engine failure robbed Clark of victory in France, but Clark won in Britain, leading home Hill's BRM and the Ferrari of Surtees, who had posted just one second place in the preceding races but was about to mount a title challenge.

Victories for Surtees in Germany and Italy sandwiched a win for team-mate Bandini in Austria, a race where Hill, Surtees, and Clark all failed to finish. Hill won from Surtees in the United States to leave three drivers in with a shot at the title at the last race in Mexico.

Hill was four points ahead of Surtees with Clark nine behind, but, with Clark leading, Hill spinning out of the running, and Surtees only fourth, the Lotus driver looked set for the title. Then his engine failed one lap from the finish and, with Bandini moving over to concede second, Surtees took the title.

1965

Clark was unstoppable from the start, with a Lotus car that seemed unbreakable and a Climax engine that put the power back into the hands of the British teams. Ferrari failed to perform, while Honda arrived, luring Richie Ginther from BRM, who, in turn hired Jackie Stewart.

The season began in South Africa on New Year's Day and Clark took an easy victory ahead of champion Surtees, whose second place would be his best finish of the year. The next race was in Monaco, but after European teams had ignored the Indianapolis 500 for years when it was a championship race, Lotus decided to skip Monaco and go to America. Hill took advantage to win while Clark led Lotus to victory on the other side of the Atlantic.

When Clark returned he continued his relentless pursuit of the championship. He won in Belgium, in the wet, and in France, both times ahead of Stewart's BRM, then he took his fourth consecutive win in Britain and continued to claim victories in Holland and Germany. With only a driver's best six races counting toward the championship, the title was already his.

Clark retired from the remaining three races with engine failure, which allowed Stewart to score his maiden win in Monza, Hill to win a third race for BRM in the United States, and Ginther to claim the first-ever race victory for both Honda and tire supplier Goodyear in Mexico.

1966

An incredibly varied field lined up for the 1966 season, with the new 3-liter formula creating all sorts of engine solutions. There were five different winners in nine races, but Brabham's mid-season run in his self-named car, with a reliable and light Repco engine, put him in the driving seat for a third world title.

Stewart won the opening race in Monaco for BRM, but the second race was at a rain-hit Spa circuit in Belgium and the Scot had a terrible crash that sidelined him for two months as eight cars retired on the opening lap. Surtees won in what would be his last race for Ferrari before his switch to Cooper.

Brabham's winning run began when Lorenzo Bandini's Ferrari dropped out in France and he inherited the lead. He followed victory there with a 1-2 ahead of Denny Hulme in Britain, a third win in Holland, and a fourth in Germany—a race marred by a crash in which John Taylor, driving a Brabham-BRM, suffered burns that led to his death.

All the title contenders, including Brabham, retired from the race at Monza, handing the Australian his third world title as rookie Ludovico Scarfiotti won for Ferrari. Clark took his first win of the season in the United States and Surtees finished the year off with victory in Mexico.

1967

The arrival of the new Lotus 49 coupled with a revolutionary Cosworth DFV engine tempted Hill to join rival Clark in what many saw as the dream team for 1967. Stewart stepped into the void left by Hill at BRM while Surtees left Cooper to join Honda and Brabham retained their Antipodean line-up of Brabham and Hulme.

ABOVE: *Jim Clark (Lotus 49 Ford) on his way to victory in the 1968 South African Grand Prix.*

Pedro Rodriguez was a surprise winner of the first race, in Kayalami, and it was five months before the season continued at Monaco. In what was to be another tragic race, Bandini was leading when he lost control, crashed, and was badly burned while trapped underneath his Ferrari. He died three days later. Hulme took a hollow victory for Brabham and the championship moved on to Holland, where the Lotus 49 made its debut and Clark drove it to victory.

Reliability problems for Lotus handed Gurney the only ever win for Eagle-Weslake in Belgium and, though Clark survived to win in Britain, he and Hill suffered engine, transmission, and suspension failures that left Brabham to take 1-2 finishes in France, Germany, and Canada, where Formula One arrived for the first time.

Clark ran out of fuel while leading at Monza, handing victory to Surtees and Honda, then the Lotus finally found some reliability, which allowed Clark to lead a 1-2. But it was too little, too late, and while Clark won the season finale in Mexico, the reliable Brabhams fought it out for the title with Hulme doing enough to claim the crown.

1968

A season that should have seen a classic battle between Clark and Hill in a more reliable Lotus is now tragically remembered as the season that Formula One lost one of its greats after Clark died racing in Formula Two.

The season started well for Lotus in South Africa as Clark dominated and lead Hill in a 1-2 finish, but it was to be Clark's final victory and when the field reconvened in Spain for race two, everyone on the grid was still getting over the loss of the former champion.

Hill, now racing in a newly sponsored red, white, and gold Lotus fitted with aerodynamic wings, scored victories in Spain and Monaco. Then two new teams hit the heights, with Bruce McLaren winning for his team in Belgium and Stewart winning for the Tyrrell-run Matra team in Holland. Ferrari won in France but, tragically, Jo Schlesser was killed when his car caught fire.

Racing continued, and after Jo Siffert won in Britain in a private Lotus, Stewart took victory at Germany's Nürburgring and Hulme won in Monza and Canada, moving him level with Hill in the championship.

Victory in the United States for Stewart set up a three-way season-ending title battle in Mexico. Hulme crashed out early, but Stewart and Hill vied for the lead until the Scot suffered handling problems and dropped down the order, leaving Hill to win the title.

1969

Stewart had narrowly missed out on the title in 1968 and, after Matra joined Honda in pulling their works programs, he was hoping the French manufacturer's full support of Tyrrell would take him to the top as rival drivers switched teams and took time to settle.

The Scot started well, dominating the season opener in South Africa, then won again in Spain after Ferrari suffered

ABOVE: *Jackie Stewart (Matra MS80-Ford Cosworth) leads Jacky Ickx (Brabham BT26-Ford Cosworth) during the 1969 Canadian Grand Prix.*

engine problems and the two Lotus cars crashed heavily after failures to their high-mounted wings, which were subsequently banned from the sport.

Hill claimed his fifth win in Monaco, but it was just a minor break in Stewart's rhythm, and the Scot raced to further victories in Holland, France, and Britain, where he had to battle hard with Jochen Rindt before the Lotus, now fitted with less radical wings, was forced to the pit for repairs.

Jackie Ickx put Brabham back in the winners' circle in Germany, but Stewart secured the title with a sixth and final win of the year after a massive slipstreaming battle at Monza, with the top four split by just 0.2 seconds.

Ickx won in Canada after knocking Stewart out of the race and Rindt won in the United States, in a race marred by a major accident that saw Hill break both legs. He missed the season finale in Mexico, which was won by Hulme for McLaren.

Jack Brabham

Brabham was a shrewd racer with a business mind and an engineering education, and he used all three of these talents to become the only ever driver to win a world championship in a car of his own making. He was a determined character who spanned two eras in the sport, enjoying a variety of successes that eventually saw him become the first knight of motorsport.

A second-generation Australian, Brabham drove in Formula One for an incredible 16 years, making his debut in 1955 and finishing at the age of 44. During his 126 starts, he only achieved 13 poles, 31 podiums, and 14 wins but, crucially, those victories spanned the three years in which he won his three world titles.

ABOVE: *Jack Brabham (right) talking with Team Lotus boss Colin Chapman (left) during the 1969 Formula One season.*

EARLY YEARS

Born in the outskirts of Sydney in 1926, Brabham learned to drive his dad's trucks at the age of 12 and soon began racing midget cars on the dirt tracks of Australia while studying engineering and working in a garage. He spent two years in the Australian Air Force as a flight mechanic before moving into professional Speedway and Speedcar racing, winning several championships in the late 1940s.

A move to tarmac racing beckoned, and after a few years in Australia and New Zealand he was lured over to Europe in early 1955, where he began to mix with the top drivers while working at Cooper, and raced his own version of their machines in national events. It was inevitable that he would soon step up to the top level.

MAKING A MARK

Brabham made his Formula One debut with one race in Britain in the 1955 season and, after another outing the following year, he was given a full season of racing in 1957. Cooper developed a revolutionary mid-engined car and, after two building years Brabham, with a powerful new Climax

ABOVE: *Jack Brabham (Brabham BT33 Ford) leads Jean-Pierre Beltoise (Matra-Simca MS120) and Jacky Ickx (Ferrari 312B) into Casino Square at the 1970 Monaco Grand Prix.*

ABOVE: *Jack Brabham (Brabham BT19 Repco)—who won the race—leads Denny Hulme (Brabham BT20 Repco), Jim Clark (Lotus 33 Climax), and Graham Hill (BRM P261) during the 1966 Dutch Grand Prix.*

engine, took two wins and three further podiums to beat Ferrari to the title.

He was joined by fellow engineering fan Bruce McLaren in an all-Antipodean line-up at Cooper the following year and the pair dominated, with the Australian securing his second title in a row, thanks to a run of five consecutive victories in the middle of the season. Ironically, the pair would eventually fight each other as race-car manufacturers a few years down the line.

As the 1960s arrived, Lotus and BRM led the British attack and Cooper's star faded. Brabham retired from six of the eight races and put up a disastrous title defence with Cooper so he entered his own team in 1962, first using Lotus machines then—with the help of friend Ron Turanac—introducing the first Brabham-designed car. The BT3, BT7, and BT11 machines failed to perform, but with the arrival of 1966 things were about to change.

END OF AN ERA

When a new 3-liter engine formula came into force, Brabham thought outside the box and helped Australian company Repco develop an engine that, while not the most powerful, was lightweight and reliable. It created a perfect package with his new BT19 machine. The first-ever manufacturer-driver victory came in France, then three more wins in a consistent campaign resulted in a third and final world crown.

Brabham continued to develop successful cars the following year, but was beaten to the title by team-mate Denis Hulme, who enjoyed better reliability. Brabham had a disastrous season the following year, then had to watch Jacky Ickx lead the team after seriously injuring his foot in a testing crash then, in a dangerous period of racing and with pressure coming to stop before disaster struck, he sold his stake in the team and retired at the end of the 1970 season.

Graham Hill

A supreme racing talent with a love for the glamorous parties of the swinging sixties, Hill represented a great British talent in an exciting era. His slicked back hair, neatly trimmed moustache, and clipped newsreader accent reflected his roots as a stockbroker's son, but his battles with Jim Clark were legendary and results showed his ability was matched only by his supreme level of commitment.

Decked out in the blue and white racing colors of his beloved London Rowing Club, Hill spent 17 years in Formula One and in 176 starts he took 13 poles, 36 podiums, and 14 wins. He won two world titles and was the only driver to take the Triple Crown of motorsport with victories in the Indy 500, Le Mans, and the Monaco Grand Prix. He also fathered a son, Damon, who would go on to race in his father's colors, becoming the first next-generation racer to follow in his father's footsteps.

ABOVE: *Graham Hill celebrates winning the 1965 United States Grand Prix at Watkins Glen.*

PREVIOUS SPREAD: *Graham Hill leads Jo Siffert (both Lotus 49B Ford) and Jackie Stewart (Matra MS10 Ford) during the 1968 Mexican Grand Prix. They finished in first, sixth, and seventh positions respectively.*

BELOW: *Graham Hill (BRM P57) on his way to winning both the race and the World Championship at the 1962 South African Grand Prix.*

ABOVE: *Graham Hill (Lotus 49B-Ford Cosworth) leads Jean-Pierre Beltoise (Matra MS80-Ford Cosworth) during his victorious drive in the 1969 Monaco Grand Prix.*

EARLY YEARS

Born Norman Graham Hill, in Hampstead, London, in 1929, the boy who would become one of Britain's biggest sporting names first concentrated on school work, studying at Hendon Tech, then served in the Royal Navy. He also had a passion for rowing rather than racing, winning at Henley Regatta as a stroke in the LRC Eight in 1950.

Motorsport came into his life at the age of 24, when he attended a racing school at Brands Hatch. He quickly joined as a mechanic and driver then moved to Lotus, where he built his own club racing car and secured drives in Cooper and Lotus sports cars. When Lotus stepped up to Formula One in 1958, Hill went with them.

MAKING A MARK

In an inauspicious start, Hill retired from his first seven races in Formula One and failed to score a championship point in two years with Lotus. He joined BRM in the hope of something better and instead he had a terrible time, his underpowered car allowing him just seven points in two years.

The determined driver always knew things would turn around, and when a new V8 engine arrived at BRM in 1962, they did just that. He opened the year with a win and added three more, and two second places, to beat Lotus—and great rival Jim Clark—to the title as Britain began to rule the Formula One roost.

Three successful, but frustrating, years as championship runner-up followed as Hill and BRM were twice beaten by Clark and Lotus and once by Ferrari when John Surtees won on counted results. After another tough year at BRM in 1966, boosted only by victory in the Indy 500, he signed with Lotus to create a dream team alongside Clark.

END OF AN ERA

The Lotus was fast but fragile in 1967 and Hill retired from eight of 11 races. The following season was set for the long-awaited battle of Britain but, when Clark died in a Formula Two race after winning the season opener, Hill had to lead Lotus back to glory and took his second and final title in honor of his late friend.

Jochen Rindt came in to replace Clark and Hill could not match the Austrian's pace, a then-record fifth victory at Monaco the highlight of a season that ended with a leg-breaking crash at Watkins Glen. He came back to grab a championship runners-up spot with Brabham in 1971 but things fell apart when he set up Embassy Racing as his Shadow and Lola cars, and his own Hill GH1, failed to perform.

Hill retired in 1975, to concentrate on team management, but on the way back from a test session in France in the November of that year, with promise forming around new driver Tony Brise, Hill lost control of his light aircraft, killing six onboard, and Formula One lost a legend.

Jackie Stewart

A clear-thinking Scot with an instinct for business and marketing that matched his talents on track, Stewart was instrumental in leading Formula One into a new era. His three titles put him among the greats as a racer, but his legacy to the sport remains his endless campaigns for safety and the way he led drivers to celebrity status.

Stewart was a disciplined racer and his composed mental approach saw him take 27 wins and 43 podiums from 99 starts during a nine-year career. He went on to become an excellent businessman, forming a strong relationship with Ford, and tasted Formula One success again when he created a winning team in the late 1990s.

ABOVE: *Jackie Stewart at the 1967 Mexican Grand Prix.*

ABOVE: *Jackie Stewart (Matra MS80-Ford Cosworth) in action during his winning race at the 1969 French Grand Prix.*

EARLY YEARS

Born John Young Stewart in Milton, Scotland, in 1939, the 'Flying Scot' always seemed destined to follow in the footsteps of his father Robert, an amateur motorbike racer, and his older brother Jimmy, who was an aspiring racer and drove for the Ecurie Ecosse team in the 1953 British Grand Prix before a career-ending crash at Le Mans.

Stewart worked as a mechanic in his father's Jaguar business, but was initially discouraged from motorsport and instead chose shooting, where he represented Scotland before turning to the track. He made his racing debut in sports and GT cars in 1961 and joined Ecurie Ecosse before Ken Tyrrell signed him up for Formula Three and he began carefully working his way up the ladder.

MAKING A MARK

Stewart stepped up to Formula One in 1965, joining BRM as Tyrrell did not yet have a team in the top level. He was an instant success, scoring points in his first race, finishing on the podium in

ABOVE: *Jackie Stewart (BRM P261) on his way to victory in the 1966 Monaco Grand Prix.*

his second, and taking victory in his eighth on the way to third in the championship.

He opened his second season with victory in Monaco, but at the second race, in Belgium, he rolled his car and was trapped underneath for 25 minutes, his collarbone fractured and his race suit soaked in gasoline. He came out unscathed, but the crash alerted him to the dangers in the sport and he began his endless campaign for safety improvements.

After a tough season with BRM in 1967, with just two finishes from 11 races, he reunited with Tyrrell, who arrived in Formula One to run the Matra team. It was an impressive debut for the outfit and Stewart took a championship second with three wins. The next year he took his first title, with six wins from 11 races.

END OF AN ERA

Tyrrell went on his own in 1970, using a March chassis before bringing in his own Tyrrell 001 for the final three races. In a season that saw Lotus and Ferrari dominate, however, Stewart could only manage fifth in the championship after eight retirements, including three in three with the team's new car.

Things went much better in 1971 and the new Tyrrell 003 was in a class of its own, with Stewart racing to six victories and a second world championship. He won four more races the following year but missed one race becuase of a stomach ulcer and was beaten to the title by Emmerson Fittipaldi.

His final title came in 1973, with another five victories, but his retirement came one race early when he pulled out of that year's United States Grand Prix, following the death of team-mate François Cevert.

He continued to campaign for Formula One safety while working as a television commentator and an ambassador for major car brands, then returned to the sport when he and his son Paul set up Stewart Grand Prix. The team claimed second in Monaco in their first year and won the European Grand Prix in 1999, before it was sold to Jaguar.

THE 1970s

Danger was still a real concern for motorsport at the start of the 1970s, but until the incumbent Formula One champion Jackie Stewart retired and began his campaign for improvements, death was almost considered an unfortunate but unavoidable part of the sport.

The 1970s saw some great racing, but it was overshadowed year after year by the loss of some great names, including the decade's opening champion Jochen Rindt, popular Mexican Pedro Rodriguez, Swede Ronnie Peterson, and three-time World Champion Graham Hill.

Developments focused on speed and the advancement of aerodynamics was dramatic, changing the look of the cars significantly from the cigar tube shape of the 1960s to high-speed full ground-effect super cars with wings and wide, slick tires by the end of the decade. Innovation was king as sidepods appeared, air boxes sprouted above the driver, wings became more complex, suspension was overhauled, and six wheels appeared. But it was Lotus' ground-effect, channelling air under the car to create suction, that had the most success.

Drivers from five different nations and four different teams became World Champion during the decade and the calendar continued to expand, increasing to between 16 and 17 races, with Brazil and Japan arriving to make the series increasingly more global.

1970

Tyrrell took a gamble on a new British firm to supply the car for reigning champion Stewart in 1970, with Matra replaced by March, while Ferrari had great confidence in their new 312B and Lotus pinned their hopes on the new, wedge-shaped, 72, which would be introduced five races into the season.

Stewart put the new March on pole at the season opener in South Africa, but dropped to third as Brabham stormed through to claim victory in the race itself. Stewart gave March their debut win in their second race, however, when he took a fighting win in Spain.

Brabham returned to form in Monaco only to see his heroic defence of first place end on

LEFT: *Jacques Laffite (no. 26, Ligier JS5-Matra) is involved in a pile up during the 1976 British Grand Prix.*

ABOVE: *Jackie Stewart (March 701 Ford) on his way to victory in the 1970 Spanish Grand Prix.*

the final corner when he crashed and allowed Rindt through to take the win. Soon after, Formula One lost one of its biggest names when Bruce McLaren was killed testing a Can-Am car at Goodwood.

Petro Rodriguez won for BRM in Belgium, but then Lotus introduced the 72 and it was game over. Rindt took victory on the car's debut in Holland then won in France, Britain, and Germany before Ickx hit back with a win for Ferrari on Austrian Rindt's home soil.

A tragic practice crash claimed the life of 28-year-old Rindt ahead of the next race, in Italy, and Clay Regazzoni took a hollow victory for Ferrari. As the season progressed Ickx won in Canada, but a retirement in the last but one race in the United States ended his title chances and Rindt was named the sport's first posthumous champion.

1971

Tyrrell decided to go it alone after a promising test for his own car at the end of the previous season and it proved to be a wise decision, as Stewart dominated and the rest of the field failed to produce a consistently strong contender.

Ferrari newcomer, American Mario Andretti, won the opening race in South Africa as Stewart had to fight his way from seventh to second, but the Scot hit back in the next two races, with strong victories in Spain and Monaco.

Safety issues forced the Belgian race to be cancelled and when the field reconvened in a rain-soaked Holland, Stewart struggled and Ickx drove his Ferrari to a stunning victory, lapping the Scot five times. Pedro Rodriguez claimed second for BRM, but he soon became the next Formula One fatality after crashing in a sports car race.

Stewart won in France, Britain, and Germany, twice leading team-mate François Cevert home in a 1-2 for Tyrrell. BRM managed to stop his run of success when Jo Siffert won in Austria, but when Ickx retired from the race the championship went to Stewart.

Peter Gethin snatched victory from Peterson by 0.01s in Italy as the top five cars crossed the line within 0.61s of each other. Stewart retired with engine failure in Monza, but won in Canada while his team-mate Cevery claimed his first win at the season finale in the United States.

1972

In an updated version of the Lotus 72, young Brazilian Emerson Fittipaldi excelled and put the British team back in contention for the championship. An increase in sponsorship helped to change the face of Formula One. Lotus now ran the black and yellow of John Player Special, while Marlboro funding allowed BRM to run five cars and Yardley stepped over to McLaren.

Bernie Ecclestone became team manager of Brabham and when Formula One returned to Argentina for race one, his home driver Carlos Reutermann took pole, though reigning champion Stewart raced past to win for Tyrrell.

Denny Hulme won for McLaren in South Africa, Fittipaldi drove his Lotus to victory in Spain, and Jean-Pierre Beltoise took BRM's last ever win in treacherous conditions at Monaco, making it four different winners from the four opening races. However, Fittipaldi would soon stamp his authority with victory in four of the following six races.

The Brazilian won in Belgium, with Stewart sidelined by a stomach ulcer, and though the Scot came back victorious in France, Fittipaldi won again in Britain. Ickx led a Ferrari 1-2 in

Germany, but the consistent Fittipaldi extended his title lead over Stewart by winning in Austria then sealed the crown with victory in Monza. A new car helped Stewart win the last two races, but it was all too late.

1973

Lotus hoped to dominate when Peterson joined Fittipaldi in the 'dream team' and, though McLaren, Brabham, and March were all in the mix, it was the resurgent Stewart, in his Tyrrell, who led the fight to stop them.

Fittipaldi started well, with victories in Argentina and the new round in Brazil, but Stewart took an easy victory in South Africa after an heroic act of bravery saw Mike Hailwood pull Clay Regazzoni from a blazing car when the pair collided on lap three.

Fittipaldi made it three from four with victory in Spain, but fuel pressure problems handed Stewart the win in Belgium and the Tyrrell driver won again in a hard fight at Monaco. Six races in, it was three-a-piece.

The next race, in Sweden, saw Hulme win for McLaren but also marked the start of six tough races for Fittipaldi in which he scored just one points finish and retired on four occasions. In that time, Peterson won in France, a pile-up allowed Peter Revson to win for McLaren in Britain, and Stewart led Cevert to two 1-2 finishes in Holland and Germany.

Lotus returned to form in Austria, where Peterson waved Fittipaldi through for the sake of the title only for the Brazilian to retire. The pair finished 1-2 in Italy, but the title battle was over. The season wasn't, and after Revson won in the Canadian rain Cevert was killed in practice in the United States. Peterson won, but the death of Stewart's team-mate vindicated the Scot's decision to quit.

1974

Fittipaldi moved from Lotus to McLaren when the team lured the major Marlboro sponsorship funding away from BRM, while Tyrrell, who had lost the late Cevert and retired Stewart, brought in Jody Scheckter and Patrick Depallier. There was change at Ferrari, too, with a brand new car and the arrival of Regazzoni and Niki Lauda.

The first blood of the season went to McLaren, with Hulme showing his new team-mate the way in Argentina before Fittipaldi won in Brazil. Formula One was soon struck once again with tragedy, though. The next race, in South Africa, saw another fatality, when Peter Revson crashed in practice, but the race ran and Reutermann won for Brabham.

After Lauda's Ferrari victory in Spain, McLaren took two wins, with Fittipaldi in Belgium and Peterson in Monaco. Tyrrell claimed a 1-2 in Sweden, then Ferrari did the same in Holland and, with six different winners in eight races, the drivers' title was wide open.

Peterson and Scheckter took second victories in France and Britain respectively before Regazzoni finally won for Ferrari in Germany. Lauda had been the Ferrari star so far, but Regazzoni's consistency put him in with a title shout.

Reutermann won in Austria and Peterson in Italy but, after finishing first and second in Canada, Regazzoni and Fittipaldi fought for the title in the United States finale. They were level on points, but a disappointing finish saw Regazzoni drop down the field with handling problems, leaving Fittipaldi finishing fourth to claim the title.

ABOVE: *François Cevert (Tyrrell 006 Ford Cosworth) in action during the 1973 British Grand Prix.*

1975

After several years of British success, Ferrari introduced the new longitudinal gearboxed 312T and was ready to return to form. Lauda grew into a fine team leader, but a season to savour for the Italian giants was hit by more fatalities, making it a sad year for everyone involved in Formula One.

Jean-Pierre Jarier gave Shadow a surprisingly strong start with pole positions in Argentina and Brazil, but, both times, his car failed him and Fittipaldi won the first for McLaren with compatriot Carlos Pace, in a Brabham, leading him to home in the second.

Scheckter won at home in South Africa for Tyrrell, but when the series moved to Spain there was disaster. After a threatened boycott the race went on, but when a crash killed five spectators, it was stopped, with Mass declared the winner.

Lauda had an important run when he won in the wet in Monaco, then claimed wins in Belgium, Sweden, and France, with James Hunt beating him to victory in Holland as he took his and Hesketh's first win.

The British race saw a multiple pile-up take out 15 and Fittipaldi was declared the winner after the race was stopped. Reutermann won in Germany as punctures decimated the field, then American Mark Donohue died in practice for the Austrian race, which saw Vittorio Brambilla another red-flag winner after rain stopped play.

Regazzoni won in Monza while Lauda finished third to take the title for Ferrari before finishing the season off in style with a win in the United States. But in a tragic end to the year, Graham Hill, who had retired at the start of the season, died in a plane crash.

1976

Ferrari's champion Lauda faced a tough challenge from James Hunt in 1976 after the Briton replaced Fittipaldi at McLaren. In a nail-biting battle, Lauda suffered a serious accident but came back to take the championship right down to the wire.

Hunt started strongly, putting his McLaren on pole in Argentina and South Africa, but both times he lost out to Lauda in the race, then Regazzoni made it three for Ferrari with victory at a new Long Beach street race in the United States.

Hunt finally won in Spain, but was then disqualified and Lauda took full points again. Lauda extended his lead with wins in Belgium and Monaco as Hunt failed to score in either, then Scheckter led a Tyrrell 1-2 in their unique six-wheel car in Sweden.

There was a double celebration for Hunt in France when he won and Lauda retired, after which his Spanish win was reinstated after appeal. Ironically, at the next race in Britain Hunt was disqualified and Lauda was handed victory after the Briton

was deemed to have illegally taken the restart after the race was stopped on lap one.

Lauda was well on course for the title when he crashed in Germany and suffered severe burns. Hunt won the race and Lauda missed the next two races, which both went to Hunt, but, remarkably, returned in Italy, where he finished fourth as Peterson won for March.

Hunt moved to within three points of the lead, winning in Canada and the United States then, when Lauda pulled out of the last race in Japan on safety grounds after a torrential downpour, Hunt raced on and claimed the third place he needed to take the title.

1977

Ferrari and Lauda put together a consistent campaign in a season that saw eight different winners from the 17 races. Significant technical developments were also made, with ground-effect aerodynamics arriving on the Lotus 78 while turbo engines were introduced by Renault. However, the year was again tainted by driver and spectator deaths.

The opening race in Argentina saw Scheckter hand his new Wolf team a debut win before Ferrari resumed normal service and won twice, with Reutermann in Brazil and Lauda in South Africa. An horrific accident at that race killed Tom Pryce and a track marshal. The loss was compounded when Pace died in a plane crash before the next race.

Andretti drove the new 78 to wins in the United States and Spain, then Scheckter won again in Monaco. A dramatic wet Belgian race saw Nilsson take victory for Lotus before Hunt, who struggled in his title defence, won on home soil after a dramatic fight with Jean-Pierre Jabouille, as Renault debuted their new turbocharged machine.

Lauda won for Ferrari in Germany and Holland and took second places in Austria, where Alan Jones gave Shadow a first win, and Italy, where Andretti finished first for Lotus. Lauda had been third or better in all but one of the races he had finished and he secured the title with fourth place in the United States, a race won by Hunt.

Lauda immediately left Ferrari, the Italian team having announced Jacques Villeneuve would replace him in 1978, and the new World Champion did not take part in the final two races in Canada and Japan, which were won by Scheckter and Hunt respectively.

RIGHT: *Action from the 1976 Monaco Grand Prix as the field passes through the Grand Hotel Hairpin.*

1978

Ferrari introduced the new 312T3 in a bid to retain their superiority, but Lotus took another step forward with the revolutionary 79 and soon began to dominate the season. Their success, however, was soured by the tragic death of Ronnie Peterson.

Lotus started strongly with wins in Argentina, for Andretti, and South Africa, for Peterson—the latter after Patrese's new Arrows car dropped out of the lead with engine failure. Ferrari won with Reutermann in Brazil and again in the United States, where Villeneuve hit a backmarker and crashed out of the lead.

Depallier won for Tyrrell in Monaco, but then the Lotus 79 arrived and the team dominated, with 1-2 finishes in Belgium,

Spain, and France, separated only by victory in Sweden for Lauda in Brabham's radical, but subsequently banned, fan car.

A double Lotus retirement let Reutermann win for Ferrari in Britain, but Lotus then won in Germany, Austria, and Holland; the latter being their fourth 1-2 of the year as Peterson was forced to play second fiddle to Andretti. Only Peterson could beat Andretti to the title, but a fiery start-line crash in Italy saw him suffer terrible burns and, despite being quickly dragged from the wreckage by Hunt, Regazzoni, and Depallier, he died the following day.

Andretti was crowned Champion, but it was the Ferraris of Reutermann and Villeneuve that went on to win the last two races, in the United States and Canada.

ABOVE: *1978 Belgian Grand Prix: Mario Andretti (Lotus 79 Ford) on his way to victory and the first of three consecutive 1-2 finishes for the new Lotus 79.*

ABOVE: *Jody Scheckter (Ferrari 312T4) on his way to victory in the 1979 Italian Grand Prix.*

1979

Reutermann left Ferrari to fill Peterson's place at Lotus, but when the team tried to take the ground-effect concept to the next level they failed and Ferrari, who brought in Scheckter to join Villeneuve, benefitted from the introduction of a reliable new car that had the right balance between power and aerodynamics.

The season started with victories for Laffitte's Ligier in Argentina and Brazil, but Ferrari introduced their new car for race three and Villeneuve led 1-2 finishes in South Africa and the United States. Ligier won again with Depallier in Spain, but Scheckter got his first Ferrari win in Belgium and followed it up with victory in Monaco.

Formula One history was made at Dijon in France, when the usually unreliable Renault made it across the finish line to claim the first-ever turbo-powered victory, with Jean-Pierre Jabouille leading home Arnoux after a dramatic wheel-to-wheel battle.

The new Williams FW07 had been competitive ever since its Belgian debut and in Britain Jones put it on pole before Regazzoni secured the team their first-ever victory. Nevertheless, Jones then had a run of dominant form that saw him win in Germany, Austria, and the Netherlands though it was not enough for him to catch the Ferraris.

Scheckter took what would be Ferrari's last title for 21 years when he won in Italy, finishing just 0.46s ahead of Villeneuve in a Ferrari 1-2 as team tactics came into play. And the season was concluded with two exciting battles between Jones and Villeneuve, with Williams winning in Canada and Ferrari taking the spoils in the United States.

Emerson Fittipaldi

With one of the longest and most successful careers in motorsport, Fittipaldi was the youngest Formula One World Champion in his day and went on to become one of the oldest drivers on the CART circuit in a top-flight professional racing career that lasted more than a quarter of a century.

Fittipaldi, a member of a racing family, spent a full decade racing in Formula One, beginning in 1970 and ending in 1980, and achieved 35 podiums and 14 wins in 144 starts before moving into American racing, where he won the CART title and the Indianapolis 500 before retiring from the sport.

EARLY YEARS

Born in São Paolo, Brazil, in 1946, Emerson Fittipaldi was the younger of motorsport journalist Wilson Fittipaldi's two sons and spent his early days racing bikes with his elder brother, also named Wilson, before the pair built and raced karts,

ABOVE: *Emerson Fittipaldi (McLaren) on the podium following his victory in the 1975 British Grand Prix at Silverstone.*

BELOW: *Emerson Fittipaldi crosses the finish line ahead of Niki Lauda, to take the win at the 1974 Belgian Grand Prix.*

then moved into Brazilian Formula Vee, where Emerson won the title.

He headed to Europe, in 1969, to race in Formula Ford and, after being promoted by the Jim Russell driving school, he was signed by Colin Chapman to compete in Formula Two for Lotus in 1970. Fittipaldi did not have long to impress in that series, however, as he was soon fast-tracked up to the top tier in the middle of that season.

MAKING A MARK

Fittipaldi made his Grand Prix debut in the 1970 British Grand Prix and was quickly promoted to team leader when Jochen Rindt lost his life, the Brazilian's first win coming after just four race starts when, in the United States, he halted Jacky Ickx's efforts to overhaul the late Austrian in the championship table.

His promising start took a blow when an accident in 1972 ruined his form and he ended a winless season sixth in the championship. He returned to form the following year and raced to five victories and three podiums on his way to his first title.

The good form continued at the beginning of 1973, with Fittipaldi winning three of the first four races, but the pressure from new team-mate Ronnie Peterson began to tell. Peterson went on to win four races that year, while Fittipaldi did not add any further victories to his three early wins. Jackie Stewart beat him to the title and he left to join McLaren, where three victories and consistent finishes in other races saw him secure his second and final world title in 1974.

END OF AN ERA

The following season saw political battles damage the sport and though Fittipaldi won two races and took four second places on his way to a World Championship runner-up spot, he quit McLaren to join his brother Wilson, as they set up their own Formula One team named after sponsors Copersucar.

The team struggled and Fittipaldi even failed to qualify in one race, finishing the new team's debut season in 17th place as his former McLaren team took the title with James Hunt. He stuck with the team for a total of five seasons, but one solitary second place finish, at home in Brazil in 1978, was his best result and he retired from racing in 1980.

The team folded two years later, but Fittipaldi returned to racing in 1984, joining the American CART series at the age of 38. He won the championship and the Indy 500 in 1989 and took the Indianapolis race victory again in 1993, beating reigning Formula One champion Nigel Mansell. He finally retired in 1996 when a crash at the Michigan International Speedway ended his career.

ABOVE: *Emerson Fittipaldi (McLaren M23-Ford) in the pits at the 1974 Monaco Grand Prix.*

Niki Lauda

Lauda was a brave and confident racer whose success came through clever, calculated performances more than pure out-and-out pace. During a dramatic career he came back twice, once from a fiery crash and once from early retirement, to become one of the few Formula One drivers to claim three world titles.

Supremely self-confident both on and off the track, Lauda spent 13 seasons in Formula One and started 131 races. He took 24 poles, 25 wins, and 54 podiums between 1971 and 1985 and in retirement he went on to become a successful airline businessman, a modern Formula One team principal, and a television commentator.

EARLY YEARS

Born Andreas Nikolas Lauda in Vienna, in 1949, the Austrian hailed from a wealthy family who helped to fund his way into Formula One despite his father's resistance. Lauda's first race,

ABOVE: *Niki Lauda (McLaren Ford) on the podium, celebrating his victory in the 1982 British Grand Prix.*

BELOW: *Niki Lauda (Ferrari 312T2) battles with Mario Andretti (Lotus 78 Ford) on his way to winning the 1977 Dutch Grand Prix.*

ABOVE: *Niki Lauda (Ferrari 312T2) in action during the 1977 Monaco Grand Prix, he went on to finish in second place.*

a hill climb, ended with a second place finish, and he continued to impress when he stepped up to join Formula Vee and then Formula Three.

He spent some time driving private Porsche and Chevron sports cars before securing a large bank loan to fund a seat with the March Formula Two team in 1971, a move that proved effective. Lauda was promoted to the top tier the following year, when he raced in both Formula Two and Formula One.

MAKING A MARK

After making his debut in a one-off appearance at his home race in 1971, a disappointing season with March saw Lauda take another loan to join Brabham, where he did enough to impress Ferrari into handing him a seat for the 1974 season. He took his first win in the Spanish Grand Prix that year, but eight race retirements stalled his title challenge and he finished the season in fourth place.

The 1975 season saw him clinch his first title with five wins and a further three podiums and he was in control the following year, with five wins, before an horrific crash at the Nürburgring saw him hit the barriers and then collide with a backmarker. The car burst into flames and Lauda was dragged from the wreckage with toxic fume inhalation and severe burns that put him into a coma.

Astonishingly, he was back in the car in just 30 days, but handed the title to rival James Hunt when he pulled out of the rain-hit Japanese Grand Prix claiming conditions were undriveable. The following year, a run of six second places added to his three victories and secured his second and last title with Ferrari.

END OF AN ERA

Lauda quit Ferrari to join Brabham in 1978, winning with the radical fan car in Sweden and again in Italy, but quit the sport after two seasons with the team when, at the Canadian Grand Prix, after a disastrous season that saw him retire 11 times from 13 races, he decided he no longer wanted to race for a living.

He spent two years working on his airline business before returning to the track, for financial reasons, with McLaren in 1982. He failed to mount a serious title challenge that year, despite winning his third race, but after a winless 1983 he was joined by Alain Prost and the pair dominated.

Lauda took the 1984 title by just half a point, with five wins and four crucial second place finishes but, when Prost took the upper hand in 1985, Lauda left, his final win coming in Holland that year. He returned to his airline business while also consulting for Ferrari in Formula One before a foray into team management with Jaguar Racing and, later, a move into television.

James Hunt

Hunt was the epitomy of the sport during the glamor-filled 1970s, managing to maintain an admirable combination of hard racing and hard partying during his career. He grew a reputation as a quick-witted maverick with a love for women, cigarettes, and alcohol—but inside a car he was as talented and committed a racer as anyone on the grid.

Known as 'Hunt the Shunt' when he arrived in Formula One, the British driver shook off that tag in a seven-year Grand Prix career that saw him take 10 wins from 92 starts. His world title came in 1976, and his success coupled with his charm and charisma brought a whole new audience to Formula One.

ABOVE: *James Hunt celebrates winning the 1976 French Grand Prix.*

PREVIOUS SPREAD: *James Hunt (McLaren M23 Ford) locks up and takes off over the front wheel of John Watson's Brabham BT45B Alfa Romeo, in the chain reaction of collisions at Cooks Corner on the first lap of the 1977 United States Grand Prix.*

ABOVE: *James Hunt (McLaren M23 Ford) leads John Watson (Penske PC4 Ford) on his way to victory in the 1976 Dutch Grand Prix.*

EARLY YEARS

Born in Belmont, England in 1947, James Simon Wallis Hunt was a stockbroker's son with a variety of talents that saw him play junior tennis at Wimbledon and train to become a doctor before making his foray into motorsport driving a self-made racing mini.

He graduated through Formula Ford and Formula Three, developing an entertaining driving style that was sometimes spectacular and often ended in accidents. He stepped up to Formula Two with the works March team and, when that collapsed, he raced a privately-entered Hesketh March before graduating to Formula One.

MAKING A MARK

The Hesketh team gave Hunt his debut in 1973 at the Monaco Grand Prix. He retired from the race due to engine trouble, but his first points arrived at the very next race and at the end of the season, in the United States Grand Prix, he raced to second place and the team started to gain respect.

ABOVE: *James Hunt (McLaren M23-Ford) on his way to victory in the 1976 German Grand Prix at Nürburgring.*

A lack of reliability plagued Hesketh the following year, with Hunt retiring from more than half the races he entered, but things began to look up when a debut victory came in Holland in 1975. It was a short burst of sunshine for the team, however, and with funds run drying up rapidly Hesketh pulled out of the sport at the end of the year, leaving Hunt without a drive for 1976.

Hesketh's departure proved fortuitous, however, as Hunt stepped into the McLaren seat vacated by Emerson Fittipaldi and had an instant chance to race at the front. He took his first win for the team in only his fourth race and after a season-long battle with Niki Lauda, which saw the Austrian sidelined for two races due to a crash, he chased down a 17-point deficit in the final three rounds to win the world title by a solitary point.

END OF AN ERA

Hunt continued with McLaren in 1977, but Lauda was back on top of his game and the Briton could manage only fifth in the championship as eight retirements overshadowed his three victories (including his last ever, in Japan) and hampered his challenge. Lauda took control for Ferrari that year before the Lotus ground-effect cars began to dominate in 1978 and Hunt's McLaren team were left standing.

A move to the promising Wolf team beckoned in 1979 as Hunt tried to re-ignite his career, but their ground-effect car was inferior to those of their rivals. The Briton retired from six of the seven races he entered and walked away from racing after the Monaco Grand Prix in the middle of the season.

His on-track Formula One career had lasted just six seasons, but his off-track involvement would last significantly longer as he took up a position in the commentary booth alongside Murray Walker, offering an open—and often very frank—viewpoint and a talented take on reading a race. Sadly, his life was cut short when, at the age of 45, he died at his Wimbledon home after suffering a heart attack.

8

THE
1980s

The start of the decade was overshadowed by political rows as the manufacturer teams and the privateers vied for supremacy. The manufacturers, led by Ferrari, Renault, and Alfa Romeo, were pushing for a limitation in the use of ground-effect aerodynamics, to help make the most of their turbo engines, while the smaller teams wanted no restrictions because they could not afford the cost of developing the new high-power engines.

The disputes were resolved with a ban on ground-effect skirts and a move to flat-bottom cars as turbo engines became the norm and carbon fibre chassis became the lead innovation of the day. Limitations to the power of the turbo led to a return to normally aspirated engines being standard again by the end of the decade.

Inside the cars, new names emerged. Tragic accidents in the early 80s cut short the career of Didier Pironi and cost Gilles Villeneuve his life, leaving Brazilians Ayrton Senna and Nelson Piquet, Frenchman Alain Prost, and Briton Nigel Mansell as the men to watch.

1980

Williams built on the form they showed at the end of the 1970s while champions Ferrari lost their way and even failed to qualify for one race. Alfa Romeo returned and Brabham stepped up to the front. Safety continued to be an issue with several top drivers either killed, paralysed, or lucky to escape.

Jones took a dominant win at the season-opener in Argentina but it was Arnoux in the turbocharged Renault who took the next two wins, in Brazil and South Africa, the latter seeing Prost break his wrist and Marc Surer severely damage both legs in two separate crashes.

Regazzoni's career was ended at the next race in the United States when he hit an

LEFT: *Gerhard Berger (Ferrari F187/88C) holds off Alain Prost (McLaren MP4/4 Honda) as they race through Casino Square during the 1988 Monaco Grand Prix. Prost went on to win the race.*

ABOVE: *Alan Jones (Williams FW07B-Ford Cosworth) in action during his winning race at the 1980 British Grand Prix.*

abandoned car, flew into a concrete barrier, and was paralysed. Piquet scored his first victory in that race, for Brabham, then Pironi took his maiden win, for Ligier, in Belgium. Williams then began a run of victories when Reutermann took the spoils in Monaco and though Jones' victory in Spain was declared void after the turbo teams refused to take part, he went on to win in France and Britain.

Depallier died in a testing crash before the German race, which was won by Laffite, then Jean-Pierre Jabouille won for Renault in Austria.

The championship was decided in the next three races, with Piquet taking the lead by a point after wins in Holland and Italy and setting up a dramatic race in Canada. Jones and Piquet collided on the first lap, causing a race stoppage, but Piquet retired from the restart and Jones won the race then finished off in style with victory in the United States.

1981

Williams and Brabham led the way in 1981, but off-track disputes made more headlines than the racing as FISA and FOCA went to war. The season got off to a false start when the FISA teams pulled out of the first round in South Africa, and the championship proper started in the United States instead.

Ground-effect skirts were banned for the first race and Jones won for Williams. Brabham introduced a controversial suspension system in Brazil, but Piquet slipped up in the wet and Reutermann led a Williams 1-2 despite being told to let team-mate Jones past.

Piquet won in Argentina and San Marino but,t in Belgium, a mechanic died after being hit by a car in practice and another mechanic had his legs broken while working on Patrese's stalled Arrows on the grid. Reutermann won the race after Piquet and Jones collided.

Villeneuve took surprise wins for Ferrari in Monaco and Spain then, in France, Renault driver Prost took his first victory in a rain-affected race of two halves. Briton John Watson was victorious on home soil for McLaren, Piquet won in Germany, and Laffitte became the seventh different winner in 11 races with victory in Austria.

Prost took a second win for Renault, in Holland, while Piquet's second place put him level with Reutermann in the table. Prost won again in Italy then Laffite won in Canada to put himself in with a chance of the championship. The final race went to Jones but in the title race Piquet picked up the points he needed to take the crown.

1982

The off-track arguments came to a head in a tragic, incident-filled season of strikes, deaths, and drama. Lauda came out of retirement to race for McLaren while Jones made way for Keke Rosberg at Williams, who triumphed through consistency as 11 different drivers took wins in the 16 races.

The season began with a drivers' strike in South Africa, but Prost went on to dominate, coming back to win after a puncture dropped him from first to eighth. He was awarded victory in Brazil after top two Piquet and Rosberg were disqualified, then Lauda won the United States West race after 12 cars crashed out.

Arguments over the Brazil disqualifications caused seven teams to boycott San Marino and Ferrari took a 1-2 as Pironi began a bitter feud by overtaking Villeneuve on the final lap. Villeneuve was dead before the next race, killed in Belgium while qualifying as he pushed to beat his team-mate. Ferrari pulled out and Watson won for McLaren.

Patrese won a dramatic Monaco race after leader Prost crashed with three laps remaining. Watson took his second win, in the United States, and Piquet won in Canada, but Riccardo Paletti died when he crashed into Pironi's stalled Ferrari on the grid.

Pironi took victory in Holland and Lauda won in Britain, but Pironi's career was ended by a terrible leg-breaking accident in Germany. Tambay gave Ferrari a hollow win there, then Elio de Angelis won for Lotus in Austria and Rosberg took his only victory of the year in Switzerland.

The season came to a climax in a Las Vegas car park when, after Arnoux took victory in Italy, the title was between Watson and Rosberg. Watson finished second behind Alboreto's Tyrrell, but Rosberg's fifth place was enough to take the title.

1983

In stark contrast to the previous year, 1983 was all about the on-track action. Flat-bottom cars cancelled out ground-effect and turbos were on top, with the arrival of Arnoux allowing a rejuvenated Ferrari to take the fight to Renault and Brabham-BMW. Williams and McLaren, meanwhile, struggled on with non-turbo machinery and Lotus was rocked by the death of legendary team chief Colin Champman.

Piquet won the first race in Brazil, but Watson stormed through the field in the non-turbo McLaren to win from 22nd in the United States West. Renault won in France with Prost, and Ferrari won in Italy with Tambay then Rosberg gave his non-turbo Williams the glory in Monaco.

ABOVE: *Nelson Piquet (Brabham BT52B BMW) on his way to victory in the 1983 European Grand Prix.*

Prost won in Belgium then Alboreto scored the Cosworth DFV's last win in a United States race that suited non-turbo cars. Frenchmen Prost and Arnoux then traded win for win, with Prost taking victory in Britain and Austria and Arnoux triumphant in Canada, Germany, and Holland, the latter race seeing Prost collide with Piquet.

Prost looked comfortable, 14 points ahead, but he failed to finish in Italy, where consistent podium finisher Piquet won, and Piquet beat him to victory at the European Grand Prix in Britain, leaving just two points between them ahead of the South African season finale.

Piquet led early on but, when Prost retired, the Brabham driver needed fourth or better to win the title, so slowed to protect his car. He allowed Patrese through to win, but secured the points he needed for title number two.

1984

Refuelling was banned for the new season, but the biggest news was the departure of Prost from Renault. Disillusioned by the management, he formed a dream team with Lauda at TAG-Porsche powered McLaren and they were in a class of their own.

Prost won on his McLaren debut, with Rosberg second in the Honda-powered Williams, but Lauda led a McLaren domination in South Africa, with Prost racing through the pack from the back to finish second.

Alboreto won for Ferrari in Belgium, but it was the only non-McLaren victory in the first six races as Prost took San Marino, Lauda won France, and Prost finished ahead in Monaco, scoring half points after Mansell crashed out of the lead and the race was stopped early.

McLaren suffered a blip in form across the Atlantic as Brabham driver Piquet won the Canadian and United States East races and Rosberg won the United States West race for Williams, with Mansell collapsing as he tried to push his Lotus across the line after a gearbox failure.

Back in Europe, McLaren were unbeatable and won all seven remaining races. Lauda won in Britain when Prost's gearbox failed, Prost led a 1-2 in Germany, but in Austria he spun off to hand Lauda victory. Prost led another 1-2 in Holland, but his engine blew in Italy and Lauda won.

Prost won the European Grand Prix to make it six wins to Lauda's five, but his team-mate had more points due to more finishes and in the final race of the year, in Portugal, Prost won but Lauda came second to win the title by just half a point.

1985

After narrowly losing out on the last two occasions Prost was hoping for third time lucky in 1985, but he faced strong competition as Rosberg was joined by Mansell at Williams, Senna took the Briton's place at Lotus, and Alboreto led the Ferrari charge after Arnoux quit the team one race into the season.

Prost started well, winning in Brazil, but Senna mastered the rain in Portugal to turn pole into a dominant win. The young Brazilian took pole in San Marino, but ran out of fuel two laps from home. New leader Johansson also stopped and Prost finished first but was underweight so Elio de Angeles took the win.

Prost won in Monaco, with Alboreto claiming his third second place of the year. The Italian then led a Ferrari 1-2 in Canada before Rosberg won for Williams in the United States as Senna, Mansell, and Prost all crashed out. Piquet won for Brabham in France, but Prost was back on top in Britain, lapping second-placed Alboreto.

Alboreto won in Germany, despite hitting Ferrari team-mate Johansson on lap one, but Prost took more points with a podium there and a win in Austria. Off-form champion Lauda found his speed to take a final victory in Holland before Prost's sixth win of the year in Italy.

Senna won in Belgium then Mansell took win number one in Britain as Prost came in fourth to take the title. Mansell triumphed again in South Africa and Rosberg closed the season, winning at the new race in Australia, but it was Prost's consistency, with podiums in all his 11 scoring races, that won the title.

1986

It was a classic year-long battle for the title in 1986. Rosberg replaced the retired Lauda at McLaren, but he was outshone by Prost with the Williams-Hondas of Mansell and Piquet, who arrived from Brabham, and Senna's Lotus; making it a four way fight that went to the wire at a spectacular season-ending race.

Piquet won on home ground in Brazil on his Williams debut, but it was Brazilian Senna who took victory in Spain, finishing 0.014s ahead of Mansell in an epic battle. Prost took his first win of the year in San Marino, then won Monaco, though Formula One was shocked by a now rare driver death when de Angeles was killed testing his Lotus.

Mansell won four of the next five races, his victories in Belgium, Canada, France, and Britain split only by Senna's pole-to-flag victory in the United States. Piquet hit back in the next four, with wins in Italy, Germany—where both McLarens ran out of fuel on the final lap—and the new race in Hungary, while Prost won in Austria. Mansell won in Portugal then Berger took Benetton's first victory when Formula One returned to Mexico.

At the final race in Australia, Mansell had a seven-point lead, but it was still possible that either Piquet or Prost could steal the title. Mansell took pole, but dropped out the race when his tire blew. Williams pulled Piquet in for a safety check and Prost—who had suffered a puncture himself—stormed through to take the title by two points.

1987

The field was split between turbo and non-turbo cars in preparation for a turbo ban in 1989, but Williams kept their high powered Honda engine and dominated. Increasingly bitter rivalry developed between team-mates Mansell and Piquet and a dramatic battle for the title went down to the penultimate race of the season.

Mansell took pole in Brazil, but Prost won ahead of Piquet in a race full of overtaking at the front. Mansell won in San Marino, with Piquet sidelined by a practice crash, but the Briton had a double fight coming together with Senna in Belgium, first in cars on the track then with fists in the paddock, as Prost led a McLaren 1-2.

Senna won from Piquet at Monaco after Mansell's engine blew and the Lotus driver won again in the United States after Mansell suffered cramp. The next six races went to Williams, with Mansell and Piquet taking three each, the Briton scoring a popular home win after a spectacular overtake on his team-mate at Silverstone.

During this period, however, Mansell suffered some significant retirements, with his engine failing in Germany and a wheel nut falling off in Hungary. His title bid took another dent when he retired in Portugal with Piquet third as Prost took the win.

Mansell won in Spain, with Piquet fourth, and led a Williams 1-2 in Mexico, but injured his back in a practice crash in Japan. His title bid was over. Piquet failed to finish again as Berger won in Japan and Australia, but he had already done enough.

1988

McLaren took Honda from Williams for 1988 and Senna joined Prost in a new super team that completely crushed the opposition, winning 15 of the 16 races as Williams descended from dominant champions to mid-grid mediocrity.

Senna claimed a season-opening pole in Brazil, but a problem forced him to the pits. Prost took win number one after Senna raced from 21st to second in 20 laps, only to be disqualified for using the spare car.

Senna hit back in San Marino with a pole-to-flag victory and was dominating Monaco when he inexplicably crashed into the barriers to hand Prost victory. The next four races saw McLaren 1-2s, with Prost leading in Mexico and France, Senna in Canada and the United States.

Heavy rain at Silverstone saw Prost stop on safety grounds as Senna won ahead of Mansell in a shock second. Senna then took a hat-trick of wins in Germany, Hungary, and Belgium before his domination was stopped by a backmarker in Italy and Ferrari scored a poignant 1-2 just weeks after Enzo Ferrari passed away.

Prost won in Portugal and Spain, battling the March of Ivan Capelli as Senna finished sixth and fourth. Prost then looked set for victory in Japan when Senna dropped to 14th at the start but Senna raced back and overtook Prost to win.

Prost won the final race to amass 107 points but, with only the best 11 finishes counting toward the championship, his tally was adjusted to 87 and Senna—with 90 points and eight wins—had done enough to win his first title.

ABOVE: *Andrea de Cesaris of Italy in action in his Brabham BMW as it catches fire during the 1987 British Grand Prix.*

ABOVE: *Ayrton Senna(McLaren MP4/4 Honda) leads the field as they approach St. Devote during the 1988 Monaco Grand Prix.*

ABOVE: *Ayrton Senna leads into the first corner followed by team-mate Alain Prost (both McLaren MP4/5 Honda) during the 1989 Belgian Grand Prix. Senna finished in first place and Prost in second.*

1989

A move to the new 3.5-liter non-turbo formula failed to stop another season of McLaren domination, but the rivalry between Senna and Prost boiled over as they tried to out-do each other in every way. Mansell joined Ferrari with instant success, but the Italian team was not strong enough to mount a title challenge.

An incredible 38 cars entered the opening race, necessitating a new pre-qualifying session, but the season started in shock when Philippe Strieff was paralysed in a crash in testing.

Mansell and Ferrari won in Brazil, but San Marino saw his team-mate Berger suffer a fiery crash. The race was stopped and restarted, at which point Senna overtook Prost and broke a gentlemen's agreement. Senna led home a McLaren 1-2 with Prost left fuming.

Senna went on to dominant wins in Monaco and Mexico, but it was not to last and he suffered four retirements as Prost won in the United States, Boutsen broke McLaren's domination with a Williams 1-2 in Canada, and Prost won again in France and Britain.

Senna capitalized on Prost's gearbox problem to win in Germany, but Mansell secured a stunning victory in Hungary. Senna won in Belgium as his old team Lotus failed to qualify, though engine failure in Italy forced him to retire again as Prost won his fourth race of the season.

Berger won in Portugal after Mansell took out Senna, leaving Prost with a 24-point lead. Senna would not give up and won in Spain then battled Prost for victory in Japan. The pair collided, putting Prost out, but Senna came back to win only to be disqualified, handing victory to Nannini's Benetton and the title to Prost.

Nelson Piquet

A colorful character and a consistent racer, Piquet was as committed as they come and his impressive successes came during one of the most intense eras of tight competition ever seen. He was praised as a cunning champion, well aware of how to make the most out of both car and team, but was equally criticized for his sometimes irreverent approach to life.

Piquet had an impressive victory record, winning races in all but four of the 14 seasons he raced in Formula One. During 204 Grand Prix starts, he took 24 pole positions, 23 wins, and 60 podiums, clocking up three World Championship titles despite racing against the likes of Ayrton Senna, Alain Prost, Keke Rosberg, and Nigel Mansell.

ABOVE: *Nelson Piquet before the 1983 European Grand Prix at Brands Hatch.*

ABOVE: *Nelson Piquet (Brabham BT49C-Ford Cosworth) on his way to fifth position, and the World Championship win, in the 1981 Las Vegas Grand Prix.*

EARLY YEARS

Born Nelson Souto Maior, in Rio de Janeiro in 1952, Piquet took his mother's surname when he began racing karts at the age of 14 to hide his actions from his politician father, who was against him following a career in motorsport.

A champion karter, he moved into Formula Super Vee in Brazil before heading to Europe, where he made an instant impact in the British Formula Three championship, winning twice in 1977, then securing the title with a record number of victories the following year. Soon after that, he stepped up to Formula One.

MAKING A MARK

Everyone wanted a piece of Piquet in 1978 and, after his debut at the German Grand Prix in a one-off drive for Ensign, which resulted in race retirement, he raced a private McLaren three times, then tried out for Brabham in the final race of the year, impressing the team and earning a full seat alongside Niki Lauda for 1979.

Piquet was right on the pace, but nine retirements meant the results did not reflect his true performance. The following year, when Lauda retired, Piquet led the team with three wins but finished runner-up to Alan Jones in the title race before finally securing the title in 1981, beating Carlos Reutermann in a thrilling season-ending race.

The following year was one of disappointment with an unreliable Brabham, but a return to form in 1984 saw three wins and five more podiums. Piquet beat Prost to win a second title. He remained loyal to Brabham for two more years but, after just three wins, he made a move in search of a healthy wage and more success.

END OF AN ERA

Piquet began a new era at Williams in 1986, creating a bitter rivalry with team-mate Mansell. He won three times and narrowly missed out to Prost in a tight three-way title battle, but the following year saw him take his third crown taking three wins and seven second places during a season-long fight with Mansell.

Williams lost Honda power for 1988 and, when they decided to run a normally aspirated engine against the more powerful turbo machines, Piquet joined Lotus who continued with Honda. His two seasons with the team proved to be a disaster, however, and with three third place finishes his main reward, his career looked to be coming to an end.

He was saved from the scrapheap by Benetton, who took him on for two more years, and the Brazilian returned to the top step of the podium in 1990 with victories in Japan and Australia moving him up to third in the drivers' championship behind the duel between Alain Prost and Ayrton Senna.

His final season saw one win and two further podiums, but the arrival of Michael Schumacher made him look like a man nearing the end of his career and he retired with fourth at his final race, in Adelaide. Not finished with racing, he took on the Indy 500 twice, with his first outing ending in a heavy crash, but then retired to concentrate on helping his son Nelsinho climb the racing ladder.

ABOVE: *Nelson Piquet (Williams FW11 Honda) crosses the line and takes the checkered flag to win the 1986 Brazilian Grand Prix.*

Alain Prost

Prost is in the record books as of the greatest achievers in Formula One, thanks to a combination of a smooth driving style, calculated performances, and a complete commitment to all elements of racing, both on the track and in the garage. Nicknamed 'Le Professeur' for his analytical approach to racing, he was a nervous nail biter outside the car, but a polished performer when he hit the track.

Prost struck up a great, but often bitter, rivalry with his Brazilian nemesis Ayrton Senna, though his results spoke for themselves: four championships from 13 seasons in the sport. In an incredible career he won 51 races from 199 starts, taking 33 pole positions, 106 podiums, and 798.5 points—almost four per race.

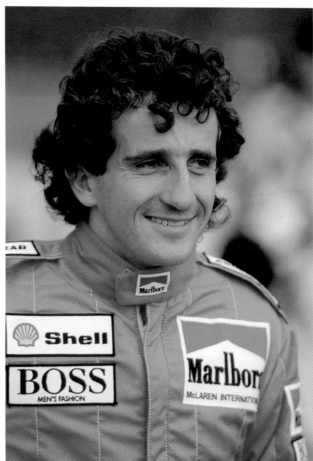

ABOVE: *Alain Prost at the 1986 Brazilian Grand Prix at Jacarepaguá.*

EARLY YEARS

Born in Lorette, France, in 1955, Alain Marie Pascal Prost was the son of a middle-class couple. He wanted to play football professionally, before discovering Formula One on a trip to Monaco in 1970 and, after his first racing experience, with his brother Daniel in a kart at an amusement park whilst on vacation, he was hooked.

He bought his own kart with money earned from working in his father's shop while still at college, then moved into cars with a stint at the Winfield racing school before stepping up to French Formula Renault, where he won all but one race in 1976. He won the Euro title the next year and Euro Formula Three two years later, after which he got the call from McLaren.

MAKING A MARK

Prost scored points for McLaren on his Grand Prix debut in Argentina, but left the team after two crashes to join Renault in 1981. His first win came in France that year, but the car was fragile and, though he was on the podium every time he finished, nine retirements in 15 races ruined his title challenge.

ABOVE: *Alain Prost (McLaren MP4/2B TAG Porsche) on his way to winning the 1985 Austrian Grand Prix.*

ABOVE: *Alain Prost (McLaren MP4/4 Honda) celebrates his victory in the 1988 Australian Grand Prix at Adelaide.*

NEXT SPREAD: *Alain Prost leads René Arnoux (both Renault RE30B) and the rest of the field at the start of the 1982 Dutch Grand Prix.*

It was a similar story in 1982, with two wins and seven retirements, but the following year saw him finish as championship runner-up, with four wins. A move to McLaren in 1984 began a successful six-year stint with the team and, in his first season Prost narrowly missed out to experienced team-mate Niki Lauda, who took the title by just half a point.

Prost outperformed his former champion team-mates Lauda and Rosberg, taking back-to-back titles in 1985 and 1986, but after a dominant year for Williams in 1987, he was faced with his greatest challenge when Senna arrived in 1988. He lost out to the Brazilian as McLaren dominated the season, but beat him to the crown after a controversial collision at the season-ending Japanese Grand Prix in 1989.

END OF AN ERA

Prost's relationship with Senna had soured that season and he left McLaren, after taking 30 wins in 96 races, to join Ferrari.

The pair battled again in 1990, with Senna taking the title after another controversial season-ending collision, then Ferrari lost their way and after his first winless season in 11 years, he was sacked before the last race for criticizing the management.

After a sabbatical he returned with Williams and, in a car that was the class of the field, he won his fourth title with seven victories before retiring to avoid teaming up with the incoming Senna for 1994. As a French TV pundit, he watched as his former rival perished in a tragic accident the following year, and vowed never to race again.

He moved into team management, buying Ligier in 1997 and re-naming it Prost Grand Prix. The team scored points on its debut and finished sixth in the championship using Mugen-Honda engines, but a switch to Peugeot for the following three years brought nothing but disaster and the team folded at the start of 2002.

Ayrton Senna

A blisteringly fast driver with a passionate temperament, Senna was one of the sport's greatest racers, described by many as both an enigma and a true genius. Shy, thoughtful, and supremely intelligent, he was constantly learning, certain that each new piece of information would help him push his car even closer to the edge.

Senna raced in 10 full seasons before his life was cut short in a tragic accident at the San Marino Grand Prix in 1994. He finished on the podium in almost half his 161 starts, taking 41 wins on the way to three world titles, but he will always be remembered for the astonishing last-gasp qualifying laps that won him 65 pole positions.

EARLY YEARS

Born into a wealthy family in São Paolo in 1960, Ayrton Senna da Silva first got behind the wheel at the age of four and raced karts before moving to England in 1981 to step into single-seaters. He won the Formula Ford championship that year with 12 race victories, then dominated Formula Ford 2000 the next year with 21 wins from 27 starts.

A move to Formula Three in 1983 saw him dominate the first half of the season before a mid-season slump almost threw the title away and Martin Brundle fought back. But Senna won the final round to take the title, then proved his talent further when he raced to victory in the prestigious Macau Grand Prix at the end of the year.

MAKING A MARK

Formula One had noticed the young Brazilian and, following tests with Williams and McLaren, Toleman gave him his debut in 1984. He retired from his first race, in Brazil, but after finishing second in only his sixth outing a lack of results, due to poor reliability, made him decide to join Lotus the following year.

His first victory came in the wet in Portugal, in the second race of the 1985 season, but with McLaren and Williams producing the best cars, Senna's three seasons at Lotus saw him win just six races. His best finish in the championship was third, in 1987 and, with top spot in his targets, he made a switch to the more successful McLaren team.

ABOVE: *Ayrton Senna at his race debut for Team Lotus at the 1985 Brazilian Grand Prix.*

That season saw the start of an intense rivalry with Prost, with Senna winning a straight fight against his new two-time World Champion team-mate as the Honda-powered MP4/4 dominated the season. Senna scored eight wins and won his first title with a great comeback victory in the wet in Japan.

Senna won six more races in 1989, but the pair collided in Japan and Prost's consistent results gave him the title. The Frenchman joined Ferrari in 1990, but the battle continued, with Senna taking six wins and a second title after taking Prost off in Japan. He then fended off Nigel Mansell's challenge to take the crown a third time in 1991.

END OF AN ERA

Senna's chances of further championships were dented when Williams dominated in 1992 and, with McLaren off the boil, he won three times and finished only fourth. The next year,

ABOVE: *Ayrton Senna (Toleman TG184 Hart) in action during the 1984 Monaco Grand Prix.*

ABOVE: *Ayrton Senna (Williams FW16 Renault) during the 1994 Italian Grand Prix. He was tragically killed after an accident on the start of lap seven.*

uncertain of McLaren's pace, he agreed to compete on a race-by-race basis and won the European Grand Prix at Donington with an incredible performance in wet-dry conditions, then took a record sixth victory at Monaco. With Prost now the target at Williams, he was inspired to see out the entire season and finished second as his old rival took the title and retired.

Senna joined Williams in 1994 and was expected to dominate, but the form team—which had moved to the front with a technologically advanced car—lost their way when driver aids were eliminated and Senna failed to finish the first two races. Then came the blackest weekend of them all.

After Brazilian Rubens Barrichello escaped from a dramatic crash in Friday practice came Roland Ratzenberger's accident on Saturday . The Austrian's death brought Senna to tears and, one day later, the great champion himself was lost after his car ploughed into a concrete wall at the Tamburello corner.

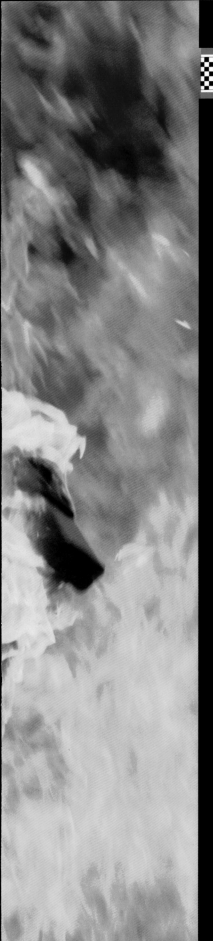

8

THE 1990s

The decade began with the separation of one of the sport's strongest-ever driver line-ups as Prost left Senna at McLaren to join Ferrari. The pair continued to fight for supremacy both on and off the track, battling for wins while vying with each other to get the best seat at Williams as their technologically advanced cars moved to the front. But everything was to change at Imola in 1994 in one of the most shocking weekends Formula One has ever seen.

Improvements in safety had made the sport complacent and the deaths of Senna and Roland Ratzenberger, who both perished at San Marino, instigated fundamental change. The following seasons saw stringent new crash structures introduced into Formula One design while tracks were improved and electronic aids were reduced.

Much changed, but much had stayed the same. Cars were significantly safer, new raised-nose aerodynamics changed their look, and the commercial side of the sport underwent major expansion. Williams had their day in the middle of the decade, but by the end, while the names of Prost and Senna had been replaced by Michael Schumacher and Mika Häkkinen, it was Ferrari and McLaren leading the way once again.

1990

After his controversial clash with Prost in Japan in 1989, Senna was facing a ban. He received a late reprieve and lined up with Berger at McLaren, with Prost now at Ferrari, but the end of the season proved a leopard cannot change its spots.

Senna started with victory in Phoenix ahead of newcomer Jean Alesi's surprisingly strong Tyrrell, the first to sport a raised-nose design that would radically change the look of Formula One. But Prost then took his first Ferrari win in Brazil, on Senna's home soil.

Patrese won for Williams in San Marino then Senna mastered Monaco and also won in Canada before Prost took wins in Mexico, where he led Mansell in a Ferrari 1-2; France, where he overtook surprise leader Ivan Capelli's Leyton

LEFT: *Benetton mechanic Paul Seaby is engulfed in flames during a disastrous Jos Verstappen pit stop at the 1994 German Grand Prix. Amazingly, Seaby survived the accident with only minor burns.*

ABOVE: *Jean Alesi (Tyrrell 018 Ford) laps backmarker Michele Alboreto (Arrows A11B Ford) with Ayrton Senna (Mclaren MP4/5B Honda) hot on his heels behind at the 1990 United States Grand Prix.*

House with three laps to go; and Britain.

Senna won in Germany and, after losing to Boutsen in Hungary, beat Prost to victory in Belgium and then, crucially, on Ferrari home soil in Italy. Mansell then won in Portugal, with Senna beating Prost to second.

The sport lost two talented drivers when Allesandro Nannini severed his hand in a helicopter accident and Martin Donnelly had an horrendous crash during qualifying for the Spanish race. Donnelly suffered multiple injuries that he later recovered from, but which ended his Formula One career.

Prost won in Spain, and then came Japan. The pair lined up on row one, but when Senna started slowly he refused to concede the corner. They collided and Senna won the title. Piquet won the race for Benetton, as he did in Australia, but the Japan collision tarnished Senna's reputation.

1991

Reigning champion Senna was concerned by the pace of his new McLaren, but a great opening run put him in the driving seat early on. Ferrari faltered as Alesi joined Prost and Williams. Nigel

Mansell, back in his famous 'Red 5' machine, took the fight to McLaren, and a new name arrived to change the sport forever.

Senna took pole and victories in the first four races, including his first in on home soil, but Piquet and Benetton broke the stranglehold in Canada when he raced past a slowing Mansell, who lost the win when his engine cut out on the final lap as he waved to the crowd.

Patrese gave Williams their first victory of the year in Mexico then Mansell took wins in France, Britain, and Germany, eating into Senna's lead as the Brazilian twice ran out of fuel on the final lap. But Senna's mastery of qualifying gave him pole and victory in Hungary.

Spa saw the debut of Michael Schumacher who, driving for the new Jordan team, qualified seventh but retired on lap one. Senna won, despite gearbox problems, but Mansell hit back in Italy, where Schumacher scored his first points in fifth after moving to Benetton.

The wheel literally fell off Mansell's title challenge in Portugal when a wheel nut came loose after a pit stop and he was disqualified. He battled on, winning the next race in Spain as

Senna finished fifth, but when he crashed in Japan it was all over. Senna won the title and handed victory in Japan to team-mate Berger before winning a shortened race in terrible conditions in Australia.

1992

There was no stopping the dominant Williams cars this time, with some of the most technologically advanced equipment seen in the sport helping Mansell and Patrese to win after win. Prost was gone, sacked by Ferrari and on sabbatical waiting for a spare seat at Williams, and while Senna battled hard for McLaren it was Michael Schumacher who came closest to the leading duo.

Mansell went one better than Senna's start the previous year, winning the first five races from pole in dominant fashion, with Patrese second four times. Schumacher took his first podium in Mexico, but it was Senna who broke the Williams deadlock after holding Mansell off for lap after lap to win in Monaco.

Berger won in Canada after the lead contenders failed to finish, but Mansell won again in a rain-hit French race that saw Patrese wave him through. He then won at home, to became Britain's most victorious driver, and in Germany. Senna won in Hungary, but Mansell clinched the title with second place.

Schumacher scored a canny maiden victory in Belgium by picking the right strategy in variable wet-dry conditions then Senna won in Italy, just days after Honda confirmed they would pull out of the sport at the end of the year. Mansell won in Portugal to break the record number of wins in a season, then Patrese and Berger won in Japan and Australia to bring the season to an end.

ABOVE: *1992 San Marino Grand Prix: Nigel Mansell (Williams FW14B Renault) on his way to setting a new record of winning five consecutive Grand Prix from the start of the season.*

ABOVE:*Ayrton Senna (Williams FW16 Renault) at the 1994 San Marino Grand Prix, before he was tragically killed in an accident on the start of lap seven.*

1993

Williams continued to dominate, with Prost and Damon Hill teaming up for the 1993 season after Mansell moved to the United States to uniquely add the IndyCar title to his Formula One crown. Senna took the fight to his old rival in the Ford-powered McLaren after deciding to drive on a race-by-race basis.

The battle was back on from the start as Prost and Senna lined up alongside each other on the grid in South Africa. Prost won there, but Senna won in a wet Brazil then drove the race of his life to win the European Grand Prix, lapping Prost in Donington's wet-dry conditions.

Prost was back in the groove in San Marino, winning in the dry, and he won again in Spain before Senna took his sixth Monaco win, benefiting from Prost's stop-go penalty and Schumacher's retirement to finish ahead of Hill, whose father won five races in the principality.

Williams then won seven in a row, Prost taking a run of four as Hill missed out twice through engine and tire failure before the Briton finally got his first win in Hungary and followed it with two more in Belgium and Italy, when Prost's engine failed five laps from the end.

Schumacher won in Portugal, but Prost finished close behind in second and, on winning the title, announced his retirement. Senna won in Japan, with Häkkinen taking a podium after joining McLaren as a replacement for the disappointing Michael Andretti, and finished the season off with another victory in Australia.

1994

Senna joined Williams to create one of the most hotly anticipated car-driver combinations, but the car suffered from a ban on driver aids. Three races in, Senna was killed and Schumacher, despite running a Bennetton-Ford car inferior to the Williams-Renault, was left to take over the mantle of a legend. Senna took pole in the Brazilian and Pacific Grand Prix, but Schumacher won both after Senna spun in the first and collided with Häkkinen in the second. Then came San Marino.

The sport was shocked when Roland Ratzenberger died after crashing in Saturday practice then Senna crashed during the race. Schumacher continued on to victory, but then news came through that Senna had died from his injuries.

Schumacher won in Monaco as the FIA made immediate safety changes, but then Karl Wendlinger crashed and went into a coma in practice. He recovered, but the drivers called for temporary chicanes to slow the cars at the next race in Spain.

Hill won for Williams, with Schumacher second after getting stuck in fifth gear, then the German won in Canada and France before Hill took victory in Britain after Schumacher was disqualified for ignoring a black flag.

Berger took Ferrari's first win in 58 races in Germany after an dramatic 11-car pile-up and a pit-lane fuel fire on Verstappen's Benetton. Schumacher took victory in Hungary but Hill then won three in a row, with Schumacher disqualified in Spa and suspended in Italy and Portugal.

Schumacher won the European Grand Prix, but Hill won in Japan. At the final race in Australia, with one point between them, the pair collided and Schumacher won his first title as the returning Mansell took his final race victory.

1995

The FIA introduced significant safety improvements to the cars after the tragic 1994 season, including reducing engine capacity to 3-liters and raising ride height with a stepped bottom, but the Williams-Renault cars remained the class of the field. It was a very British front of the grid as Johnny Herbert joined Benetton, Williams made David Coulthard permanent alongside Damon Hill, and McLaren—now with Mercedes engines—took on Nigel Mansell to partner Mika Häkkinen. Hill had the best shot at Schumacher, but the German, now also powered by Renault, proved tough to take on.

Hill started strongly and, though his suspension failure handed Schumacher victory in Brazil, he dominated Argentina and San Marino. Schumacher crashed at Imola, but was back in Spain for a Benetton 1-2 after hydraulics problems hit both Williams cars. That race saw Mansell retire for good after a disastrous time with McLaren.

Superior strategy saw Schumacher steal victory from Hill in Monaco, but gearbox problems stopped him winning in Canada as Alesi took his first. Hill lost to Schumacher strategy again in France, then Herbert took a first win, in Britain, after Hill hit Schumacher in an ambitious overtake.

Just before the German race, legendary Juan Manuel Fangio died aged 84, and it was fitting that Schumacher, who eventually beat Fangio's titles record, took a home win. Hill crashed there, but led a Williams' 1-2 in Hungary. Schumacher took Belgium and Herbert inherited Italy after Hill hit Schumacher and both Ferraris failed.

Coulthard dominated Portugal with a maiden win but Schumacher won the European Grand Prix after knocking out Hill and passing Alesi three laps from home. He sealed the title with a Pacific Grand Prix win and celebrated with victory in Japan before Hill took a consolation prize in Australia, winning by two laps as just eight drivers finished.

ABOVE: *Olivier Panis (Ligier JS43 Mugen-Honda) drives around the streets with the tricolour, celebrating his victory in the 1996 Monaco Grand Prix.*

1996

Schumacher took on a new challenge at Ferrari in 1996 as he and Eddie Irvine replaced Benetton-bound Berger and Alesi. It took time for the German to move the struggling team to the front and, with a lack of opposition for the dominant Williams cars, Damon Hill only had his new team-mate Jacques Villeneuve to beat.

Villeneuve was not going to make it easy and he should have won from pole on his debut, but an oil leak forced him to hand victory to Hill, who also took wins in Brazil and Argentina. Villeneueve got his first by beating Schumacher in a tight European Grand Prix and Hill won again in San Marino after Schumacher put his Ferrari on pole.

Wet conditions created surprise results in the next two races, with Olivier Panis leading just four finishers in Monaco and Schumacher passing an all-Williams front row to claim his first win for Ferrari in Spain as just six cars made the finish.

Williams returned to form and won the next five races: Hill led 1-2s in Canada and France and took a lucky win when Berger stopped three laps from the finish in Germany; Villeneuve won in Britain and headed a 1-2 in Hungary.

Schumacher mastered drying conditions to win a three-way battle in Belgium, then delighted the *tifosi* by winning in Italy

after Hill crashed out. Villeneve led a Williams 1-2 in Portugal to take the title to the wire but Hill, who needed just one point, won in Japan to become the first second-generation World Champion.

1997

Champion Hill was shown the door as Williams welcomed Heinz-Harald Frentzen and the Briton decided to take a gamble on Arrows-Yamaha. Villeneuve took control, but Ferrari were becoming a force and Schumacher took a 'do or die' approach as the title went to the wire.

Villeneuve crashed out on lap one in Australia, leaving Coulthard to win for McLaren, but then took dominant victories in Brazil and Argentina before Frentzen won his first for Williams in San Marino.

Schumacher dominated Monaco in the wet as the Williams and McLaren cars crashed and Stewart finished second in their fifth race. Panis challenged Villeneuve for victory in Spain, but lost and then suffered a leg-breaking crash in Canada as Schumacher raced to victory.

Schumacher took a dominant win in France, but Villeneuve gained from Häkkinen's late engine failure to win in Britain and

Berger recovered from a virus to win in Germany. Hill, who had been nowhere all season, looked set for a surprise win in Hungary, but stopped on the final lap and Villeneuve took it.

Schumacher won a wet race in Belgium as Villeneuve struggled to fifth and the title contenders were nowhere as Coulthard won in Italy. Wins in Austria and Luxembourg put Villeneuve closer, but disqualification for passing under waved yellows in Japan saw Schumacher move ahead with victory. He now just had to finish ahead of Villeneuve to take the title in the season-ending European Grand Prix. Following a controversial incident during lap 48, where Schumacher turned into Villeneuve, causing a collision, Schumacher was disqualified from the 1997 World Championship. Despite the collision Villeneuve continued and claimed the title, finishing third as Häkkinen won his first race.

1998

The season saw cars narrowed and grooved tires introduced to reduce increasing speeds. McLaren were quick to get on top of the rules. Williams lost Renault factory engines and tires were significant as Bridgestone helped McLaren in the fight with Goodyear-shod Ferrari.

McLaren stunned in Australia as their two cars lapped the field, Häkkinen leading Coulthard in a dominant 1-2. It was the same in Brazil and though Schumacher won in Argentina, his challenge would not be sustained as Coulthard beat Häkkinen in San Marino, vice-versa in Spain, and Häkkinen won alone in Monaco.

Schumacher began a hat-trick of wins when both McLarens failed in Canada. He won fair and square in France, then took a confused victory in Britain, ahead of Häkkinen, after the FIA failed to add a time penalty for pit-line speeding.

Häkkinen fought back to lead McLaren 1-2s in Austria and Germany, but Schumacher took a strategic victory in Hungary. He excelled in wet conditions in Belgium, but hit Coulthard and crashed out of the lead to hand his old Jordan team a maiden win, with Hill leading a 1-2.

Schumacher led a 1-2 for Ferrari in Italy after champion Villeneuve, still without a win, spun out of the lead. Häkkinen beat Schumacher in Luxembourg. By now his lead was four points with only Japan to go. Schumacher had to fight from the back after stalling on the grid, but his hopes went when a tire failed, leaving Häkkinen to win the race and the title.

1999

The decade closed as it began, with a clear battle between McLaren and Ferrari, but mid-season disaster for Schumacher left Irvine taking Ferrari's charge to the wire. Williams faltered and Jordan stepped up, with Frentzen joining Hill to become real contenders, while Villeneuve's promising new BAR team failed to deliver.

Irvine won his first race as Häkkinen retired and Schumacher finished last in Australia. Häkkinen won round two ahead of Schumacher, but handed the German victory in San Marino when he crashed into the barriers. Schumacher won Monaco again then Häkkinen took victories in Spain and Canada, then was beaten by Frentzen's Jordan in France.

Schumacher's title challenge hit the skids in Britain when a leg-breaking crash put him out for six races. Coulthard won after pit mistakes for Häkkinen and Irvine, and when the McLaren pair collided at the start in Austria, Irvine took the win.

He won again in Germany, then handed victory to Ferrari sub Mika Salo, but the next two races saw McLaren 1-2s, with Häkkinen ahead in Hungary and Coulthard in Belgium, a race which saw Villenuve finally post his first finish of a disastrous season.

Frentzen won for Jordan in Italy, then Herbert took Stewart's first victory in a wet European Grand Prix. Schumacher returned for the new Malaysia race and fended off Häkkinen as Irvine led a Ferrari 1-2, but the Ulsterman failed at the final hurdle in Japan. Häkkinen took the title with a win as Irvine managed only third. Nevertheless, Ferrari were the constructors' champions as Formula One headed toward a new era.

ABOVE: *1999 Malaysian Grand Prix: Eddie Irvine (Ferrari F399) closely followed by Mika Hakkinen (McLaren MP4/14 Mercedes). They finished in first and third positions respectively.*

Michael Schumacher

Schumacher was an uncompromising driver with a natural talent and a stand-out ability to mould a team around him. His career was constantly dogged by controversy, but there was never any doubting his resilience, as he steamed through a record-breaking career with Benetton and Ferrari.

The best driver, by results, ever seen in Formula One, Schumacher started 248 races over 16 years and tops out every vital statistic. He won 91 times, 40 more than Alain Prost's previous record, and started on pole 68 times, beating Ayrton Senna by three. He took 154 podium finishes, 48 more than Prost, and almost doubled Prost's previous top points total with a tally of 1,369.

EARLY YEARS

Born in Hürth-Hermülheim, Germany, in 1969, Schumacher was the eldest son of a bricklayer and began driving karts at

ABOVE: *Michael Schumacher celebrates first position and his maiden Grand Prix win on the podium at the 1992 Belgian Grand Prix.*

BELOW: *Michael Schumacher (Ferrari F300) on his way to victory in the 1998 Canadian Grand Prix.*

ABOVE: *Michael Schumacher (Benetton B194 Ford) crashes at a chicane during a practice session for the 1994 Australian Grand Prix.*

NEXT SPREAD: *Michael Schumacher (Benetton B195 Renault) takes the checkered flag to win the 1995 French Grand Prix at Magny-Cours.*

a local circuit at the age of six, obtaining a racing licence aged 12. To pay for his son's karting, Schumacher's father, Rolf, repaired karts at the track and his mother Elisabeth manned the canteen.

In 1988, Schumacher began to race cars, competing in German Formula Ford and Formula König. He was signed by his future manager Willi Weber to race German Formula Three in 1989, winning the title the following year before joining Heinz-Harald Frentzen and Karl Wendlinger in the Mercedes 'wunderkind' world sports cars team.

MAKING A MARK

Schumacher arrived in Formula One in the middle of the 1991 season, when Eddie Jordan brought him in for Belgium after regular driver Betrand Gachot had been jailed for an altercation with a London taxi driver. Schumacher qualified seventh but retired with clutch failure on lap one and promptly moved to the more competitive Benetton team.

There, in a car designed by Ross Brawn and Rory Byrne, he took his first points in his second race and, in the following season, won his first race, in Belgium, a year after his debut. He finished third that season and fourth in 1993, before a tragic 2004 saw him graduate to the top of Formula One.

Schumacher had already won twice before Ayrton Senna crashed at Imola and, oblivious to the consequences, he raced on to notch up his third win before being told the Brazilian had lost his life. Schumacher won his first title that year, despite two disqualifications and a two-race ban, and took a second in 1995, with a further nine wins.

END OF AN ERA

Schumacher brought his Benetton era to a close with a move to Ferrari in 1996, convinced by boss Jean Todt that, with the design team of Brawn and Byrne, who came with him, they could put the struggling Italian giants back where they belonged.

The first win came quickly, in Spain that year, but Williams were dominant and Damon Hill won the title. In 1997, Jacques Villeneuve won for Williams after Schumacher failed in a blatant effort to knock off his rival and the German's results were wiped from the record books.

Schumacher was left waiting again in 1998, when McLaren rose to prominence, and a leg-breaking crash forced him out of six races in 1999, handing the title to Häkkinen despite a valiant effort from Ferrari team-mate Eddie Irvine to take it to Ferrari.

Finally, in 2000, Schumacher took his third title with nine race wins and began an incredible era of supremacy. The following four years brought four championships with 39 wins from 68 races as Ferrari put all their efforts into Schumacher's campaign and, controversially at times, asked his team-mate Rubens Barrichello to step aside.

In 2002 Schumacher scored 11 victories in one season, two more than the previous record, and won by the largest margin after finishing every race on the podium. In 2004, he bettered that with a record 148 points in a season and 13 race wins from a possible 18.

Ferrari faded in 2005, with Michelin winning the tire war against Bridgestone, as Alonso broke Schumacher's title-winning run. The next year, after winning in Italy, Schumacher announced his retirement and ended his career with fourth in Brazil.

Damon Hill

A determined and hard-working driver, Hill's level-headed approach to racing saw him become the first second-generation World Champion, following in the footsteps of his father Graham. His mild-mannered nature appealed to everyone in the paddock while his grit and integrity proved an admirable combination on the track.

Hill was a late starter and spent just eight seasons in Formula One, bringing speed and commitment to the racetrack. In 115 starts he took 20 pole positions, finished on the podium 42 times, and achieved 22 wins, making him the fourth most victorious British driver in history.

ABOVE: *Damon Hill celebrates on the podium after winning the 1996 Japanese Grand Prix.*

ABOVE: *Damon Hill (Jordan 198 Mugen Honda) leads Michael Schumacher (Ferrari F300) through the chicane on his way to victory in the 1998 Belgian Grand Prix.*

EARLY YEARS

Born in Hampstead, London, in 1960, Hill was just 15 years old when his two-time World Champion father died in a plane crash. Initially against a career in cars, Hill began racing bikes, funded by a job as a motorcycle courier, then got a taste for four wheels when he first drove a Formula Ford car in 1983.

Wearing the same London Rowing Club helmet design as his father, he had limited success in Formula Ford before moving up to Formula Three in 1986, finishing third after two seasons. Lack of funding prevented an immediate move into F3000, but he eventually secured a place in a backmarker team in 1989 and did enough to join a front-running outfit in 1990, when he led five races but never won.

MAKING A MARK

Williams took note and signed Hill up as test driver in 1991, a role that saw him play an integral behind-the-scenes part of the team's return to championship success. Hill was given the chance to mix his test driving with a race seat at Brabham and in 1992 he did well to qualify the uncompetitive car, with his debut coming on

ABOVE: *Damon Hill (Williams FW18 Renault) on his way to victory in the 1996 Canadian Grand Prix.*

home ground when 'Mansell Mania' saw the track stormed by thousands of fans.

When Mansell left for IndyCars in 1993, Hill stepped up to race with Alain Prost and, after overcoming early season errors, he notched up his first success with a hat-trick of victories. Prost left and Senna arrived for 1994, but with just two races gone the Brazilian died in a crash at Imola and Hill had to take control as the team regrouped.

He lost out to Michael Schumacher in a tight title battle tarnished by the Benetton driver's misdemeanours in Britain, where he ignored black flags; Belgium, where his car was declared illegal; and Australia, when a collision between the pair in the final race handed Schumacher his first title.

Hill was beaten by Schumacher again the following year, despite four wins and five other podium finishes, but he took the title in 1996 after winning eight of the 16 races in a year of Williams domination that saw him pushed all the way by team-mate Jacques Villeneuve.

END OF AN ERA

The victory was not enough for Williams, and an out of favor Hill was replaced by Heinz-Harald Frentzen in 1997. Left without a front-line drive, Hill joined Arrows, but failed to start his first race and retired from the next five. His only moment of glory came when he ran within a whisker of victory in Hungary, only for the car to fail him on the closing laps and drop him to second.

He was lured to Jordan for 1998 after their strong performances the previous year, but the first half of the season was a disaster. The team turned things around midway through, however, and after winning his first point of the year in Germany he led his team-mate Ralf Schumacher to a 1-2 in Belgium, taking Jordan's first-ever victory.

His resurgence was brief, however, and when new team-mate Frentzen outpaced him in 1999, he fast-tracked his retirement plans and quit the sport after failing to finish in the British Grand Prix. He walked away from the sport, but returned to become president of the British Racing Drivers' Club, as well as making occasional media appearances.

Mika Häkkinen

A naturally fast Finn with a shy and reserved paddock personality, Häkkinen had achieved little of his potential until a life-threatening crash kick-started his career. He displayed incredible determination and bravery to come back from the brink and his loyalty to McLaren saw him fulfil the potential he had always promised.

In a brief period between two eras of Michael Schumacher success, Häkkinen seized the moment to take two titles, scoring 13 of his 20 victories between 1998 and 1999. During his 11-year career he made 161 starts and finished on the podium in almost a third of his races, achieving his 420 points with just two teams.

ABOVE: *Mika Häkkinen celebrates winning the 1998 Australian Grand Prix.*

ABOVE: *Mika Häkkinen crosses the line ahead of team-mate David Coulthard (both McLaren MP4/12 Mercedes) to win the 1997 European Grand Prix.*

EARLY YEARS

Born in Finland in 1968, Häkkinen, the son of a harbormaster, showed early potential and gained guidance from former World Champion Keke Rosberg, who would eventually be his manager. After a spell in karts he began an impressive career in the junior formulae with victory in the 1987 Finnish, Swedish, and Nordic Formula Ford 1600 championships.

He followed that with victory in the Opel Lotus Euroseries in 1998 and, after an off year with an inexperienced team in British Formula Three, he won the title in 1990 with 12 race wins. He was set to win the prestigious Macau Formula Three race that year, but a last-lap crash handed victory to future Formula One rival Michael Schumacher.

MAKING A MARK

Lotus handed Häkkinen his Formula One break in 1991 and though he repaid them with a points finish in only his third race, the season was a disappointment with the car failing to make the most of its driver's potential. Improvements came the following year, but only enough to turn Häkkinen into a regular points scorer and he knew he had to make a move to further his career and chase his first victory.

He joined McLaren in 1993, arriving as a reserve in case Ayrton Senna decided not to race the full season. Häkkinen sat on the sidelines for most of the year, but was given his chance when Michael Andretti was dropped for the final three races. He needed just two to secure his first-ever podium finish.

Häkkinen took six more podiums in 1994 but, at the end of a tough 1995, he almost lost his life when a practice crash in Australia left him in a coma. He was back for the start of 1996 but, despite several further podium finishes, his maiden victory did not come until the final race of the year, at the European Grand Prix in Jerez.

The 1998 season brought sweeping rule changes and, with top designer Adrian Newey onboard, McLaren moved to the front. Eight victories that season secured Häkkinen his first title and, when Michael Schumacher was injured and Eddie Irvine struggled to lead the Ferrari challenge, Häkkinen sealed a second crown the following year.

END OF AN ERA

Hakkinen was keen to make it a hat-trick of titles in 2000, but Schumacher was now back to full fitness and, though the McLaren driver made it a close fight with four wins and seven second places, his Ferrari rival proved too tough to beat, with 19 points separating the pair at the end of the year.

Häkkinen suffered another big crash in Australia at the start of the following season and it seemed to affect his motivation as his team-mate David Coulthard stepped up to take the fight to Ferrari. Häkkinen lost a certain win in Spain when his car failed just a few corners from the finish and a podium in Canada. Wins in Britain and the United States were his only highlights.

He announced he would be taking a sabbatical at the end of the season but never came back. He made a successful return to the track in 2005, racing in the DTM for Mercedes alongside several of his old Formula One rivals but, after taking three wins during his three seasons in the series, he retired again and moved into driver management.

ABOVE: *Mika Häkkinen in action during his winning race at the 1998 Monaco Grand Prix.*

ABOVE: *David Coulthard leads Mika Häkkinen (both McLaren MP4/15 Mercedes) at the 2000 British Grand Prix. They finished in first and second positions respectively*

2001

Schumacher was dominant in his title defence during a year in which traction control returned and Fernando Alonso and Kimi Räikkönen made significant debuts.

At the Australian Grand Prix Schumacher won from pole then led a dominant Ferrari 1-2 in the wet in Malaysia before Coulthard won in Brazil.

Williams returned to the top step with Ralf Schumacher in San Marino, but Michael won for Ferrari in Spain. Coulthard won in Austria, but Schumacher was controversially handed second when Barrichello was given team orders.

Schumacher won in Monaco, where retirements gave Jaguar their first podium, then Ralf led the first Schumacher 1-2 in Canada. In the European Grand Prix, Michael led home Montoya then scored a second Schumacher 1-2 in France.

Häkkinen and McLaren returned to form in Britain and Ralf Schumacher won in Germany but, when Michael won the next race in Hungary, the title was his. He won again in Belgium and the season wrapped up with Montoya finally taking

his maiden win in Italy, Häkkinen winning his last race in the United States, and Schumacher winning from pole in Japan to finish the season with almost twice the points of closest rival Coulthard.

2002

Ferrari created an exclusive leading-team partnership with Bridgestone Tires and they were in a class of their own, both on pace and reliability. Schumacher finished every race, winning 11, with podiums in the rest. However, team orders caused controversy, first in Austria where Barrichello was forced to move over for Schumacher. He did so in the most obvious way and to Ferrari's shame; the pair were booed by the crowd on the podium.

Ferrari shamed themselves again in the United States, when Schumacher slowed to cross the line alongside Barrichello and the Brazilian accidentally overtook him to win, but they finished the season in style with their ninth 1-2 finish in Japan.

2003

New rules including one-lap qualifying and a points structure were introduced to make the sport more entertaining, but all it needed was improved performance from Michelin runners McLaren and Williams to create a title battle that went down to the wire.

Coulthard won for McLaren in Australia, with Ferrari off the podium for the first time since 1999. Malaysia then saw the youngsters shine with Alonso on pole and Räikkönen victorious then Fisichella won for Jordan in Brazil.

Schumacher returned to form in San Marino, Spain, Austria, and Canada, separated by Montoya's Monaco victory. Räikkönen had been second in four out of six races and Montoya continued a run of 50 points from a possible 60 with victory in Germany.

The top three contenders were separated by two points with three races to run, but then Schumacher led a Ferrari resurgence, winning in Italy and the United States, and got the point he needed to take the title in a rain-hit finale in Japan.

2004

The drama of 2003 was replaced by dull domination as Ferrari and Bridgestone made Schumacher awe-inspiringly unstoppable, winning 12 of the first 13 races with Barrichello backing him up again. Williams, meanwhile, had a terrible run as their drivers collided in Europe, were disqualified in Canada, and had Ralf Schumacher out for six races after a crash in the United States.

Räikkönen's win in Belgium for the out-of-form McLaren ended Schumacher's run, but second was enough to seal a record seventh driver's crown. Barrichello then won in Italy and the first China race, with Schumacher in a career-low 12th, but the German returned to win in Japan and Montoya finished the season with a consolation victory in a rainy Brazil.

2005

Ferrari faced a backlash after a dominant 2004 and, in a season with the most races ever, Renault enjoyed a consistent campaign and McLaren-Mercedes produced a fast but fragile car to give Räikkönen and new team-mate Montoya joy and despair in equal measure.

Renault claimed early advantage when Fisichella won with Alonso third in Australia. Alonso took dominant wins in Malaysia and Bahrain before McLaren launched a come-back with victories for Räikkönen in Spain and Monaco.

Schumacher's dismal season was hardly brightened by victory in a farcical United States Grand Prix after all Michelin runners pulled out on safety grounds. Back in Europe, Alonso's consistency continued with victory in France, second in Britain, and another victory in Germany.

Räikkönen clawed 10 points back by winning in Hungary, but while McLaren then dominated with wins for Räikkönen in Turkey, Belgium, and Japan and Montoya in Italy, Alonso was crowned champion when he finished third behind a McLaren 1-2 in Brazil.

ABOVE: *Fernando Alonso (Renault R24) forces an error from Felipe Massa (Sauber Petronas C23) during the 2004 Bahrain Grand Prix.*

2006

Bidding for an eighth title, Schumacher matched Alonso at the head of the field, the pair filling the top two places in eight of 18 races as the old champion took the new one right down to the wire. The season saw the arrival of BMW, Honda, Toro Rosso, and Super Aguri while Jordan became Midland then Spyker.

Renault won the first three races, but Schumacher won in San Marino and Europe before Alonso embarked on a run of four wins in Spain, Monaco—where Schumacher deliberately crashed to block him in qualifying—Britain and Canada. But Ferrari and Schumacher fought back in the United States, then won again in France and Germany.

Button took his maiden win for Honda in Hungary then Massa won his first for Ferrari at the new race in Turkey. Schumacher closed the title gap with wins in Italy, where Alonso retired, and China, but retired in Japan and his long shot at the title went when Alonso won it with second in Brazil as Renault took the constructors' crown.

ABOVE: *Fernando Alonso (Renault R26) leads Michael Schumacher (Ferrari 248) and Giancarlo Fisichella (Renault R26) on his way to victory in the 2006 Brazilian Grand Prix.*

2007

Alonso left Renault to create a turbulent partnership with team protegée Lewis Hamilton at McLaren, and Räikkönen filled Schumacher's big boots at Ferrari. A new knock-out qualifying format was introduced and these three fought the closest title battle in two decades. McLaren lost all constructors' points due to a spy scandal, leaving Ferrari ahead as BMW continued to build a strong campaign, while Renault and Williams dropped off the pace and Honda's promise turned to disaster.

Räikkönen and Alonso started the season well and were dominant until Hamilton took his first victory in a stop-start crash-hit race in Canada. Hamilton won again in the United States before Räikkönen's season came back to life with wins in France and Britain. The leading teams shared the honors in the middle part of the season, before Hamilton won in torrential rain in Japan. He then threw his advantage away as he crashed in the pit-lane in China to hand Räikkönen the win. The Ferrari driver had been 17 points behind before that race, but he went on to win in Brazil and take the title by a point as Hamilton struggled to seventh.

2008

McLaren and Ferrari renewed their rivalry as Hamilton and Massa raced to another nail-bitingly tight title decider as Alonso returned to Renault in a season that welcomed a new street circuit in Valencia and a night race in Singapore.

Hamilton won in Australia before Ferrari struck a run of form, with Räikkönen winning in Malaysia and Spain and Massa winning in Bahrain and Turkey. Hamilton came back and won a wet Monaco race before Kubica took BMW's first win with in Canada.

Hamilton was penalised and left out of the points as Massa led a Ferrari 1-2 in France, but the Briton dominated his home race and followed up with a win in Germany.

Kovalainen won in Hungary, but Massa dominated in Valencia and won again in the Belgian rain after Hamilton was disqualified for an illegal move in a battle with Räikkönen.

Italy saw a shock victory for Toro Rosso and Sebastian Vettel then Alonso won the night race in Singapore and the Japan Grand Prix where Massa and Hamilton collided.

Hamilton won from pole in China with Massa second, leaving them seven points apart with one to run. Massa won a thrilling race in Brazil and thought he had the title when Hamilton was sixth on the last lap, but the Briton made a last-gasp pass and stole the title by a point.

RIGHT: *Sebastian Vettel (Toro Rosso STR03 Ferrari) on his way to victory in the 2008 Italian Grand Prix.*

Fernando Alonso

Groomed for success from an early age, Alonso is a man out of the Schumacher mould, determined to work the team around him to give him greater chance of success. Composed and consistent performances have been the hallmark for his seasons of success while occasional sulky outbursts have also played an important part in his less successful years.

Alonso was the driver who brought the Schumacher era to a close, and by the end of 2008 he had achieved 21 victories and 52 podiums in seven seasons of racing. He became the youngest-ever race winner in 2003, then the youngest champion in 2005, but saw both records surpassed when Lewis Hamilton and Sebastian Vettel joined the scene.

EARLY YEARS
Born Fernando Alonso Diaz in Oviedo, Spain, in 1981, Alonso was put in a kart by his motorsport-mad father at around three years of age. He had to wait a few years before hitting the race tracks but, when he did he was spectacular, winning almost everything he entered.

He was given his first single-seater drive by former Minardi driver Adrian Campos in the 1999 Spanish Euro Open MoviStar by Nissan, winning his second race and taking the title. He stepped straight into Formula 3000 and, with one win and fourth in the championship, he was soon fast-tracked into Formula One.

MAKING A MARK
Alonso, now managed by Renault boss Flavio Briatore, was handed a drive with Minardi in 2001. He was never expected to score points—the car was too unreliable and too slow—but he regularly outpaced his team-mates and was rewarded with a Renault test drive the following year, with the promise of a race drive in the future.

Briatore's careful schooling of his young prodigy paid dividends and when Alonso stepped up to the race seat in 2003, he took pole position in only his second race with the team, in Malaysia, and won his first race in Hungary later in the year, though he ended his season with a heavy crash in the wet in Brazil.

ABOVE: *Fernando Alonso celebrates on the podium after winning the 2008 Singapore Grand Prix.*

The following year was another builder, with Ferrari dominating from start to finish and Alonso's podium finishes in four races securing fourth place in the championship. Ferrari tire supplier Bridgestone failed to match the Michelin rubber of McLaren and Renault in 2005 and the sport took a dramatic turn as Ferrari faltered. A season-long battle between McLaren and Renault saw Alonso take the title, thanks to superior reliability.

Alonso had a good start to the 2006 season, taking six wins and three second places in the first nine races to build up a comfortable cushion at the top of the table. The second half of the season saw his Renault team take their foot off the throttle, winning just one more race, but his points tally proved too tough to beat and he eased his way to a second title.

ABOVE: *Fernando Alonso (Renault R23) leads the race on the way to his maiden victory in the 2003 Hungarian Grand Prix.*

ABOVE: *Fernando Alonso (Renault R28) on his way to victory in the 2008 Japanese Grand Prix.*

END OF AN ERA

Alonso ended his relationship with Renault, moving to McLaren for the 2007 season and expecting to enjoy a privileged relationship as the two-time World Champion racing alongside rookie Lewis Hamilton. But team boss Ron Dennis' prodigy had different ideas, and Alonso's season was destined to be a challenging one.

It started well, with Alonso taking his first McLaren win in Malaysia in only his second race. He won two more races, but then fell out with the team after Hamilton broke a gentlemen's agreement in Hungary and he blocked his qualifying run in return. The pair finished level on points, just one point behind title winner Kimi Räikkönen, but the relationship was damaged beyond repair.

Alonso returned home when he rejoined Renault in 2008, but the team was not at the level they were when he left and he struggled through the first half of the season before a step-change in performance saw him win in Singapore and Japan, leaving him fifth in the championship as Hamilton won the title for McLaren.

Lewis Hamilton

Groomed for success by McLaren from the age of 12, Hamilton has been built into the complete package for the modern era, his supreme speed and control in a race car matched by his well-schooled approach to public relations and marketing.

The raw talent that Hamilton undoubtedly possessed as a youth was always matched by a steely determination to succeed that has ensured that on the track he has lived up to expectations every step of the way. After just two seasons in Formula One he had won nine times and achieved 207 points, finishing on the podium in 22 of his 35 races, and in 2008 he was crowned the youngest-ever champion.

ABOVE: *Lewis Hamilton celebrates after winning the championship on November 2, 2008, at Interlagos in Brazil.*

EARLY YEARS

Born Lewis Carl Davidson Hamilton in Stevenage in 1985, he was named after the American sprinter Carl Lewis and soon showed his own speed on the racetrack, first with remote controlled cars and then in karts. His father, Anthony, who worked in his own IT business, took control of his career from the start and soon put his son's future on track.

Hamilton was also a talented footballer and cricketer, but preferred karts, and after winning the British title aged 10, he met McLaren boss Ron Dennis and famously said he would like to drive for him one day. He was part of the team's driver development program less than three years later and began racing cars in Formula Renault in 2001.

Starting a career-long trend that would see him have one building year before winning the championship, he started in the winter series and won the Formula Renault title in his second full season. His first foray into Formula Three, at the end of 2003, ended in a trip to hospital after a crash, but things would soon run to form.

ABOVE: *Lewis Hamilton (McLaren MP4-23 Mercedes) on his way to victory at the 2008 British Grand Prix.*

ABOVE: *Hamilton takes the checkered flag to claim his maiden victory at the 2007 Canadian Grand Prix.*

After a brief split with McLaren, he returned to the fold and they placed him in Formula Three Euroseries for 2004, where he finished fifth, then dominated his second season to take the title. He moved up to GP2 in 2005 and this time needed only one chance. He beat Nelson Piquet and Timo Glock to the title and McLaren decided he was ready for Formula One.

MAKING A MARK

Hamilton made his debut alongside reigning World Champion Fernando Alonso and finished on the podium in his first race in Australia. He followed it up with four consecutive second places before scoring his maiden pole and victory in Canada in only his sixth-ever race, with his second win coming one race later in the United States.

Alonso was under pressure and building team tension came to a head in Hungary, when Hamilton broke a gentleman's agreement and Alonso blocked his qualifying run in response. Relations between the pair broke down completely, but Hamilton

won the race and took the upper hand with victory in Japan three races from the finish.

Hamilton made a mistake in China when he slid on a wet track while entering the pit-lane. Although he ended his race in the gravel he was still four and seven points ahead of closest rivals Alonso and Kimi Räikkönen, but a rash start and a mysterious gearbox problem in the final race in Brazil allowed Räikkönen to win the title by a point.

In typical career style, Hamilton would achieve his championship goal at the second attempt when, with Alonso gone, he ruled the McLaren roost. In a tight battle with Ferrari's Felipe Massa he took five wins, with victory in the penultimate race of the season leaving him needing just fifth place to take the title.

It seemed a simple task, but a rain-affected final race in Brazil saw him sixth on the last lap and the title was slipping away again. Ferrari celebrated as Massa crossed the line in first place, but when Glock, ahead in the Toyota, slowed as the rain increased and he lost grip in wet conditions, Hamilton passed to take the place and win the title by a single point.

Individual Race Winners

1950
Great Britain, Giuseppe Farina, Alfa Romeo
Monaco, *Juan Manuel Fangio*, Alfa Romeo
Indianapolis 500, *Johnnie Parsons*, Kurtis Kraft-Offenhauser
Switzerland, *Giuseppe Farina*, Alfa Romeo
Belgium, *Juan Manuel Fangio*, Alfa Romeo
France, *Juan Manuel Fangio*, Alfa Romeo
Italy, *Giuseppe Farina*, Alfa Romeo

1951
Switzerland, Juan Manuel Fangio, Alfa Romeo
Indianapolis 500, Lee Wallard, Kurtis Kraft-Offenhauser
Belgium, Giuseppe Farina, Alfa Romeo
France, Juan Manuel Fangio, Alfa Romeo
Great Britain, José Frolián Gonzáles, Ferrari
Germany, Alberto Ascari, Ferrari
Italy, Alberto Ascari, Ferrari
Spain, Juan Manuel Fangio, Alfa Romeo

1952
Switzerland, Piero Taruffi, Ferrari
Indianapolis 500, Troy Ruttman, Kuzma-Offenhauser
Belgium, Alberto Ascari, Ferrari
France, Alberto Ascari, Ferrari
Great Britain, Alberto Ascari, Ferrari
Germany, Alberto Ascari, Ferrari
Netherlands, Alberto Ascari, Ferrari
Italy, Alberto Ascari, Ferrari

1953
Argentina, Alberto Ascari, Ferrari
Indianapolis 500, Bill Vukovich, Kurtis Kraft-Offenhauser
Netherlands, Alberto Ascari, Ferrari
Belgium, Alberto Ascari, Ferrari
France, Mike Hawthorn, Ferrari
Great Britain, Alberto Ascari, Ferrari
Germany, Giuseppe Farina, Ferrari
Switzerland, Alberto Ascari, Ferrari
Italy, Juan Manuel Fangio, Maserati

1954
Argentina, Juan Manuel Fangio, Maserati
Indianapolis 500, Bill Vukovich, Kurtis Kraft-Offenhauser
Belgium, Juan Manuel Fangio, Maserati
France, Juan Manuel Fangio, Mercedes
Great Britain, José Frolián Gonzáles, Ferrari
Germany, Juan Manuel Fangio, Mercedes
Switzerland, Juan Manuel Fangio, Mercedes
Italy, Juan Manuel Fangio, Mercedes
Spain, Mike Hawthorn, Ferrari

1955
Argentina, Juan Manuel Fangio, Mercedes
Monaco, Maurice Trintignant, Ferrari
Indianapolis 500, Bob Sweikert, Kurtis Kraft-Offenhauser
Belgium, Juan Manuel Fangio, Mercedes

Netherlands, Juan Manuel Fangio, Mercedes
Great Britain, Stirling Moss, Mercedes
Italy, Juan Manuel Fangio, Mercedes

1956
Argentina, Luigi Musso, Ferrari
Monaco, Stirling Moss, Maserati
Indianapolis 500, Pat Flaherty, Watson-Offenhauser
Belgium, Peter Collins, Ferrari
France, Peter Collins, Ferrari
Great Britain, Juan Manuel Fangio, Ferrari
Germany, Juan Manuel Fangio, Ferrari
Italy, Stirling Moss, Maserati

1957
Argentina, Juan Manuel Fangio, Maserati
Monaco, Juan Manuel Fangio, Maserati
Indianapolis 500, Sam Hanks, Epperly-Offenhauser
France, Juan Manuel Fangio, Maserati
Great Britain, Stirling Moss, Vanwall
Germany, Juan Manuel Fangio, Maserati
Pescara, Stirling Moss, Vanwall
Italy, Stirling Moss, Vanwall

1958
Argentina, Stirling Moss, Cooper-Climax
Monaco, Maurice Trintignant, Cooper-Climax
Netherlands, Stirling Moss, Vanwall
Indianapolis 500, Jimmy Bryan, Epperly-Offenhauser
Belgium, Tony Brooks, Vanwall
France, Mike Hawthorn, Ferrari
Great Britain, Peter Collins, Ferrari
Germany, Tony Brooks, Vanwall
Portugal, Stirling Moss, Vanwall
Italy, Tony Brooks, Vanwall
Morocco, Stirling Moss, Vanwall

1959
Monaco, Jack Brabham, Cooper-Climax
Indianapolis 500, Rodger Ward, Watson-Offenhauser
Netherlands, Jo Bonnier, BRM
France, Tony Brooks, Ferrari
Great Britain, Jack Brabham, Cooper-Climax
Germany, Tony Brooks, Ferrari
Portugal, Stirling Moss, Cooper-Climax
Italy, Stirling Moss, Cooper-Climax
United States, Bruce McLaren, Cooper-Climax

1960
Argentina, Bruce McLaren, Cooper-Climax
Monaco, Stirling Moss, Lotus-Climax
Indianapolis 500, Jim Rathman, Watson-Offenhauser
Netherlands, Jack Brabham, Cooper-Climax
Belgium, Jack Brabham, Cooper-Climax
France, Jack Brabham, Cooper-Climax

Great Britain, Jack Brabham, Cooper-Climax
Portugal, Jack Brabham, Cooper-Climax
Italy, Phil Hill, Ferrari
United States, Stirling Moss, Lotus-Climax

1961
Monaco, Stirling Moss, Lotus-Climax
Netherlands, Wolfgang von Trips, Ferrari
Belgium, Phil Hill, Ferrari
France, Giancarlo Baghetti, Ferrari
Great Britain, Wolfgang von Trips, Ferrari
Germany, Stirling Moss, Lotus-Climax
Italy, Phil Hill, Ferrari
United States, Innes Ireland, Lotus-Climax

1962
Netherlands, Graham Hill, BRM
Monaco, Bruce McLaren, Cooper-Climax
Belgium, Jim Clark, Lotus-Climax
France, Dan Gurney, Porsche
Great Britain, Jim Clark, Lotus-Climax
Germany, Graham Hill, BRM
Italy, Graham Hill, BRM
United States, Jim Clark, Lotus-Climax
South Africa, Graham Hill, BRM

1963
Monaco, Graham Hill, BRM
Belgium, Jim Clark, Lotus-Climax
Netherlands, Jim Clark, Lotus-Climax
France, Jim Clark, Lotus-Climax
Great Britain, Jim Clark, Lotus-Climax
Germany, John Surtees, Ferrari
Italy, Jim Clark, Lotus-Climax
United States, Graham Hill, BRM
Mexico, Jim Clark, Lotus-Climax
South Africa, Jim Clark, Lotus-Climax

1964
Monaco, Graham Hill, BRM
Netherlands, Jim Clark, Lotus-Climax
Belgium, Jim Clark, Lotus-Climax
France, Dan Gurney, Brabham-Climax
Great Britain, Jim Clark, Lotus-Climax
Germany, John Surtees, Ferrari
Austria, Lorenzo Bandini, Ferrari
Italy, John Surtees, Ferrari
United States, Graham Hill, BRM
Mexico, Dan Gurney, Brabham-Climax

1965
South Africa, Jim Clark, Lotus-Climax
Monaco, Graham Hill, BRM
Belgium, Jim Clark, Lotus-Climax
France, Jim Clark, Lotus-Climax
Great Britain, Jim Clark, Lotus-Climax
Netherlands, Jim Clark, Lotus-Climax
Germany, Jim Clark, Lotus-Climax
Italy, Jackie Stewart, BRM
United States, Graham Hill, BRM
Mexico, Richie Ginther, Honda

1966
Monaco, Jackie Stewart, BRM
Belgium, John Surtees, Ferrari

France, Jack Brabham, Brabham-Repco
Great Britain, Jack Brabham, Brabham-Repco
Netherlands, Jack Brabham, Brabham-Repco
Germany, Jack Brabham, Brabham-Repco
Italy, Ludovico Scarflotti, Ferrari
United States, Jim Clark, Lotus-BRM
Mexico, John Surtees, Cooper-Maserati

1967
South Africa, Pedro Rodriguez, Cooper-Maserati
Monaco, Denny Hulme, Brabham-Repco
Netherlands, Jim Clark, Lotus-Ford
Belgium, Dan Gurney, Eagle-Weslake
France, Jack Brabham, Brabham-Repco
Great Britain, Jim Clark, Lotus-Ford
Germany, Denny Hulme, Brabham-Repco
Canada, Jack Brabham, Brabham-Repco
Italy, John Surtees, Honda
United States, Jim Clark, Lotus-Ford
Mexico, Jim Clark, Lotus-Ford

1968
South Africa, Jim Clark, Lotus-Ford
Spain, Graham Hill, Lotus-Ford
Monaco, Graham Hill, Lotus-Ford
Belgium, Bruce McLaren, McLaren-Ford
Netherlands, Jackie Stewart, Matra-Ford
France, Jacky Ickx, Ferrari
Great Britain, Jo Siffert, Lotus-Ford
Germany, Jackie Stewart, Matra-Ford
Italy, Denny Hulme, McLaren-Ford
Canada, Denny Hulme, McLaren-Ford
United States, Jackie Stewart, Matra-Ford
Mexico, Graham Hill, Lotus-Ford

1969
South Africa, Jackie Stewart, Matra-Ford
Spain, Jackie Stewart, Matra-Ford
Monaco, Graham Hill, Lotus-Ford
Netherlands, Jackie Stewart, Matra-Ford
France, Jackie Stewart, Matra-Ford
Great Britain, Jackie Stewart, Matra-Ford
Germany, Jacky Ickx, Brabham-Ford
Italy, Jackie Stewart, Matra-Ford
Canada, Jacky Ickx, Brabham-Ford
United States, Jochen Rindt, Lotus-Ford
Mexico, Denny Hulme, McLaren-Ford

1970
South Africa, Jack Brabham, Brabham-Ford
Spain, Jackie Stewart, March-Ford
Monaco, Jochen Rindt, Lotus-Ford
Belgium, Pedro Rodriguez, BRM
Netherlands, Jochen Rindt, Lotus-Ford
France, Jochen Rindt, Lotus-Ford
Great Britain, Jochen Rindt, Lotus-Ford
Germany, Jochen Rindt, Lotus-Ford
Austria, Jacky Ickx, Ferrari
Italy, Clay Regazzoni, Ferrari
Canada, Jacky Ickx, Ferrari
United States, Emerson Fittipaldi, Lotus-Ford
Mexico, Jacky Ickx, Ferrari

1971
South Africa, Mario Andretti, Ferrari
Spain, Jackie Stewart, Tyrrell-Ford
Monaco, Jackie Stewart, Tyrrell-Ford
Netherlands, Jacky Ickx, Ferrari
France, Jackie Stewart, Tyrrell-Ford
Great Britain, Jackie Stewart, Tyrrell-Ford
Germany, Jackie Stewart, Tyrrell-Ford
Austria, Jo Siffert, BRM
Italy, Peter Gethin, BRM
Canada, Jackie Stewart, Tyrrell-Ford
United States, Francois Cevert, Tyrrell-Ford

1972
Argentina, Jackie Stewart, Tyrrell-Ford
South Africa, Denny Hulme, McLaren-Ford
Spain, Emerson Fittipaldi, Lotus-Ford
Monaco, Jean Pierre Beltoise, BRM
Belgium, Emerson Fittipaldi, Lotus-Ford
France, Jackie Stewart, Tyrrell-Ford
Great Britain, Emerson Fittipaldi, Lotus-Ford
Germany, Jacky Ickx, Ferrari
Austria, Emerson Fittipaldi, Lotus-Ford
Italy, Emerson Fittipaldi, Lotus-Ford
Canada, Jackie Stewart, Tyrrell-Ford
United States, Jackie Stewart, Tyrrell-Ford

1973
Argentina, Emerson Fittipaldi, Lotus-Ford
Brazil, Emerson Fittipaldi, Lotus-Ford
South Africa, Jackie Stewart, Tyrrell-Ford
Spain, Emerson Fittipaldi, Lotus-Ford
Belgium, Jackie Stewart, Tyrrell-Ford
Monaco, Jackie Stewart, Tyrrell-Ford
Sweden, Denny Hulme, McLaren-Ford
France, Ronnie Peterson, Lotus-Ford
Great Britain, Peter Revson, McLaren-Ford
Netherlands, Jackie Stewart, Tyrrell-Ford
Germany, Jackie Stewart, Tyrrell-Ford
Austria, Ronnie Peterson, Lotus-Ford
Italy, Ronnie Peterson, Lotus-Ford
Canada, Peter Revson, McLaren-Ford
United States, Ronnie Peterson, Lotus-Ford

1974
Argentina, Denny Hulme, McLaren-Ford
Brazil, Emerson Fittipaldi, McLaren-Ford
South Africa, Carlos Reutemann, Brabham-Ford
Spain, Niki Lauda, Ferrari
Belgium, Emerson Fittipaldi, McLaren-Ford
Monaco, Ronnie Peterson, Lotus-Ford
Sweden, Jody Scheckter, Tyrrell-Ford
Netherlands, Niki Lauda, Ferrari
Switzerland, Ronnie Peterson, Lotus-Ford
Great Britain, Jody Scheckter, Tyrrell-Ford
Germany, Clay Regazzoni, Ferrari
Austria, Carlos Reutemann, Brabham-Ford
Italy, Ronnie Peterson, Lotus-Ford
Canada, Emerson Fittipaldi, McLaren-Ford
United States, Carlos Reutemann, Brabham-Ford

1975
Argentina, Emerson Fittipaldi, McLaren-Ford
Brazil, Carlos Pace, Brabham-Ford
South Africa, Jody Scheckter, Tyrrell-Ford
Spain, Jochen Mass, McLaren-Ford

Monaco, Niki Lauda, Ferrari
Belgium, Niki Lauda, Ferrari
Sweden, Niki Lauda, Ferrari
Netherlands, James Hunt, Hesketh-Ford
France, Niki Lauda, Ferrari
Great Britain, Emerson Fittipaldi, McLaren-Ford
Germany, Carlos Reutemann, Brabham-Ford
Austria, Vittorio Brambilla, March-Ford
Italy, Clay Regazzoni, Ferrari
United States, Niki Lauda, Ferrari

1976
Brazil, Niki Lauda, Ferrari
South Africa, Niki Lauda, Ferrari
USA West, Clay Regazzoni, Ferrari
Spain, James Hunt, McLaren-Ford
Belgium. Niki Lauda, Ferrari
Monaco, Niki Lauda, Ferrari
Sweden, Jody Scheckter, Tyrrell-Ford
France, James Hunt, McLaren-Ford
Great Britain, Niki Lauda, Ferrari
Germany, James Hunt, McLaren-Ford
Austria, John Watson, Penske-Ford
Netherlands, James Hunt, McLaren-Ford
Italy, Ronnie Peterson, March-Ford
Canada, James Hunt, McLaren-Ford
USA East, James Hunt, McLaren-Ford
Japan, Mario Andretti, Lotus-Ford

1977
Argentina, Jody Scheckter, Wolf-Ford
Brazil, Carlos Reutemann, Ferrari
South Africa, Niki Lauda, Ferrari
USA West, Mario Andretti, Lotus-Ford
Spain, Mario Andretti, Lotus-Ford
Monaco, Jody Scheckter, Wolf-Ford
Belgium, Gunner Nilsson, Lotus-Ford
Sweden, Jacques Laffite, Ligier-Matra
Switzerland, Mario Andretti, Lotus-Ford
Great Britain, James Hunt, McLaren-Ford
Germany, Niki Lauda, Ferrari
Austria, Alan Jones, Shadow-Ford
Netherlands, Niki Lauda, Ferrari
Italy, Mario Andretti, Lotus-Ford
USA East, James Hunt, McLaren-Ford
Canada, Jody Scheckter, Wolf-Ford
Japan, James Hunt, McLaren-Ford

1978
Argentina, Mario Andretti, Lotus-Ford
Brazil, Carlos Reutemann, Ferrari
South Africa, Ronnie Peterson, Lotus-Ford
USA West, Carlos Reutemann, Ferrari
Monaco, Patrick Depailler, Tyrrell-Ford
Belgium. Mario Andretti, Lotus-Ford
Spain, Mario Andretti, Lotus-Ford
Sweden, Niki Lauder, Brabham-Alfa Romeo
France, Mario Andretti, Lotus-Ford
Great Britain, Carlos Reutemann, Ferrari
Germany, Mario Andretti, Lotus-Ford
Austria, Ronnie Peterson, Lotus-Ford
Netherlands, Mario Andretti, Lotus-Ford
Italy, Niki Lauder, Brabham-Alfa Romeo
USA East, Carlos Reutemann, Ferrari
Canada, Gilles Villeneuve, Ferrari

1979
Argentina, Jacques Laffite, Ligier-Ford
Brazil, Jacques Laffite, Ligier-Ford
South Africa, Gilles Villeneuve, Ferrari
USA West, Gilles Villeneuve, Ferrari
Spain, Patrick Depailler, Ligier-Ford
Belgium, Jody Scheckter, Ferrari
Monaco, Jody Scheckter, Ferrari
Switzerland, Jean Pierre Jabouille, Renault
Great Britain, Clay Regazzoni, Williams-Ford
Germany, Alan Jones, Williams-Ford
Austria, Alan Jones, Williams-Ford
Netherlands, Alan Jones, Williams-Ford
Italy, Jody Scheckter, Ferrari
Canada, Alan Jones, Williams-Ford
USA East, Gilles Villeneuve, Ferrari

1980
Argentina, Alan Jones, Williams-Ford
Brazil, Rene Arnoux, Renault
South Africa, Rene Arnoux, Renault
USA West, Nelson Piquet, Brabham-Ford
Belgium, Didier Pironi, Ligier-Ford
Monaco, Carlos Reutemann, Williams-Ford
France, Alan Jones, Williams-Ford
Great Britain, Alan Jones, Williams-Ford
Germany, Jacques Laffite, Ligier-Ford
Austria, Jean Pierre Jabouille, Renault
Netherlands, Nelson Piquet, Brabham-Ford
Italy, Nelson Piquet, Brabham-Ford
Canada, Alan Jones, Williams-Ford
USA East, Alan Jones, Williams-Ford

1981
USA West, Alan Jones, Williams-Ford
Brazil, Carlos Reutemann, Williams-Ford
Argentina, Nelson Piquet, Brabham-Ford
San Marino, Nelson Piquet, Brabham-Ford
Belgium, Carlos Reutemann, Williams-Ford
Monaco, Gilles Villeneuve, Ferrari
Spain, Gilles Villeneuve, Ferrari
Switzerland, Alain Prost, Renault
Great Britain, John Watson, McLaren-Ford
Germany, Nelson Piquet, Brabham-Ford
Austria, Jacques Laffite, Ligier-Matra
Netherlands, Alain Prost, Renault
Italy, Alain Prost, Renault
Canada, Jacques Laffite, Ligier-Matra
Las Vegas, Alan Jones, Williams-Ford

1982
South Africa, Alain Prost, Renault
Brazil, Alain Prost, Renault
USA West, Niki Lauda, McLaren-Ford
San Marino, Didier Pironi, Ferrari
Belgium, John Watson, McLaren-Ford
Monaco, Riccardo Patrese, Brabham-Ford
USA East, John Watson, McLaren-Ford
Canada, Nelson Piquet, Brabham-BMW
Netherlands, Didier Pironi, Ferrari
Great Britain, Niki Lauda, McLaren-Ford
France, Rene Arnoux, Renault
Germany, Patrick Tambay, Ferrari
Austria, Elio de Angelis, Lotus-Ford
Switzerland, Keke Rosberg, Williams-Ford
Italy, Rene Arnoux, Renault
Las Vegas, Michele Alboreto, Tyrrell-Ford

1983
Brazil, Nelson Piquet, Brabham-BMW
USA West, John Watson, McLaren-Ford
France, Alain Prost, Renault
San Marino, Patrick Tambay, Ferrari
Monaco, Keke Rosberg, Williams-Ford
Belgium, Alain Prost, Renault
United States, Michele Alboreto, Tyrrell-Ford
Canada, Rene Arnoux, Ferrari
Great Britain, Alain Prost, Renault
Germany, Rene Arnoux, Ferrari
Austria, Alain Prost, Renault
Netherlands, Rene Arnoux, Ferrari
Italy, Nelson Piquet, Brabham-BMW
Europe, Nelson Piquet, Brabham-BMW
South Africa, Riccardo Patrese, Brabham-BMW

1984
Brazil, Alain Prost, McLaren-TG
South Africa, Niki Lauda, McLaren-TAG
Belgium, Michele Alboreto, Ferrari
San Marino, Alain Prost, McLaren-TAG
France, Niki Lauda, McLaren-TAG
Monaco, Alain Prost, McLaren-TAG
Canada, Nelson Piquet, Brabham-BMW
USA East, Nelson Piquet, Brabham-BMW
United States, Keke Rosberg, Williams-Honda
Great Britain, Niki Lauda, McLaren-TAG
Germany, Alain Prost, McLaren-TAG
Austria, Niki Lauda, McLaren-TAG
Netherlands, Alain Prost, McLaren-TAG
Italy, Niki Lauda, McLaren-TAG
Europe, Alain Prost, McLaren-TAG
Portugal, Alain Prost, McLaren-TAG

1985
Brazil, Alain Prost, McLaren-TAG
Portugal, Ayrton Senna, Lotus-Renault
San Marino, Elio de Angelis, Lotus-Ford
Monaco, Alain Prost, McLaren-TAG
Canada, Michele Alboreto, Ferrari
USA East, Keke Rosberg, Williams-Honda
France, Nelson Piquet, Brabham-BMW
Great Britain, Alain Prost, McLaren-TAG
Germany, Michele Alboreto, Ferrari
Austria, Alain Prost, McLaren-TAG
Netherlands, Niki Lauda, McLaren-TAG
Italy, Alain Prost, McLaren-TAG
Belgium, Ayrton Senna, Lotus-Renault
Europe, Nigel Mansell, Williams-Honda
South Africa, Nigel Mansell, Williams-Honda
Australia, Keke Rosberg, Williams-Honda

1986
Brazil, Nelson Piquet, Williams-Honda
Spain, Ayrton Senna, Lotus-Renault
San Marino, Alain Prost, McLaren-TAG
Monaco, Alain Prost, McLaren-TAG
Belgium, Nigel Mansell, Williams-Honda
Canada, Nigel Mansell, Williams-Honda
USA East, Ayrton Senna, Lotus-Renault
France, Nigel Mansell, Williams-Honda
Great Britain, Nigel Mansell, Williams-Honda
Germany, Nelson Piquet, Williams-Honda
Hungary, Nelson Piquet, Williams-Honda
Austria, Alain Prost, McLaren-TAG
Italy, Nelson Piquet, Williams-Honda
Portugal, Nigel Mansell, Williams-Honda
Mexico, Gerhard Berger, Benetton-BMW
Australia, Alain Prost, McLaren-TAG

Individual Race Winners (continued)

1987
Brazil, Alain Prost, McLaren-TAG
San Marino, Nigel Mansell, Williams-Honda
Belgium, Alain Prost, McLaren-TAG
Monaco, Ayrton Senna, Lotus-Honda
United States, Ayrton Senna, Lotus-Honda
France, Nigel Mansell, Williams-Honda
Great Britain, Nigel Mansell, Williams-Honda
Germany, Nelson Piquet, Williams-Honda
Hungary, Nelson Piquet, Williams-Honda
Austria, Nigel Mansell, Williams-Honda
Italy, Nelson Piquet, Williams-Honda
Portugal, Alain Prost, McLaren-TAG
Spain, Nigel Mansell, Williams-Honda
Mexico, Nigel Mansell, Williams-Honda
Japan, Gerhard Berger, Ferrari
Australia, Gerhard Berger, Ferrari

1988
Brazil, Alain Prost, McLaren-Honda
San Marino, Ayrton Senna, McLaren-Honda
Monaco, Alain Prost, McLaren-Honda
Mexico, Alain Prost, McLaren-Honda
Canada, Ayrton Senna, McLaren-Honda
United States, Ayrton Senna, McLaren-Honda
France, Alain Prost, McLaren-Honda
Great Britain, Ayrton Senna, McLaren-Honda
Germany, Ayrton Senna, McLaren-Honda
Hungary, Ayrton Senna, McLaren-Honda
Belgium, Ayrton Senna, McLaren-Honda
Italy, Gerhard Berger, Ferrari
Portugal, Alain Prost, McLaren-Honda
Spain, Alain Prost, McLaren-Honda
Japan, Ayrton Senna, McLaren-Honda
Australia, Alain Prost, McLaren-Honda

1989
Brazil, Nigel Mansell, Ferrari
San Marino, Ayrton Senna, McLaren-Honda
Monaco, Ayrton Senna, McLaren-Honda
Mexico, Ayrton Senna, McLaren-Honda
United States, Alain Prost, McLaren-Honda
Canada, Thierry Boutsen, Williams-Renault
France, Alain Prost, McLaren-Honda
Great Britain, Alain Prost, McLaren-Honda
Germany, Ayrton Senna, McLaren-Honda
Hungary, Nigel Mansell, Ferrari
Belgium, Ayrton Senna, McLaren-Honda
Italy, Alain Prost, McLaren-Honda
Portugal, Gerhard Berger, Ferrari
Spain, Ayrton Senna, McLaren-Honda
Japan, Alessandro Nannini, Benetton-Ford
Australia, Thierry Boutsen, Williams-Renault

1990
United States, Ayrton Senna, McLaren-Honda
Brazil, Alain Prost, Ferrari
San Marino, Riccardo Patrese, Williams-Renault
Monaco, Ayrton Senna, McLaren-Honda
Canada, Ayrton Senna, McLaren-Honda
Mexico, Alain Prost, Ferrari
France, Alain Prost, Ferrari
Great Britain, Alain Prost, Ferrari
Germany, Ayrton Senna, McLaren-Honda
Hungary, Thierry Boutsen, Williams-Renault
Belgium, Ayrton Senna, McLaren-Honda
Italy, Ayrton Senna, McLaren-Honda
Portugal, Nigel Mansell, Ferrari
Spain, Alain Prost, Ferrari
Japan, Nelson Piquet, Benetton-Ford
Australia, Nelson Piquet, Benetton-Ford

1991
United States, Ayrton Senna, McLaren-Honda
Brazil, Ayrton Senna, McLaren-Honda
San Marino, Ayrton Senna, McLaren-Honda
Monaco, Ayrton Senna, McLaren-Honda
Canada, Nelson Piquet, Benetton-Ford
Mexico, Riccardo Patrese, Williams-Renault
France, Nigel Mansell, Williams-Renault
Great Britain, Nigel Mansell, Williams-Renault
Germany, Nigel Mansell, Williams-Renault
Hungary, Ayrton Senna, McLaren-Honda
Belgium, Ayrton Senna, McLaren-Honda
Italy, Nigel Mansell, Williams-Renault
Portugal, Riccardo Patrese, Williams-Renault
Spain, Nigel Mansell, Williams-Renault
Japan, Gerhard Berger, McLaren-Honda
Australia, Ayrton Senna, McLaren-Honda

1992
South Africa, Nigel Mansell, Williams-Renault
Mexico, Nigel Mansell, Williams-Renault
Brazil, Nigel Mansell, Williams-Renault
Spain, Nigel Mansell, Williams-Renault
San Marino, Nigel Mansell, Williams-Renault
Monaco, Ayrton Senna, McLaren-Honda
Canada, Gerhard Berger, McLaren-Honda
France, Nigel Mansell, Williams-Renault
Great Britain, Nigel Mansell, Williams-Renault
Germany, Nigel Mansell, Williams-Renault
Hungary, Ayrton Senna, McLaren-Honda
Belgium, Michael Schumacher, Benetton-Ford
Italy, Ayrton Senna, McLaren-Honda
Portugal, Nigel Mansell, Williams-Renault
Japan, Riccardo Patrese, Williams-Renault
Australia, Gerhard Berger, McLaren-Honda

1993
South Africa, Alain Prost, Williams-Renault
Brazil, Ayrton Senna, McLaren-Ford
Europe, Ayrton Senna, McLaren-Ford
San Marino, Alain Prost, Williams-Renault
Spain, Alain Prost, Williams-Renault
Monaco, Ayrton Senna, McLaren-Ford
Canada, Alain Prost, Williams-Renault
France, Alain Prost, Williams-Renault
Great Britain, Alain Prost, Williams-Renault
Germany, Alain Prost, Williams-Renault
Hungary, Damon Hill, Williams-Renault
Belgium, Damon Hill, Williams-Renault
Italy, Damon Hill, Williams-Renault
Portugal, Michael Schumacher, Benetton-Ford
Japan, Ayrton Senna, McLaren-Ford
Australia, Ayrton Senna, McLaren-Ford

1994
Brazil, Michael Schumacher, Benetton-Ford
Pacific, Michael Schumacher, Benetton-Ford
San Marino, Michael Schumacher, Benetton-Ford
Monaco, Michael Schumacher, Benetton-Ford
Spain, Damon Hill, Williams-Renault
Canada, Michael Schumacher, Benetton-Ford
France, Michael Schumacher, Benetton-Ford
Great Britain, Damon Hill, Williams-Renault
Germany, Gerhard Berger, Ferrari
Hungary, Michael Schumacher, Benetton-Ford
Belgium, Damon Hill, Williams-Renault
Italy, Damon Hill, Williams-Renault
Portugal, Damon Hill, Williams-Renault
Europe, Michael Schumacher, Benetton-Ford
Japan, Damon Hill, Williams-Renault
Australia, Nigel Mansell, Williams-Renault

1995
Brazil, Michael Schumacher, Benetton-Ford
Argentina, Damon Hill, Williams-Renault
San Marino, Damon Hill, Williams-Renault
Spain, Michael Schumacher, Benetton-Ford
Monaco, Michael Schumacher, Benetton-Ford
Canada, Jean Alesi, Ferrari
France, Michael Schumacher, Benetton-Ford
Great Britain, Johnny Herbert, Benetton-Renault
Germany, Michael Schumacher, Benetton-Ford
Hungary, Damon Hill, Williams-Renault
Belgium, Michael Schumacher, Benetton-Ford
Italy, Johnny Herbert, Benetton-Renault
Portugal, David Coulthard, Williams-Renault
Europe, Michael Schumacher, Benetton-Ford
Pacific, Michael Schumacher, Benetton-Ford
Japan, Michael Schumacher, Benetton-Ford
Australia, Damon Hill, Williams-Renault

1996
Australia, Damon Hill, Williams-Renault
Brazil, Damon Hill, Williams-Renault
Argentina, Damon Hill, Williams-Renault
Europe, Jacques Villeneuve, Williams-Renault
San Marino, Damon Hill, Williams-Renault
Monaco, Oliver Panis, Ligier-Mugen-Honda
Spain, Michael Schumacher, Ferrari
Canada, Damon Hill, Williams-Renault
France, Damon Hill, Williams-Renault
Great Britain, Jacques Villeneuve, Williams-Renault
Germany, Damon Hill, Williams-Renault
Hungary, Jacques Villeneuve, Williams-Renault
Belgium, Michael Schumacher, Ferrari
Italy, Michael Schumacher, Ferrari
Portugal, Jacques Villeneuve, Williams-Renault
Japan, Damon Hill, Williams-Renault

1997
Australia, David Coulthard, McLaren-Mercedes
Brazil, Jacques Villeneuve, Williams-Renault
Argentina, Jacques Villeneuve, Williams-Renault
San Marino, Heinz-Harald Frentzen, Williams-Renault
Monaco, Michael Schumacher, Ferrari
Spain, Jacques Villeneuve, Williams-Renault
Canada, Michael Schumacher, Ferrari
France, Michael Schumacher, Ferrari
Great Britain, Jacques Villeneuve, Williams-Renault
Germany, Gerhard Berger, Benetton-Renault
Hungary, Jacques Villeneuve, Williams-Renault
Belgium, Michael Schumacher, Ferrari
Italy, David Coulthard, McLaren-Mercedes
Austria, Jacques Villeneuve, Williams-Renault
Luxembourg, Jacques Villeneuve, Williams-Renault
Japan, Michael Schumacher, Ferrari
Europe, Mika Häkkinen, McLaren-Mercedes

1998

Australia, Mika Häkkinen, McLaren-Mercedes
Brazil, Mika Häkkinen, McLaren-Mercedes
Argentina, Michael Schumacher, Ferrari
San Marino, David Coulthard, McLaren-Mercedes
Spain, Mika Häkkinen, McLaren-Mercedes
Monaco, Mika Häkkinen, McLaren-Mercedes
Canada, Michael Schumacher, Ferrari
France, Michael Schumacher, Ferrari
Great Britain, Michael Schumacher, Ferrari
Austria, Mika Häkkinen, McLaren-Mercedes
Germany, Mika Häkkinen, McLaren-Mercedes
Hungary, Michael Schumacher, Ferrari
Belgium, Damon Hill, Jordan-Mugen-Honda
Italy, Michael Schumacher, Ferrari
Luxembourg, Mika Häkkinen, McLaren-Mercedes
Japan, Mika Häkkinen, McLaren-Mercedes

1999

Australia, Eddie Irvine, Ferrari
Brazil, Mika Häkkinen, McLaren-Mercedes
San Marino, Michael Schumacher, Ferrari
Monaco, Michael Schumacher, Ferrari
Spain, Mika Häkkinen, McLaren-Mercedes
Canada, Mika Häkkinen, McLaren-Mercedes
France, Heinz-Harald Frentzen, Jordan-Mugen-Honda
Great Britain, David Coulthard, McLaren-Mercedes
Austria, Eddie Irvine, Ferrari
Germany, Eddie Irvine, Ferrari
Hungary, Mika Häkkinen, McLaren-Mercedes
Belgium, David Coulthard, McLaren-Mercedes
Italy, Heinz-Harald Frentzen, Jordan-Mugen-Honda
Europe, Johnny Herbert, Stewart-Ford
Malaysia, Eddie Irvine, Ferrari
Japan, Mika Häkkinen, McLaren-Mercedes

2000

Australia, Michael Schumacher, Ferrari
Brazil, Michael Schumacher, Ferrari
San Marino, Michael Schumacher, Ferrari
Great Britain, David Coulthard, McLaren-Mercedes
Spain, Mika Häkkinen, McLaren-Mercedes
Europe, Michael Schumacher, Ferrari
Monaco, David Coulthard, McLaren-Mercedes
Canada, Michael Schumacher, Ferrari
France, David Coulthard, McLaren-Mercedes
Austria, Mika Häkkinen, McLaren-Mercedes
Germany, Rubens Barrichello, Ferrari
Hungary, Mika Häkkinen, McLaren-Mercedes
Belgium, Mika Häkkinen, McLaren-Mercedes
Italy, Michael Schumacher, Ferrari
United States, Michael Schumacher, Ferrari
Japan, Michael Schumacher, Ferrari
Malaysia, Michael Schumacher, Ferrari

2001

Australia, Michael Schumacher, Ferrari
Malaysia, Michael Schumacher, Ferrari
Brazil, David Coulthard, McLaren-Mercedes
San Marino, Ralf Schumacher, Williams-BMW
Spain, Michael Schumacher, Ferrari
Austria, David Coulthard, McLaren-Mercedes
Monaco, Michael Schumacher, Ferrari
Canada, Ralf Schumacher, Williams-BMW
Europe, Michael Schumacher, Ferrari
France, Michael Schumacher, Ferrari
Great Britain, Mika Häkkinen, McLaren-Mercedes
Germany, Ralf Schumacher, Williams-BMW
Hungary, Michael Schumacher, Ferrari
Belgium, Michael Schumacher, Ferrari
Italy, Juan Pablo Montoya, Williams-BMW
United States, Mika Häkkinen, McLaren-Mercedes
Japan, Michael Schumacher, Ferrari

2002

Australia, Michael Schumacher, Ferrari
Malaysia, Ralf Schumacher, Williams-BMW
Brazil, Michael Schumacher, Ferrari
San Marino, Michael Schumacher, Ferrari
Spain, Michael Schumacher, Ferrari
Austria, Michael Schumacher, Ferrari
Monaco, David Coulthard, McLaren-Mercedes
Canada, Michael Schumacher, Ferrari
Europe, Rubens Barrichello, Ferrari
Great Britain, Michael Schumacher, Ferrari
France, Michael Schumacher, Ferrari
Germany, Michael Schumacher, Ferrari
Hungary, Rubens Barrichello, Ferrari
Belgium, Michael Schumacher, Ferrari
Italy, Rubens Barrichello, Ferrari
United States, Rubens Barrichello, Ferrari
Japan, Michael Schumacher, Ferrari

2003

Australia, David Coulthard, McLaren-Mercedes
Malaysia, Kimi Räikkönen, McLaren-Mercedes
Brazil, Giancarlo Fisichella, Jordan-Ford
San Marino, Michael Schumacher, Ferrari
Spain, Michael Schumacher, Ferrari
Austria, Michael Schumacher, Ferrari
Monaco, Juan Pablo Montoya, Williams-BMW
Canada, Michael Schumacher, Ferrari
Europe, Ralf Schumacher, Williams-BMW
France, Ralf Schumacher, Williams-BMW
Great Britain, Rubens Barrichello, Ferrari
Germany, Juan Pablo Montoya, Williams-BMW
Hungary, Fernando Alonso, Renault
Italy, Michael Schumacher, Ferrari
United States, Michael Schumacher, Ferrari
Japan, Rubens Barrichello, Ferrari

2004

Australia, Michael Schumacher, Ferrari
Malaysia, Michael Schumacher, Ferrari
Bahrain, Michael Schumacher, Ferrari
San Marino, Michael Schumacher, Ferrari
Spain, Michael Schumacher, Ferrari
Monaco, Jarno Trulli, Renault
Europe, Michael Schumacher, Ferrari
Canada, Michael Schumacher, Ferrari
United States, Michael Schumacher, Ferrari
France, Michael Schumacher, Ferrari
Great Britain, Michael Schumacher, Ferrari
Germany, Michael Schumacher, Ferrari
Hungary, Michael Schumacher, Ferrari
Belgium, Kimi Räikkönen, McLaren-Mercedes
Italy, Rubens Barrichello, Ferrari
China, Rubens Barrichello, Ferrari
Japan, Michael Schumacher, Ferrari
Brazil, Juan Pablo Montoya, Williams-BMW

2005

Australia, Giancarlo Fisicella, Renault
Malaysia, Fernando Alonso, Renault
Bahrain, Fernando Alonso, Renault
San Marino, Fernando Alonso, Renault
Spain, Kimi Räikkönen, McLaren-Mercedes
Monaco, Kimi Räikkönen, McLaren-Mercedes
Europe, Fernando Alonso, Renault
Canada, Kimi Räikkönen, McLaren-Mercedes
United States, Michael Schumacher, Ferrari
France, Fernando Alonso, Renault
Great Britain, Juan Pablo Montoya, McLaren-Mercedes
Germany, Fernando Alonso, Renault
Hungary, Kimi Räikkönen, McLaren-Mercedes
Turkey, Kimi Räikkönen, McLaren-Mercedes
Italy, Juan Pablo Montoya, McLaren-Mercedes
Belgium, Kimi Räikkönen, McLaren-Mercedes
Brazil, Juan Pablo Montoya, McLaren-Mercedes
Japan, Kimi Räikkönen, McLaren-Mercedes
China, Fernando Alonso, Renault

2006

Bahrain, Fernando Alonso, Renault
Malaysia, Giancarlo Fisichella, Renault
Australia, Fernando Alonso, Renault
San Marino, Michael Schumacher, Ferrari
Europe, Michael Schumacher, Ferrari
Spain, Fernando Alonso, Renault
Monaco, Fernando Alonso, Renault
Great Britain, Fernando Alonso, Renault
Canada, Fernando Alonso, Renault
United States, Michael Schumacher, Ferrari
France, Michael Schumacher, Ferrari
Germany, Michael Schumacher, Ferrari
Hungary, Jenson Button, Honda
Turkey, Felipe Massa, Ferrari
Italy, Michael Schumacher, Ferrari
China, Michael Schumacher, Ferrari
Japan, Fernando Alonso, Renault
Brazil, Felipe Massa, Ferrari

2007

Australia, Kimi Räikkönen, Ferrari
Malaysia, Fernando Alonso, McLaren-Mercedes
Bahrain, Felipe Massa, Ferrari
Spain, Felipe Massa, Ferrari
Monaco, Fernando Alonso, McLaren-Mercedes
Canada, Lewis Hamilton, McLaren-Mercedes
United States, Lewis Hamilton, McLaren-Mercedes
France, Kimi Räikkönen, Ferrari
Great Britain, Kimi Räikkönen, Ferrari
Europe, Fernando Alonso, McLaren-Mercedes
Hungary, Lewis Hamilton, McLaren-Mercedes
Turkey, Felipe Massa, Ferrari
Italy, Fernando Alonso, McLaren-Mercedes
Belgium, Kimi Räikkönen, Ferrari
Japan, Lewis Hamilton, McLaren-Mercedes
China, Kimi Räikkönen, Ferrari
Brazil, Kimi Räikkönen, Ferrari

2008

Australia, Lewis Hamilton, McLaren-Mercedes
Malaysia, Kimi Räikkönen, Ferrari
Bahrain, Felipe Massa, Ferrari
Spain, Kimi Räikkönen, Ferrari
Turkey, Felipe Massa, Ferrari
Monaco, Lewis Hamilton, McLaren-Mercedes
Canada, Robert Kubica, BMW Sauber
France, Felipe Massa, Ferrari
Great Britain, Lewis Hamilton, McLaren-Mercedes
Germany, Lewis Hamilton, McLaren-Mercedes
Hungary, Heikki Kovalinen, McLaren-Mercedes
Europe, Felipe Massa, Ferrari
Belgium, Felipe Massa, Ferrari
Italy, Sebastian Vettel, STR-Ferrari
Singapore, Fernando Alonso, Renault
Japan, Fernando Alonso, Renault
China, Lewis Hamilton, McLaren-Mercedes
Brazil, Felipe Massa, Ferrari

World Championship of Drivers

1950
1. Giuseppe Farina, Italian, Alfa Romeo, 30
2. Juan Manuel Fangio, Argentinian, Alfa Romeo, 27
3. Luigi Fagioli, Alfa Romeo, 24

1951
1. Juan Manuel Fangio, Alfa Romeo, 31
2. Alberto Ascari, Italian, Ferrari, 25
3. Jose Froilan Gonzales, Argentinian, Ferrari, 24

1952
1. Alberto Ascari, Italian, Ferrari, 36
2. Giuseppe Farina, Italian, Ferrari, 24
3. Piero Taruffi, Italian, Ferrari, 22

1953
1. Alberto Ascari, Italian, Ferrari, 34 1/2
2. Juan Manuel Fangio, Argentinian, Maserati, 28
3. Giuseppe Farina, Italian, Ferrari, 26

1954
1. Juan Manuel Fangio, Argentinian, Maserati and Mercedes Benz, 42
2. José Frolián Gonzáles, Argentinian, Ferrari, 25-1/7
3. Mike Hawthorn, British, Ferrari, 24-9/14

1955
1. Juan Manuel Fangio, Argentinian, Mercedes-Benz, 40
2. Stirling Moss, British, Mercedes-Benz, 23
3. Eugenio Castellotti, Italian, Lancia and Ferrari, 12

1956
1. Juan Manuel Fangio, Argentinian, Lancia-Ferrari, 30
2. Stirling Moss, British, Maserati, 27
3. Peter Collins, British, Lancia-Ferrari

1957
1. Juan Manuel Fangio, Argentinian, Maserati, 40
2. Stirling Moss, British, Maserati and Vanwall, 25
3. Luigi Musso, Italian, Ferrari, 16

1958
1. Mike Hawthorn, British, Ferrari, 42
2. Stirling Moss, British, Cooper-Climax and Vanwall, 41
3. Tony Brooks, British, Vanwall, 24

1959
1. Jack Brabham, Australian, Cooper-Climax, 31
2. Tony Brooks, British, Ferrari, 27
3. Stirling Moss, British, Cooper-Climax and BRM

1960
1. Jack Brabham, Australian, Cooper-Climax, 43
2. Bruce McLaren, New Zealander, Cooper-Climax, 34
3. Stirling Moss, British, Lotus-Climax, 19

1961
1. Phil Hill, American, Ferrari, 34
2. Wolfgang von Trips, German, Ferrari, 33
3. Stirling Moss, British, Lotus-Climax, 21
3. Dan Gurney, American, Porsche, 21

1962
1. Graham Hill, British, BRM, 42
2. Jim Clark, British, Lotus-Climax, 30
3. Bruce McLaren, New Zealander, Cooper-Climax, 27

1963
1. Jim Clark, British, Lotus-Climax, 54
2. Graham Hill, British, BRM, 29
3. Richie Ginther, American, BRM, 29

1964
1. John Surtees, British, Lotus-Climax, 40
2. Graham Hill, British, BRM, 39
3. Jim Clark, British, Lotus-Climax, 32

1965
1. Jim Clark, British, Lotus-Climax, 54
2. Graham Hill, British, BRM, 40
3. Jackie Stewart, British, BRM, 33

1966
1. Jack Brabham, Australian, Brabham-Repco, 42
2. John Surtees, British, Ferrari and Cooper-Maserati, 28
3. Jochen Rindt, Austrian, Cooper-Maserati, 22

1967
1. Denny Hulme, New Zealander, Brabham-Repco, 51
2. Jack Brabham, Australian, Brabham-Repco, 46
3. Jim Clark, British, Lotus-Ford

1968
1. Graham Hill, British, Lotus-Ford, 48
2. Jackie Stewart, British, Matra-Ford, 36
3. Denny Hulme, New Zealander, McLaren-BRM and McLaren-Ford, 33

1969
1. Jackie Stewart, British, Matra-Ford, 63
2. Jacky Ickx, Belgian, Brabham-Ford, 37
3. Bruce McLaren, New Zealander, McLaren-Ford, 26

1970
1. Jochen Rindt, Austrian, Lotus-Ford, 45
2. Jacky Ickx, Belgian, Ferrari, 40
3. Clay Regazzoni, Swiss, Ferrari, 33

1971
1. Jackie Stewart, British, Tyrrell-Ford, 62
2. Ronnie Peterson, Swedish, March-Ford, 33
3. Francois Cevert, French, Tyrrell-Ford, 26

1972
1. Emerson Fittipaldi, Brazilian, Lotus-Ford, 61
2. Jackie Stewart, British, Tyrrell-Ford, 45
3. Denny Hulme, New Zealander, McLaren-Ford, 39

1973
1. Jackie Stewart, British, Tyrrell-Ford, 71
2. Emerson Fittipaldi, Brazilian, Lotus-Ford, 55
3. Ronnie Peterson, Swedish, Lotus-Ford

1974
1. Emerson Fittipaldi, Brazilian, McLaren-Ford, 55
2. Clay Regazzoni, Swiss, Ferrari, 52
3. Jody Scheckter, South African, Tyrrell-Ford, 45

1975
1. Niki Lauda, Austrian, Ferrari, 64 1/2
2. Emerson Fittipaldi, Brazilian, McLaren-Ford, 45
3. Carlos Reutman, Argentinian, Brabham-Ford, 37

1976
1. James Hunt, British, McLaren, 69
2. Niki Lauda, Austrian, Ferrari, 68
3. Jody Scheker, South African, Tyrrell-Ford, 49

1977
1. Niki Lauda, Austrian, Ferrari, 72
2. Jody Schekter, South African, Wolf-Ford, 55
3. Mario Andretti, American, Lotus-Ford, 47

1978
1. Mario Andretti, American, Lotus-Ford, 64
2. Ronnie Peterson, Swedish, Lotus-Ford, 51
3. Carlos Reutmann, Argentinian, Ferrari, 48

1979
1. Jody Schekter, South African, Ferrari, 51
2. Gilles Villeneuve, Canadian, Ferrari, 47
3. Alan Jones, Australian, Williams-Ford, 40

1980
1. Alan Jones, Australian, Williams-Ford, 67
2. Nelson Piquet, Brazilian, Brabham-Ford, 54
3. Carlos Reutmann, Argentinian, Williams-Ford, 42

1981
1. Nelson Piquet, Brazilian, Brabham-Ford, 50
2. Carlos Reutmann, Argentinian, Williams-Ford, 49
3. Alan Jones, Australian, Williams-Ford, 46

1982
1. Keke Rosberg, Finnish, Williams-Ford, 44
2. Didier Pironi, French, Ferrari, 39
3. John Watson, British, McLaren-Ford, 39

1983
1. Nelson Piquet, Brazilian, Brabham-BMW, 59
2. Alain Prost, French, Renault, 57
3. Rene Arnoux, French, Ferrari, 49

1984
1. Niki Lauda, Austrian, McLaren-TAG, 72
2. Alain Prost, French, McLaren-TAG, 71 1/2
3. Elio de Angelis, Italian, Lotus-Renault, 34

1985
1. Alain Prost, French, McLaren-TAG, 73
2. Michele Alboreto, Italian, Ferrari, 53
3. Keke Rosberg, Finnish, Williams-Honda, 40

1986
1. Alain Prost, French, McLaren-TAG, 72
2. Nigel Mansell, British, Williams-Honda, 70
3. Nelson Piquet, Brazilian, Williams-Honda, 69

1987
1. Nelson Piquet, Brazilian, Williams-Honda, 73
2. Nigel Mansell, British, Williams-Honda, 61
3. Ayrton Senna, Brazilian, Lotus-Honda, 57

1988
1. Ayrton Senna, Brazilian, McLaren-Honda, 90
2. Alain Prost, French, McLaren-Honda, 87
3. Gerhard Berger, Austrian, Ferrari, 41

1989
1. Alain Prost, French, McLaren-Honda, 76
2. Ayrton Senna, Brazilian, McLaren-Honda, 60
3. Nigel Mansell, British, Ferrari, 38

1990
1. Ayrton Senna, Brazilian, McLaren-Honda, 78
2. Alain Prost, French, Ferrari, 71
3. Nelson Piquet, Brazilian, Benetton-Ford, 43

1991
1. Ayrton Senna, Brazilian, McLaren-Honda, 76
2. Nigel Mansell, British, Williams-Renault, 72
3. Riccardo Patrese, Italian, Williams-Renault, 53

1992
1. Nigel Mansell, British, Williams-Renault, 108
2. Riccardo Patrese, Italian, Williams-Renault, 56
3. Michael Schumacher, German, Benetton-Ford, 53

1993
1. Alain Prost, French, Williams-Renault, 99
2. Ayrton Senna, Brazilian, McLaren-Ford, 73
3. Damon Hill, British, Williams-Renault, 69

1994
1. Michael Schumacher, German, Benetton-Ford, 92
2. Damon Hill, British, Williams-Renault, 91
3. Gerhard Berger, Austrian, Ferrari, 41

1995
1. Michael Schumacher, German, Benetton-Ford, 102
2. Damon Hill, British, Williams-Renault, 69
3. David Coulthard, British, Williams-Renault, 49

1996
1. Damon Hill, British, Williams-Renault, 97
2. Jacques Villeneuve, Canadian, Williams-Renault, 78
3. Michael Schumacher, German, Ferrari, 59

1997
1. Jacques Villeneuve, Canadian, Williams-Renault, 81
2. Heinz-Harald Frentzen, German, Williams-Renault, 42
3. David Coulthard, British, McLaren-Mercedes, 36
3. Jean Alesi, French, Benetton-Renault, 36
* Michael Schumacher was disqualified from second place

1998
1. Mika Hakkinen, Finland, McLaren-Mercedes, 100
2. Michael Schumacher, German, Ferrari, 86
3. David Coulthard, British, McLaren-Mercedes, 56

1999
1. Mika Hakkinen, Finland, McLaren-Mercedes, 76
2. Eddie Irvine, British, Ferrari, 74
3. Heinz-Harald Frentzen, German, Jordan-Mugen Honda, 54

2000
1. Michael Schumacher, German, Ferrari, 108
2. Mika Hakkinen, Finland, McLaren-Mercedes 89
3. David Coulthard, British, McLaren-Mercedes, 73

2001
1. Michael Schumacher, German, Ferrari, 123
2. David Coulthard, British, McLaren-Mercedes, 65
3. Rubens Barrichello, Brazil, Ferrari, 56

2002
1. Michael Schumacher, German, Ferrari, 144
2. Rubens Barrichello, Brazil, Ferrari 77
3. Juan Pablo Montoya, Columbia, Williams-BMW, 50

2003
1. Michael Schumacher, German, Ferrari, 93
2. Kimi Räikkönen, Finland, McLaren-Mercedes, 91
3. Juan Pablo Montoya, Columbia, Williams-BMW, 82

2004
1. Michael Schumacher, German, Ferrari, 114
2. Rubens Barrichello, Brazil, Ferrari, 85
3. Jenson Button, British, BAR-Honda, 59

2005
1. Fernando Alonso, Spanish, Renault, 133
2. Kimi Räikkönen, Finland, McLaren-Mercedes, 112
3. Michael Schumacher, German, Ferrari, 62

2006
1. Fernando Alonso, Spanish, Renault, 134
2. Michael Schumacher, German, Ferrari, 121
3. Felipe Massa, Brazilian, Ferrari, 80

2007
1. Kimi Räikkönen, Finland, Ferrari, 110
2. Lewis Hamilton, British, McLaren-Mercedes, 109
3. Fernando Alonso, Spanish, Renault, 109

2008
1. Lewis Hamilton, British, McLaren-Mercedes, 98
2. Felipe Massa, Brazilian, Ferrari, 97
3. Kimi Räikkönen, Finland, Ferrari, 75

World Championship of Constructors

1958 Vanwall	**1975** Ferrari	**1992** Williams-Renault
1959 Cooper-Climax	**1976** Ferrari	**1993** Williams-Renault
1960 Cooper-Climax	**1977** Ferrari	**1994** Williams-Renault
1961 Ferrari	**1978** Lotus-Ford	**1995** Benetton-Renault
1962 BRM	**1979** Ferrari	**1996** Williams-Renault
1963 Lotus-Climax	**1980** Williams-Ford	**1997** Williams-Renault
1964 Ferrari	**1981** Williams-Ford	**1998** McLaren-Mercedes
1965 Lotus-Climax	**1982** Ferrari	**1999** Ferrari
1966 Brabham-Repco	**1983** Ferrari	**2000** Ferrari
1967 Brabham-Repco	**1984** McLaren-TAG	**2001** Ferrari
1968 Lotus-Ford	**1985** McLaren-TAG	**2002** Ferrari
1969 Matra-Ford	**1986** Williams-Honda	**2003** Ferrari
1970 Lotus-Ford	**1987** Williams-Honda	**2004** Ferrari
1971 Tyrrell-Ford	**1988** McLaren-Honda	**2005** Renault
1972 Lotus-Ford	**1989** McLaren-Honda	**2006** Renault
1973 Tyrrell-Ford	**1990** McLaren-Honda	**2007** Ferrari
1974 McLaren-Ford	**1991** McLaren-Honda	**2008** Ferrari

Number of Grand Prix Entered:

1. Rubens Barrichello, 271
2. Riccardo Patrese, 256
3. Michael Schumacher, 250
4. David Coulthard, 247
5. Giancarlo Fisichella, 214
6. Gerhard Berger, 210
7. Andrea de Cesaris, 208
8. Nelson Piquet, 207
9. Jarno Trulli, 202
10. Jean Alesi, 201

Number of Grand Prix Victories:

1. Michael Schumacher, 91
2. Alain Prost, 51
3. Ayrton Senna, 41
4. Nigel Mansell, 31
5. Jackie Stewart, 27
6/7. Jim Clark, 25
6/7. Niki Lauda, 25
8/9. Juan Manuel Fangio, 23
8/9. Nelson Piquet, 23
10. Damon Hill, 22

Number of Podium Finishes

1. Michael Schumacher, 154
2. Alain Prost, 106
3. Ayrton Senna, 80
4. Rubens Barrichello, 63
5. David Coulthard, 62
6. Nelson Piquet, 60
7. Nigel Mansell, 59
8. Kimi Raikkonen, 57
9. Niki Lauda, 54
10. Fernando Alonso, 52

Picture credits

The publisher would like to thank the following for permission to reproduce the following copyright material:

Getty Images
Front cover, back cover all
Page 1 AFP/Getty Images, 2 AFP/Getty Images, 4 far right, 5 far left, middle, far right, 6, 8/9, 10, 11 AFP/Getty Images, 15 AFP/Getty Images, 100 AFP/Getty Images, 101 Bongarts/Getty Images, 102/103 AFP/Getty Images, 130 AFP/Getty Images, 138/139, 141 AFP/Getty Images, 142, 154/155, 157, 159, 165, 170/171, 172, 173, 175, 176, 177, 178 top, 180 top, 181, 185 top, 195, 198 both, 204, 206, 208, 209 bottom, 210 top AFP/Getty Images, 212, 213. Back end papers

LAT Photographic
Front end papers Steven Tee/LAT Photographic
Page 4 all except far right, 5 (2 in from left) Steven Tee/LAT Photographic, (2 in from right) Glenn Dunbar/LAT Photographic, 12/13 Colin McMaster/LAT Photographic, 14, 16, 25, 18/19 Lorenzo Bellanca/LAT Photographic, 20 Lorenzo Bellanca/LAT Photographic, 21 Charles Coates/LAT Photographic, 22, 23, 24 Charles Coates/LAT Photographic, 25, 26, 27, 28, 29, 30/31 Steve Etherington/LAT Photographic, 32, 33, 34, 35, 36, 37, 38, 39, 40/41 Tim Clarke/LAT Photographic, 42 Andrew Ferraro/LAT Photographic, 43, 44, 45, 46 Glenn Dunbar/LAT Photographic, 47, 48, 49 Jeff Bloxham/LAT Photographic, 50/51 Steve Etherington/LAT Photographic, 52 Glenn Dunbar/LAT Photographic, 53, 54, 55, 56, 57, 58/59 Glenn Dunbar/LAT Photographic, 60 Tony Smythe/ LAT Photographic, 61 Charles Coates/LAT Photographic, 62 Charles Coates/LAT Photographic, 63 Charles Coates/LAT Photographic, 64 Steven Tee/LAT Photographic, 65 Charles Coates/LAT Photographic, 66 Glenn Dunbar/LAT Photographic, 67, 68/69 Steve Etherington/LAT Photographic, 70 Lorenzo Bellanca/LAT Photographic, 71, 72, 73, 74, 75, 76, 77 Charles Coates/LAT Photographic, 78/79 Steven Tee/LAT Photographic, 80 Steve Etherington/ LAT Photographic, 81, 82, 83 Andrew Ferraro/LAT Photographic, 84, 85, 86, 87, 88, 89, 90/91 Glenn Dunbar/LAT Photographic, 92 Steven Tee/LAT Photographic, 93, 94, 95, 96, 97, 98/99, 104, 105 top, 105 bottom Charles Coates/LAT Photographic, 106 both, 107, 108/109, 110 Michael Cooper/LAT Photographic, 111 top, 111 bottom Charles Coates/LAT Photographic, 112 both, 113, 114 both, 115 Charles Coates/LAT Photographic, 116, 117 top Lorenzo Bellanca/LAT Photographic, 117 bottom Glenn Dunbar/LAT Photographic, 118/119 Steven Tee/LAT Photographic, 120, 121 both, 122 both, 123, 124/125, 126/127, 128, 129, 131, 132, 133 top, 133 bottom Tony Smythe/LAT Photographic, 134/135, 136, 137, 140, 143, 144/145, 146 both, 147, 148/149, 150 both, 151, 152 both, 153, 156, 160, 161, 162 both, 163, 164 both, 166/167, 168 both, 169, 178 bottom, 179, 180 bottom, 182/183, 184, 185 bottom, 186/187 Steven Tee/LAT Photographic, 188, 189, 190, 192, 193, 194 top, 194 bottom Charles Coates/LAT Photographic, 196/197, 200 top Steve Etherington/LAT Photographic, 200 bottom, 201 Charles Coates/LAT Photographic, 202/203 LAT Photographic/Michael Cooper, 205 Steve Etherington/LAT Photographic, 207 Glenn Dunbar/LAT Photographic, 209 top, 210 bottom Glenn Dunbar/LAT Photographic, 211 Lorenzo Bellanca/LAT Photographic.

The author would like to thank Will Gray for his help with the drivers entries, and George Derrick for research on the statistics.

Index

Index